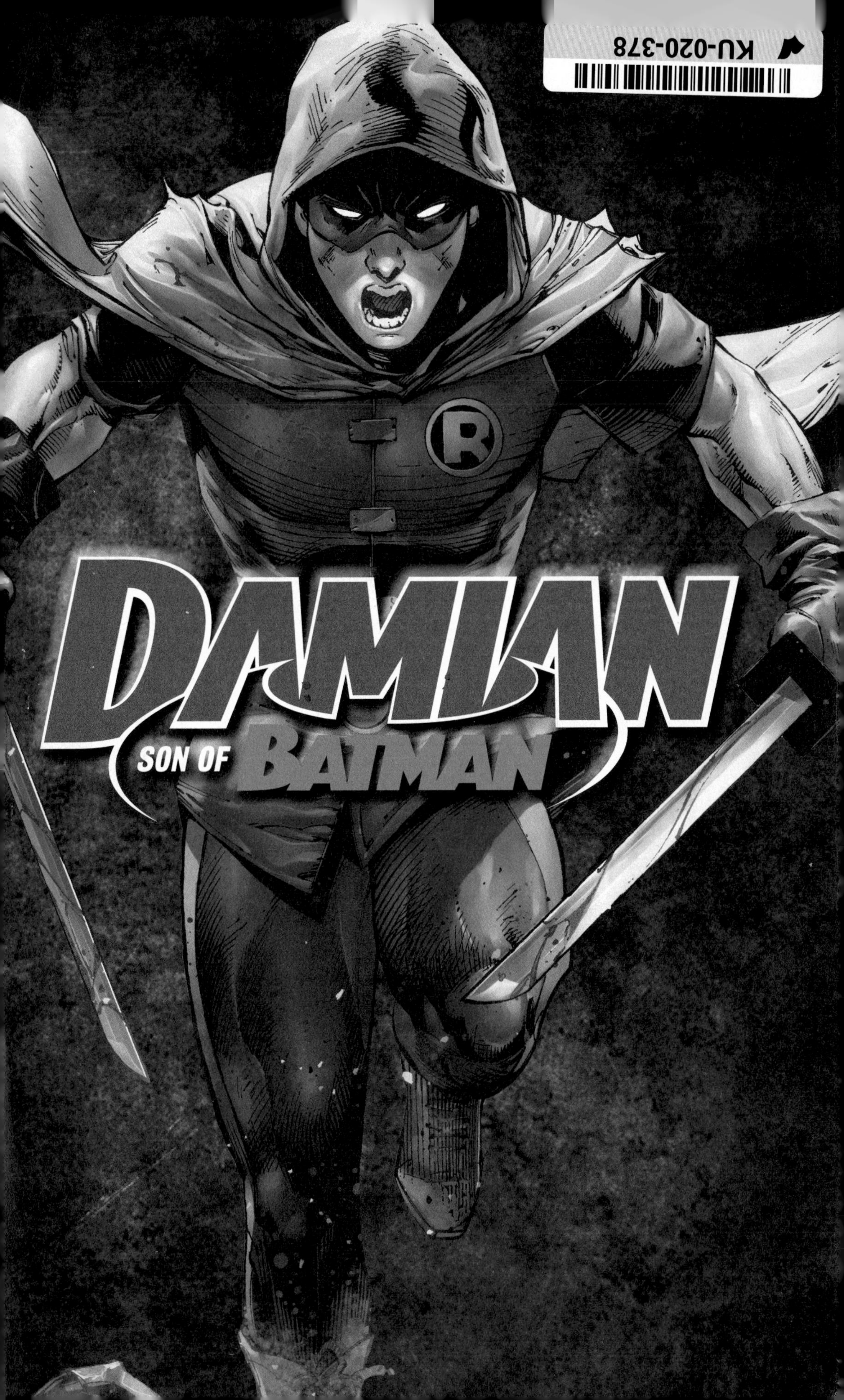
DAMIAN
SON OF BATMAN

ANDY KUBERT
WRITER & ARTIST

BRAD ANDERSON
COLORIST

NICK NAPOLITANO
LETTERER

ANDY KUBERT
&
BRAD ANDERSON
COLLECTION COVER ARTISTS

BATMAN
CREATED BY
BOB KANE

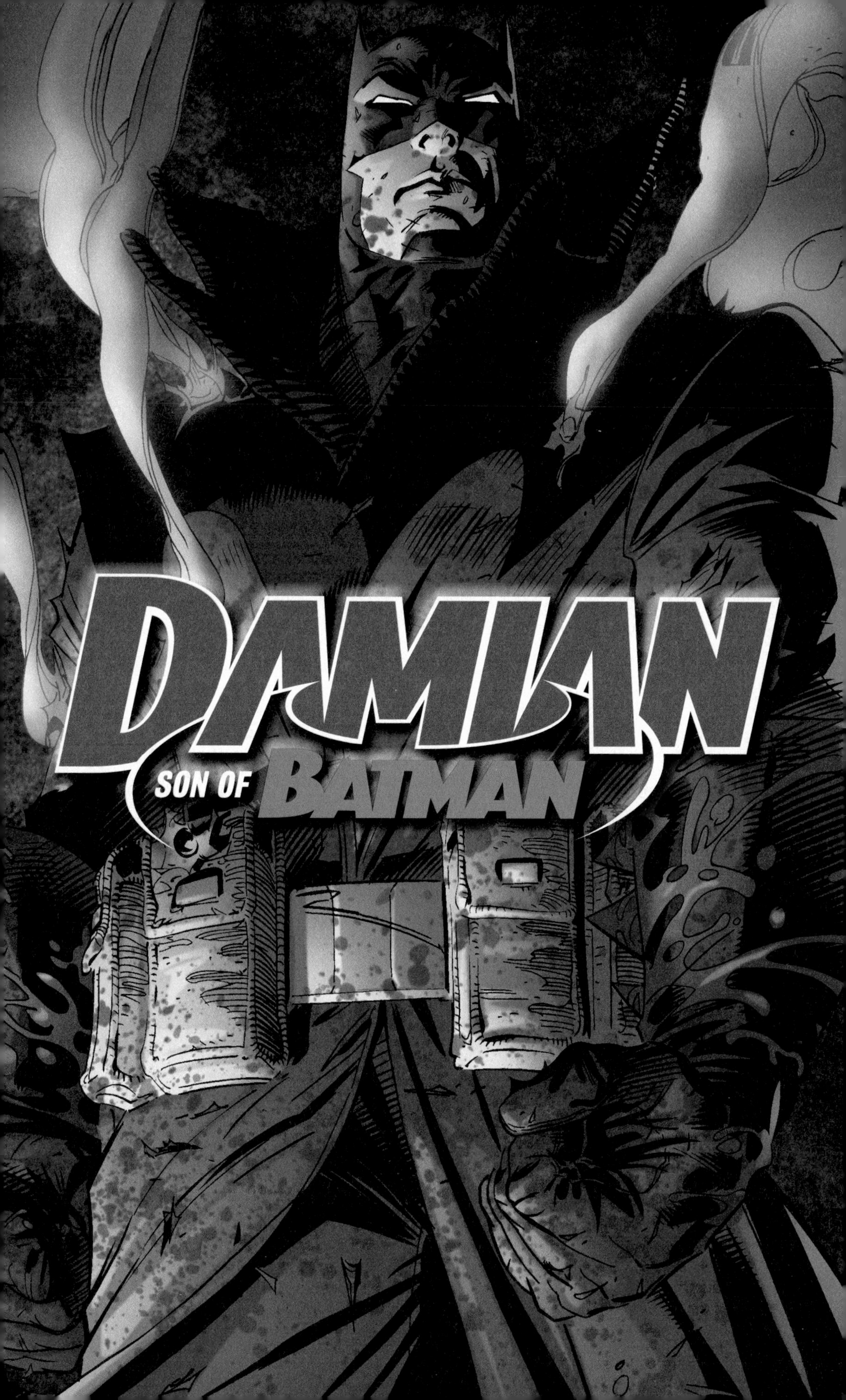
DAMIAN
SON OF BATMAN

Mike Marts Editor - Original Series
Katie Kubert Associate Editor - Original Series
Peter Hamboussi Editor
Robbin Brosterman Design Director - Books
Damian Ryland Publication Design

Bob Harras Senior VP - Editor-in-Chief, DC Comics

Diane Nelson President
Dan DiDio and **Jim Lee** Co-Publishers
Geoff Johns Chief Creative Officer
Amit Desai Senior VP - Marketing & Franchise Management
Amy Genkins Senior VP - Business & Legal Affairs
Nairi Gardiner Senior VP - Finance
Jeff Boison VP - Publishing Planning
Mark Chiarello VP - Art Direction & Design
John Cunningham VP - Marketing
Terri Cunningham VP - Editorial Administration
Larry Ganem VP - Talent Relations & Services
Alison Gill Senior VP - Manufacturing & Operations
Hank Kanalz Senior VP - Vertigo & Integrated Publishing
Jay Kogan VP - Business & Legal Affairs, Publishing
Jack Mahan VP - Business Affairs, Talent
Nick Napolitano VP - Manufacturing Administration
Sue Pohja VP - Book Sales
Fred Ruiz VP - Manufacturing Operations
Courtney Simmons Senior VP - Publicity
Bob Wayne Senior VP - Sales

DAMIAN: SON OF BATMAN

DC Comics, 1700 Broadway, New York, NY 10019
A Warner Bros. Entertainment Company.
Printed by RR Donnelley, Salem, VA, USA. 1/15/15. First Printing.

ISBN: 978-1-4012-5064-5

Library of Congress Cataloging-in-Publication Data

Kubert, Andy.
Damian, Son of Batman / Andy Kubert, Grant Morrison.
pages cm
ISBN 978-1-4012-5064-5
1. Graphic novels. I. Morrison, Grant. II. Title.

PN6728.D25K83 2014
741.5'973—dc23

2014020928

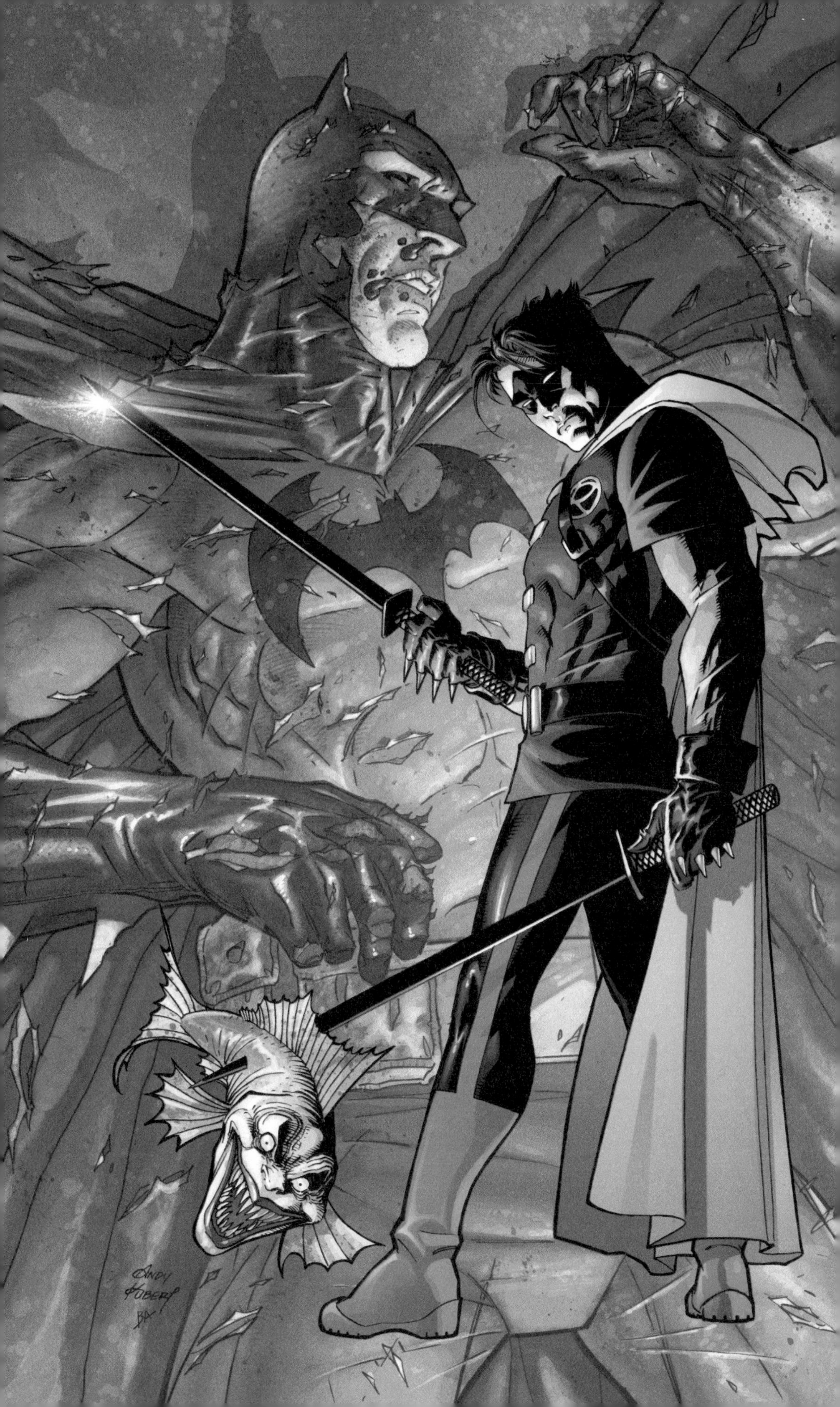

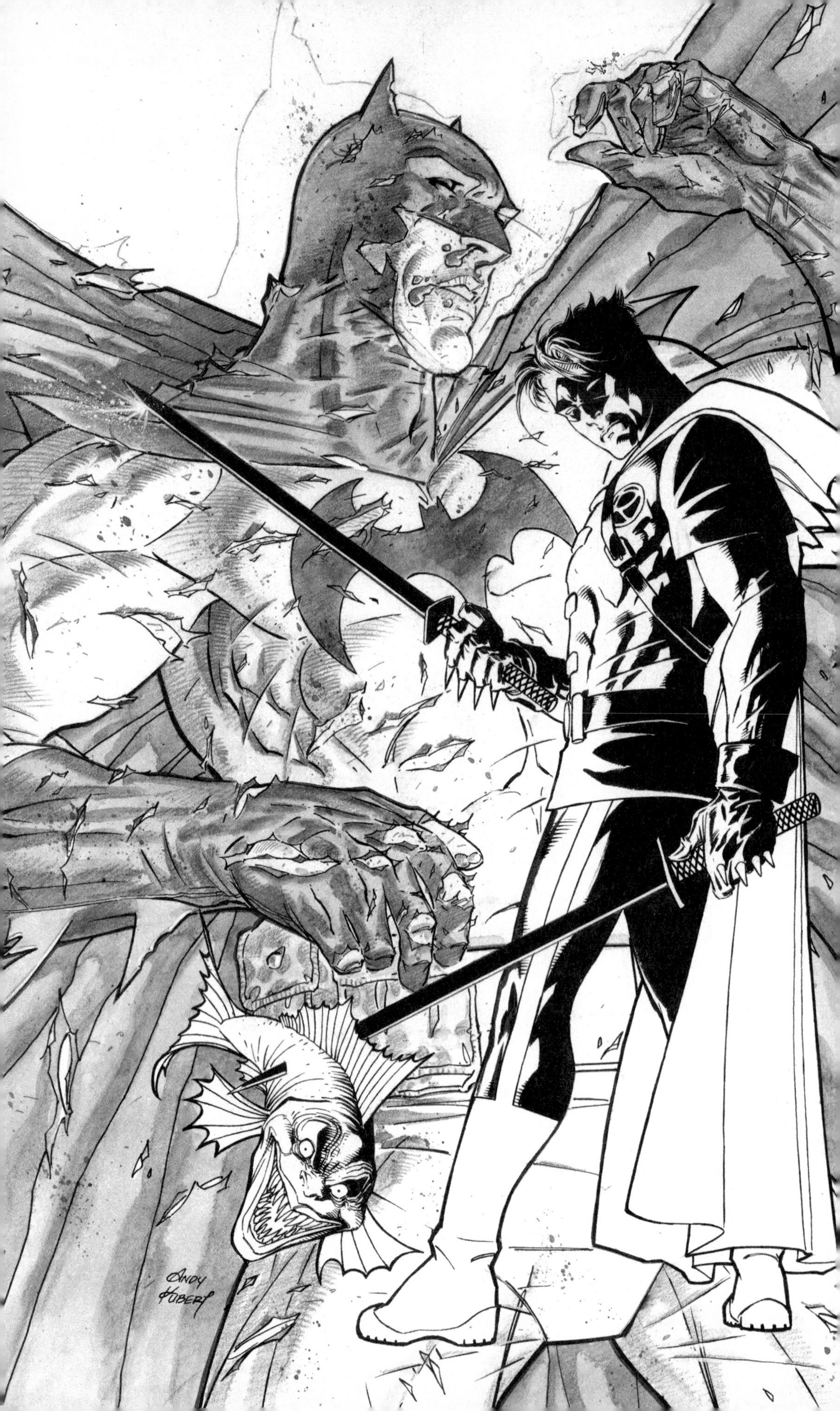
ANDY
KUBERT

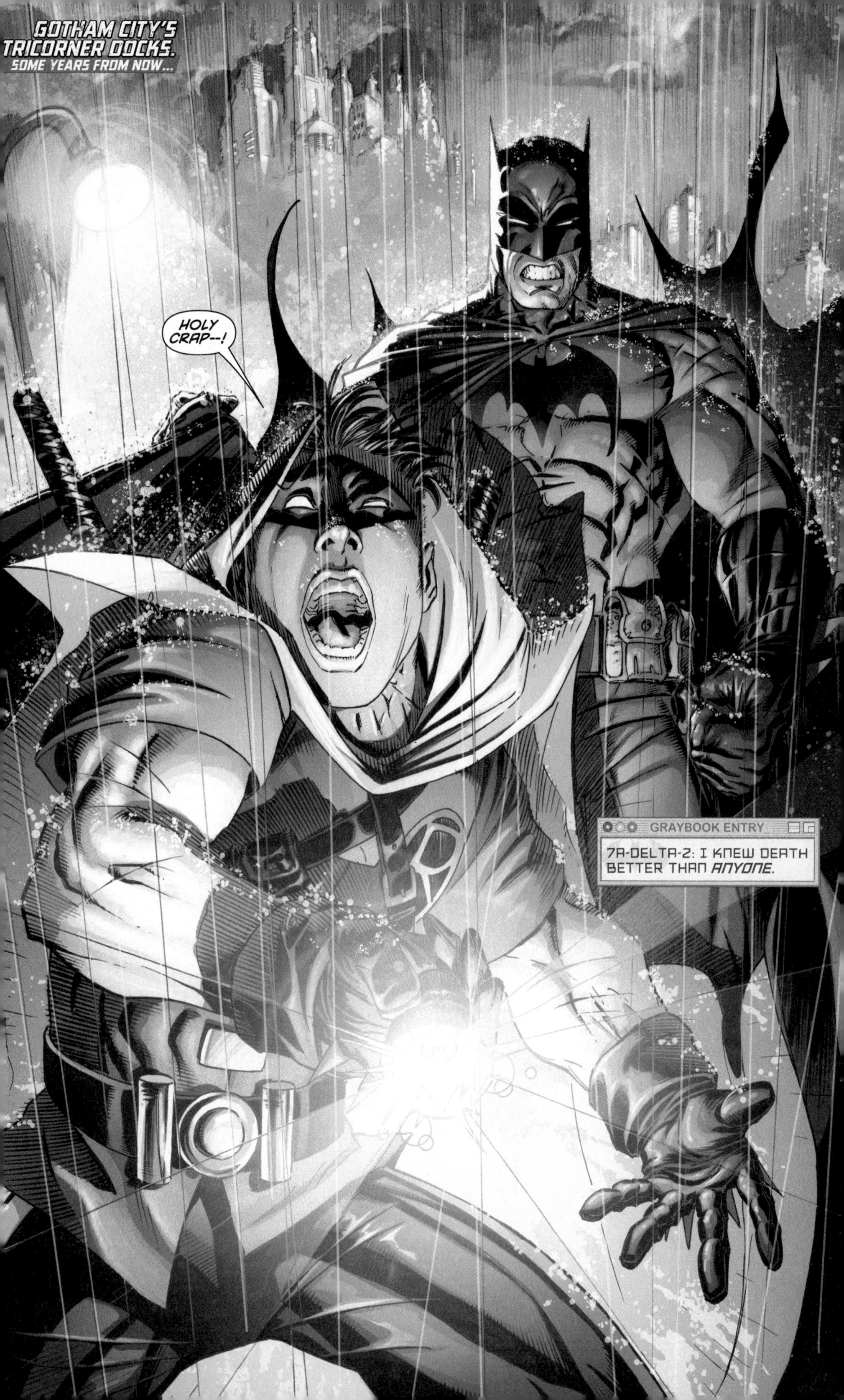
GOTHAM CITY'S TRICORNER DOCKS.
SOME YEARS FROM NOW...
HOLY CRAP--!
GRAYBOOK ENTRY
7A-DELTA-2: I KNEW DEATH BETTER THAN ANYONE.

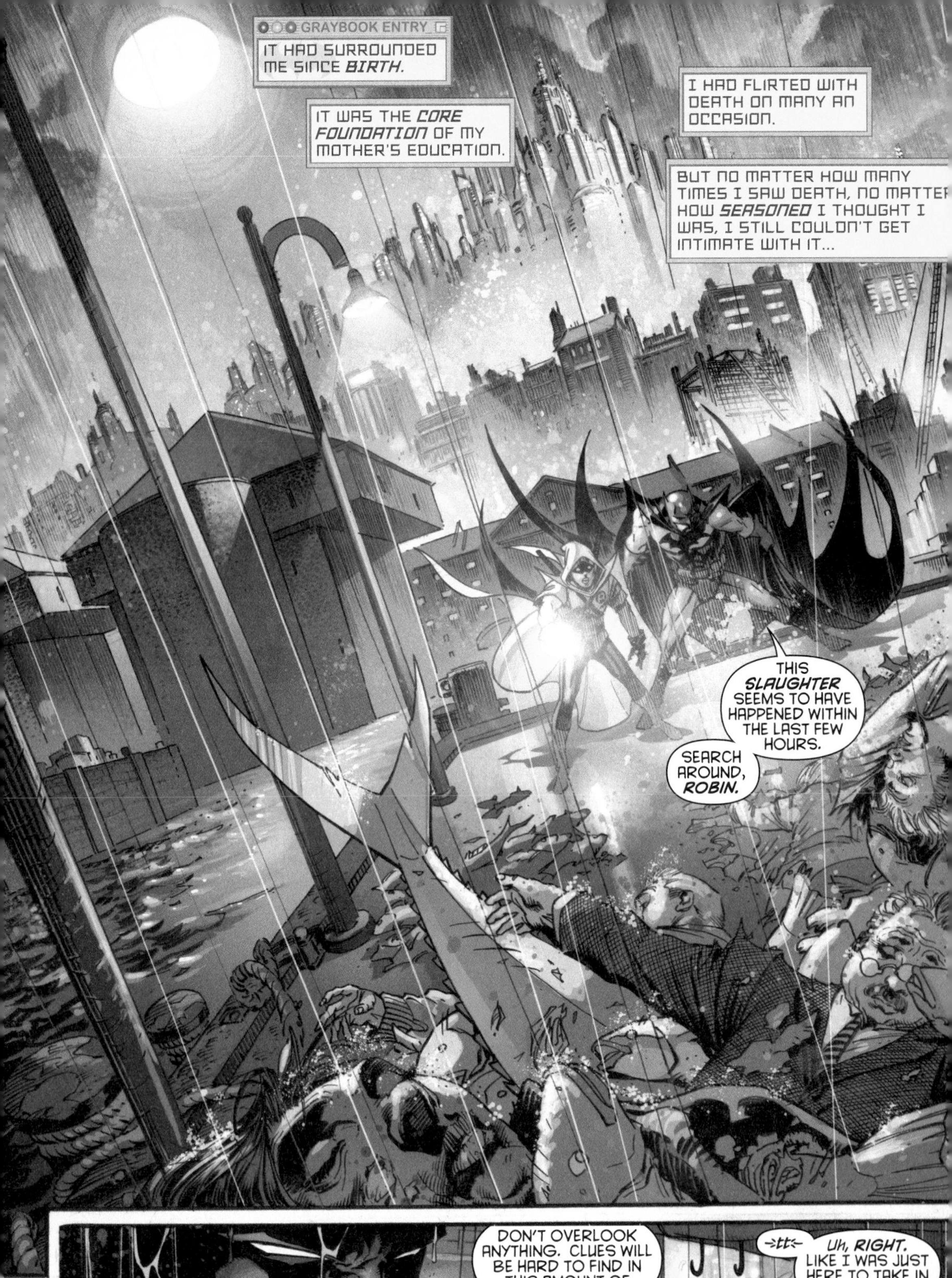
GRAYBOOK ENTRY
IT HAD SURROUNDED ME SINCE *BIRTH*.
IT WAS THE *CORE FOUNDATION* OF MY MOTHER'S EDUCATION.
I HAD FLIRTED WITH DEATH ON MANY AN OCCASION.
BUT NO MATTER HOW MANY TIMES I SAW DEATH, NO MATTER HOW *SEASONED* I THOUGHT I WAS, I STILL COULDN'T GET INTIMATE WITH IT...
THIS *SLAUGHTER* SEEMS TO HAVE HAPPENED WITHIN THE LAST FEW HOURS.
SEARCH AROUND, *ROBIN.*

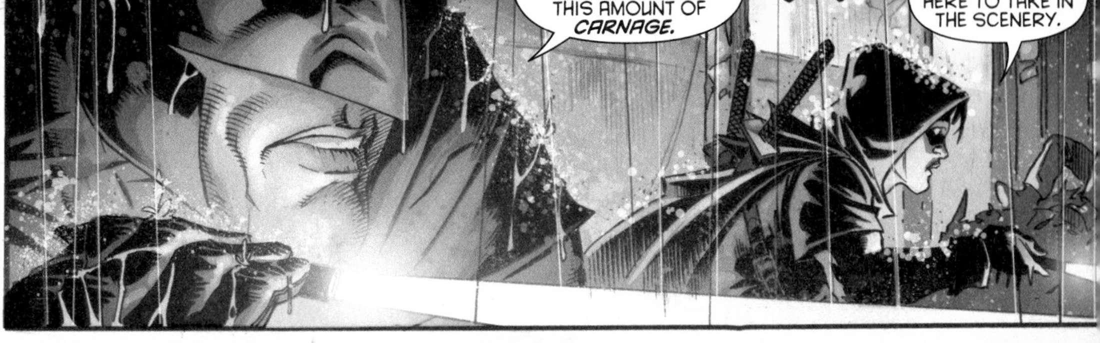
DON'T OVERLOOK ANYTHING. CLUES WILL BE HARD TO FIND IN THIS AMOUNT OF *CARNAGE.*
-tt- *Uh, RIGHT.* LIKE I WAS JUST HERE TO TAKE IN THE SCENERY.

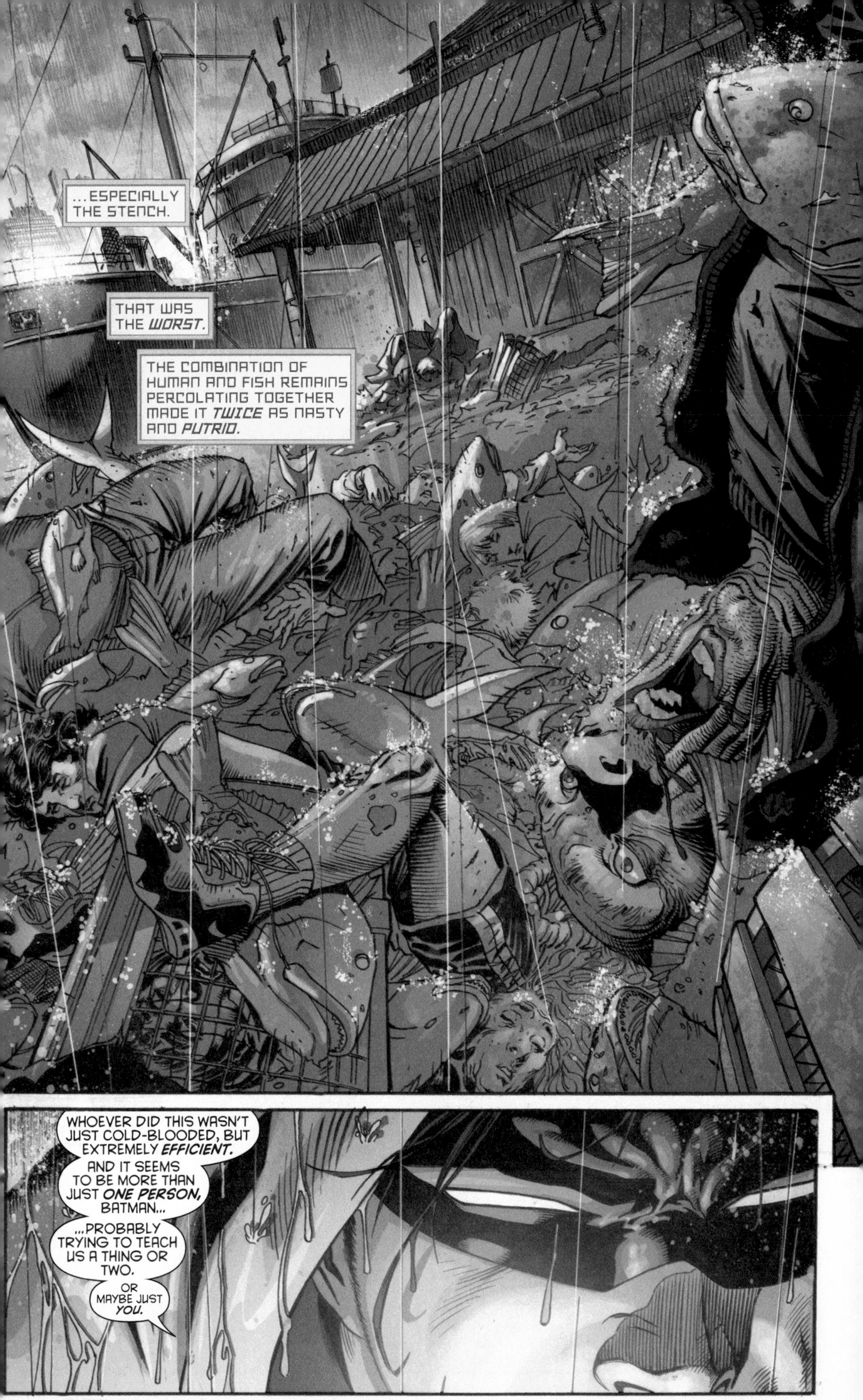
...ESPECIALLY THE STENCH.
THAT WAS THE *WORST*.
THE COMBINATION OF HUMAN AND FISH REMAINS PERCOLATING TOGETHER MADE IT *TWICE* AS NASTY AND *PUTRID*.
WHOEVER DID THIS WASN'T JUST COLD-BLOODED, BUT EXTREMELY *EFFICIENT*.
AND IT SEEMS TO BE MORE THAN JUST *ONE PERSON*, BATMAN...
...PROBABLY TRYING TO TEACH US A THING OR TWO.
OR MAYBE JUST *YOU*.

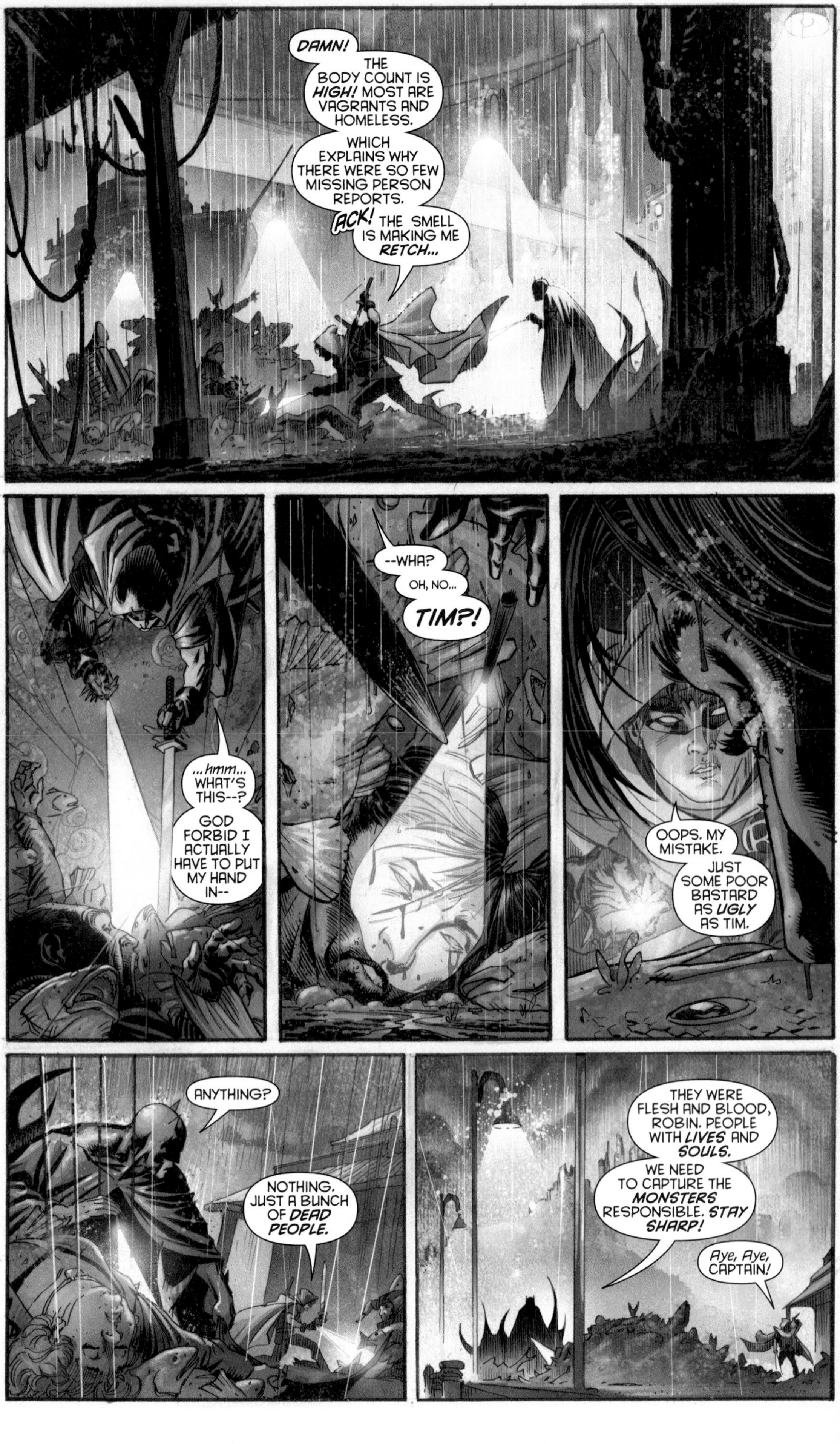
DAMN!
THE BODY COUNT IS HIGH! MOST ARE VAGRANTS AND HOMELESS.
WHICH EXPLAINS WHY THERE WERE SO FEW MISSING PERSON REPORTS.
ACK!
THE SMELL IS MAKING ME RETCH...
...hmm... WHAT'S THIS--?
GOD FORBID I ACTUALLY HAVE TO PUT MY HAND IN--
--WHA?
OH, NO...
TIM?!
OOPS. MY MISTAKE.
JUST SOME POOR BASTARD AS UGLY AS TIM.
ANYTHING?
NOTHING. JUST A BUNCH OF DEAD PEOPLE.
THEY WERE FLESH AND BLOOD, ROBIN. PEOPLE WITH LIVES AND SOULS.
WE NEED TO CAPTURE THE MONSTERS RESPONSIBLE. STAY SHARP!
Aye, Aye, CAPTAIN!

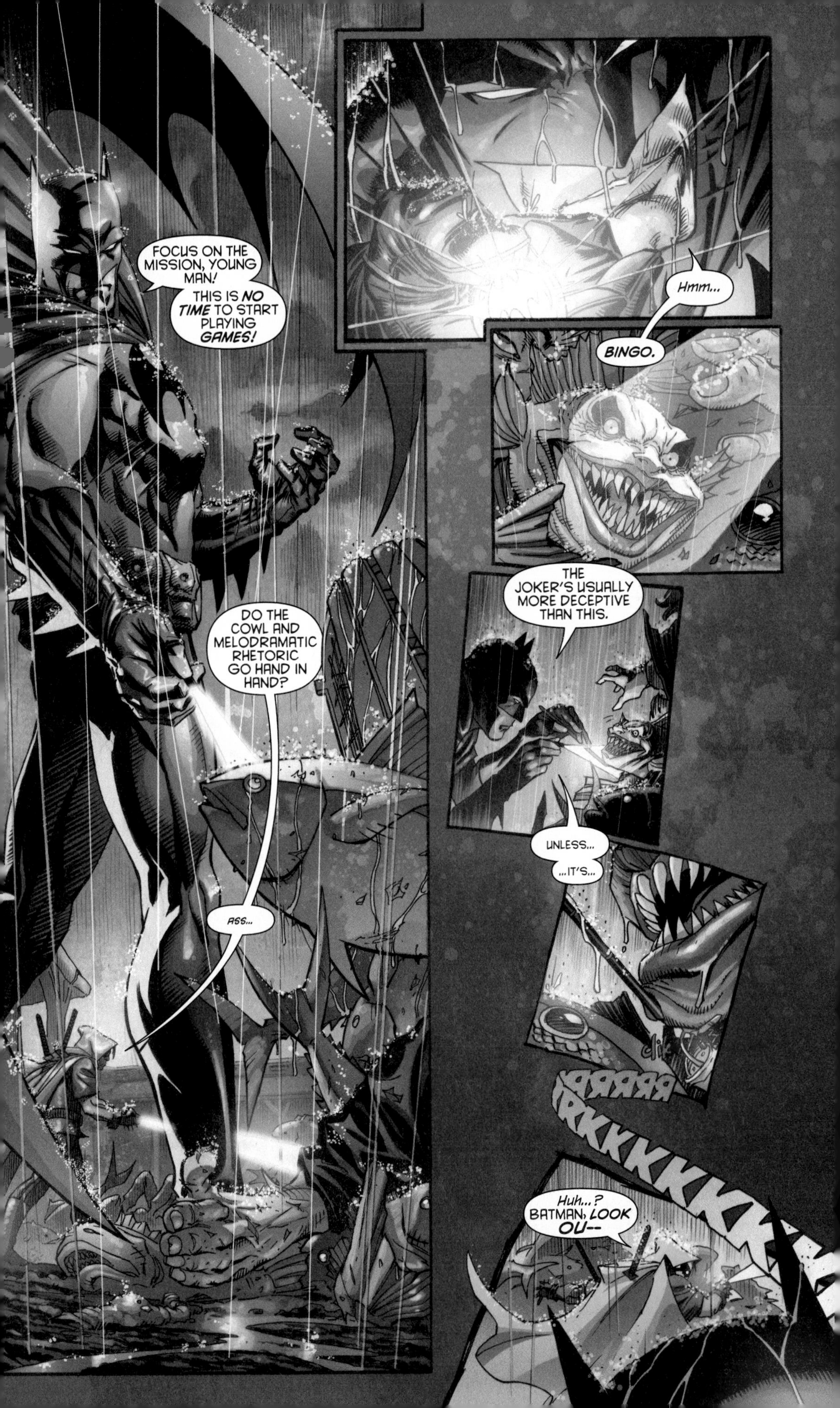
FOCUS ON THE MISSION, YOUNG MAN!
THIS IS NO TIME TO START PLAYING GAMES!
DO THE COWL AND MELODRAMATIC RHETORIC GO HAND IN HAND?
ASS...
Hmm...
BINGO.
THE JOKER'S USUALLY MORE DECEPTIVE THAN THIS.
UNLESS...
...IT'S...
clik
RRRRP
TRKKKKKKK
Huh...? BATMAN, LOOK OU--

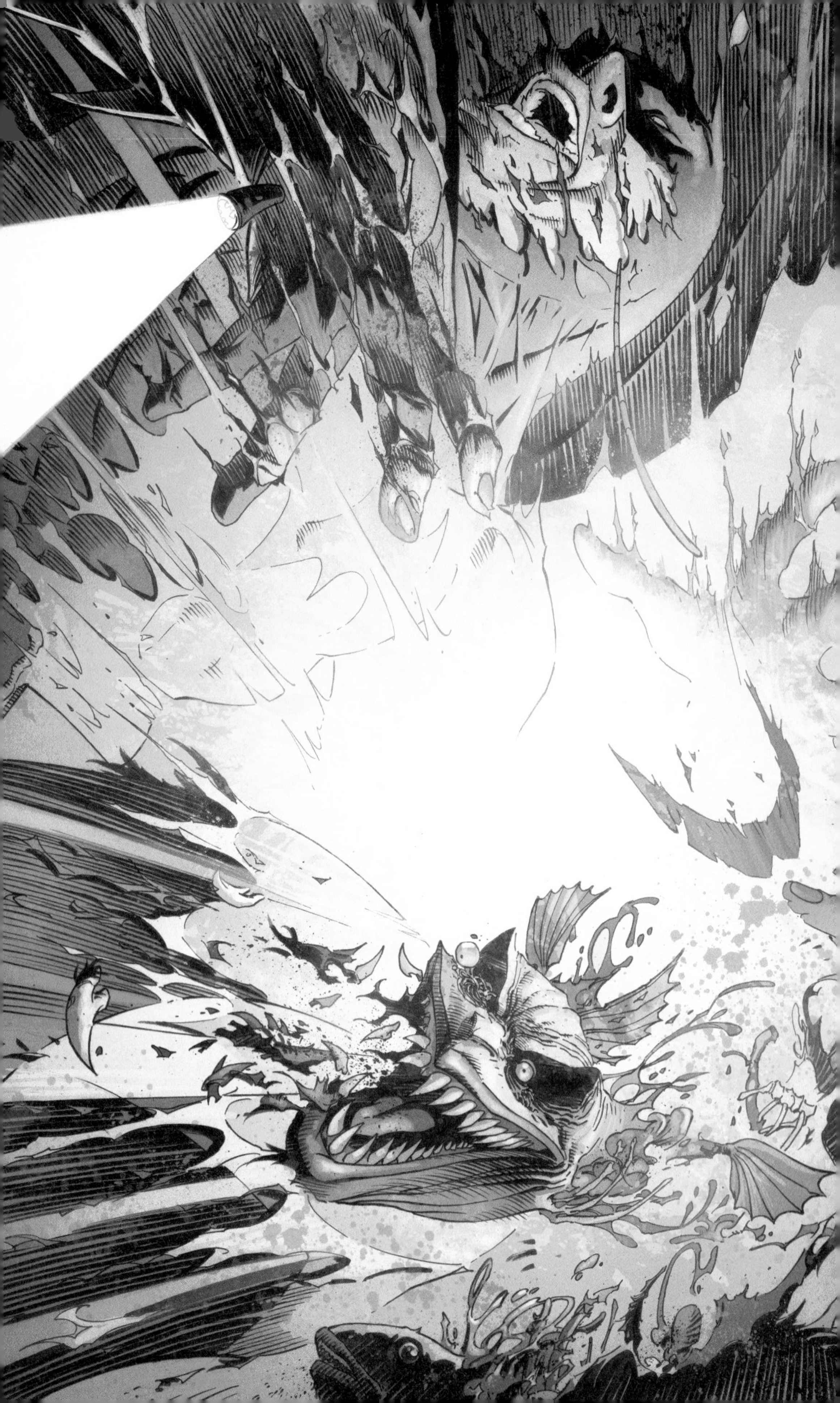

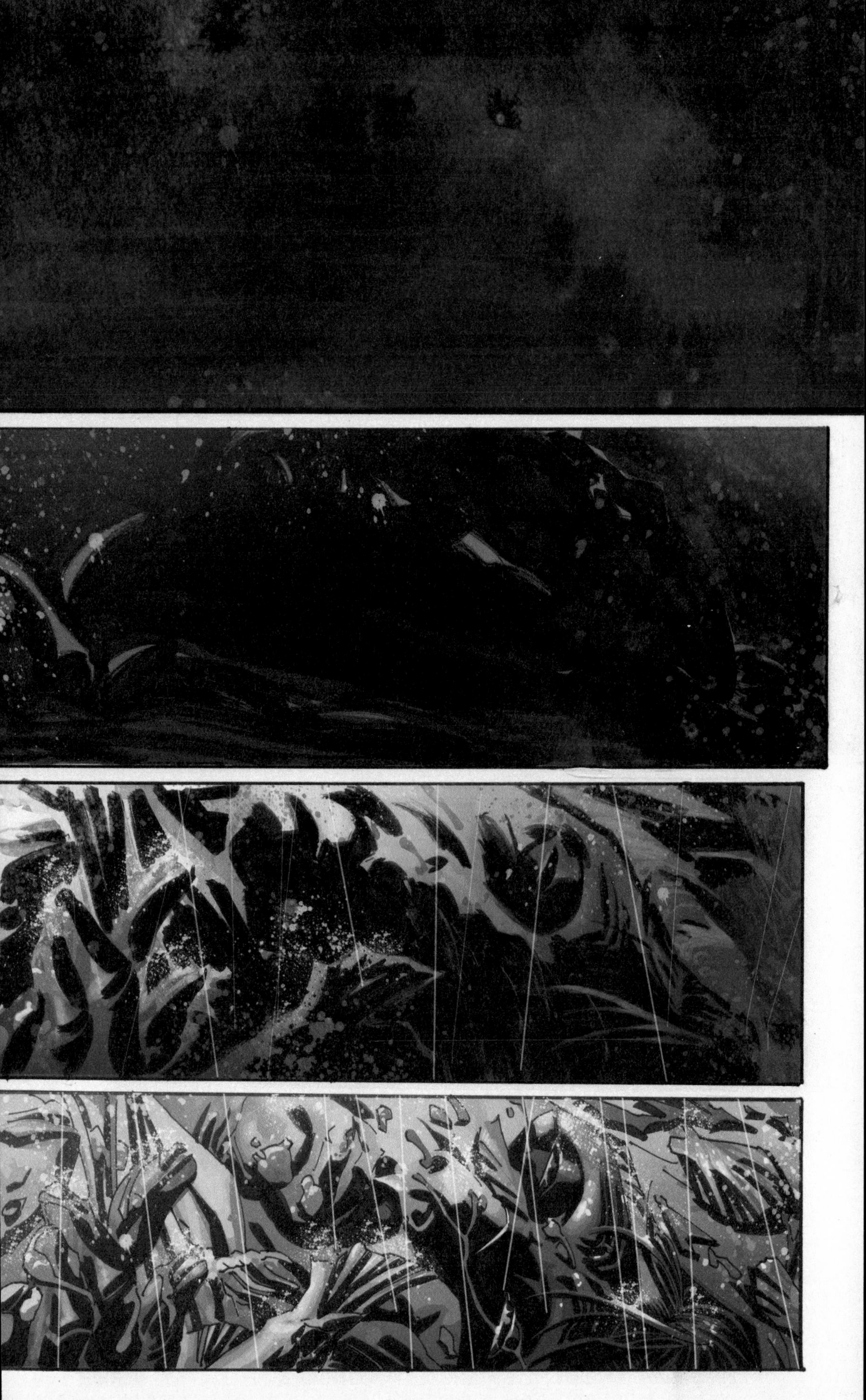

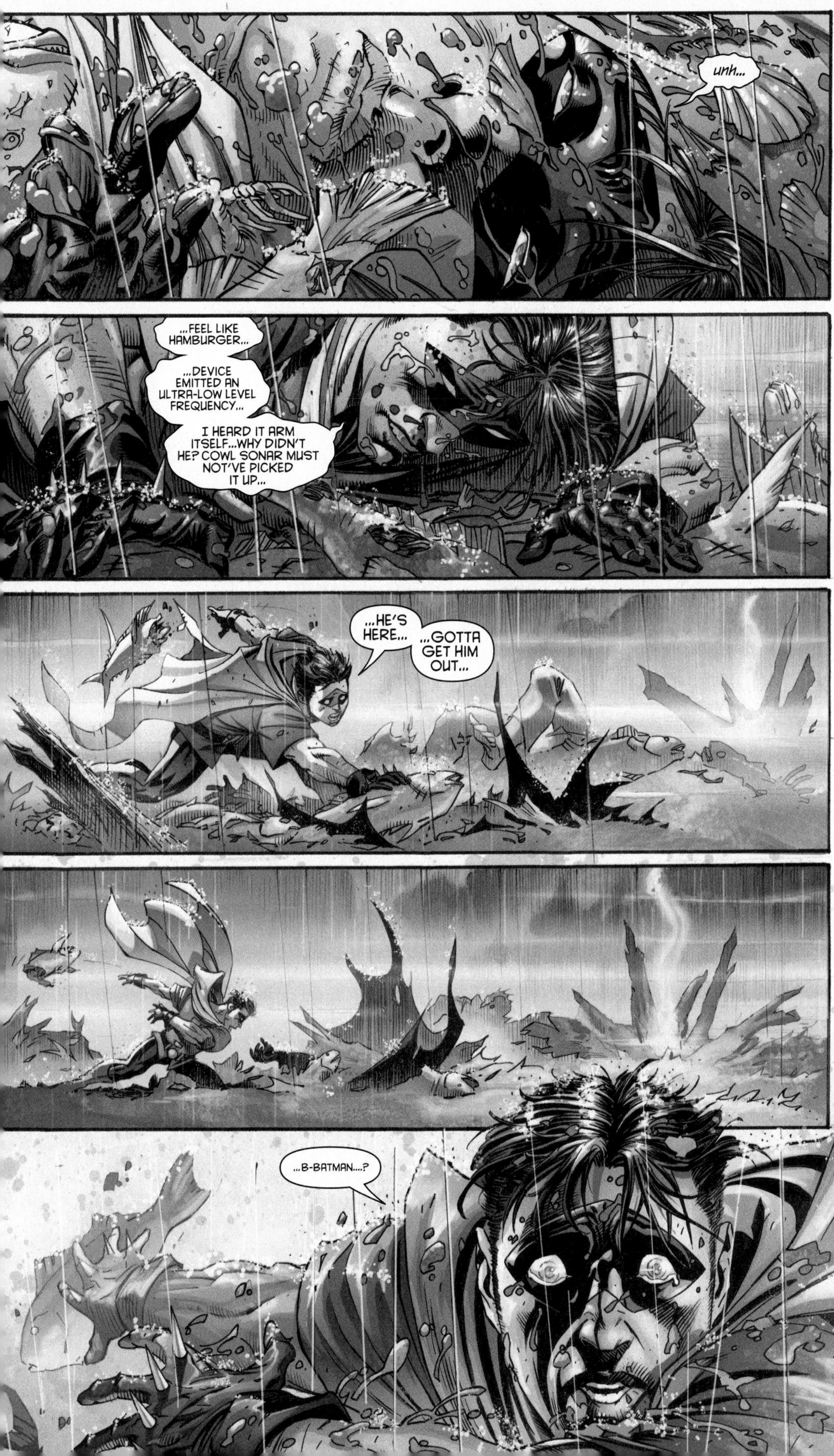
unh...
...FEEL LIKE HAMBURGER...
...DEVICE EMITTED AN ULTRA-LOW LEVEL FREQUENCY...
I HEARD IT ARM ITSELF...WHY DIDN'T HE? COWL SONAR MUST NOT'VE PICKED IT UP...
...HE'S HERE...
...GOTTA GET HIM OUT...
...B-BATMAN...?

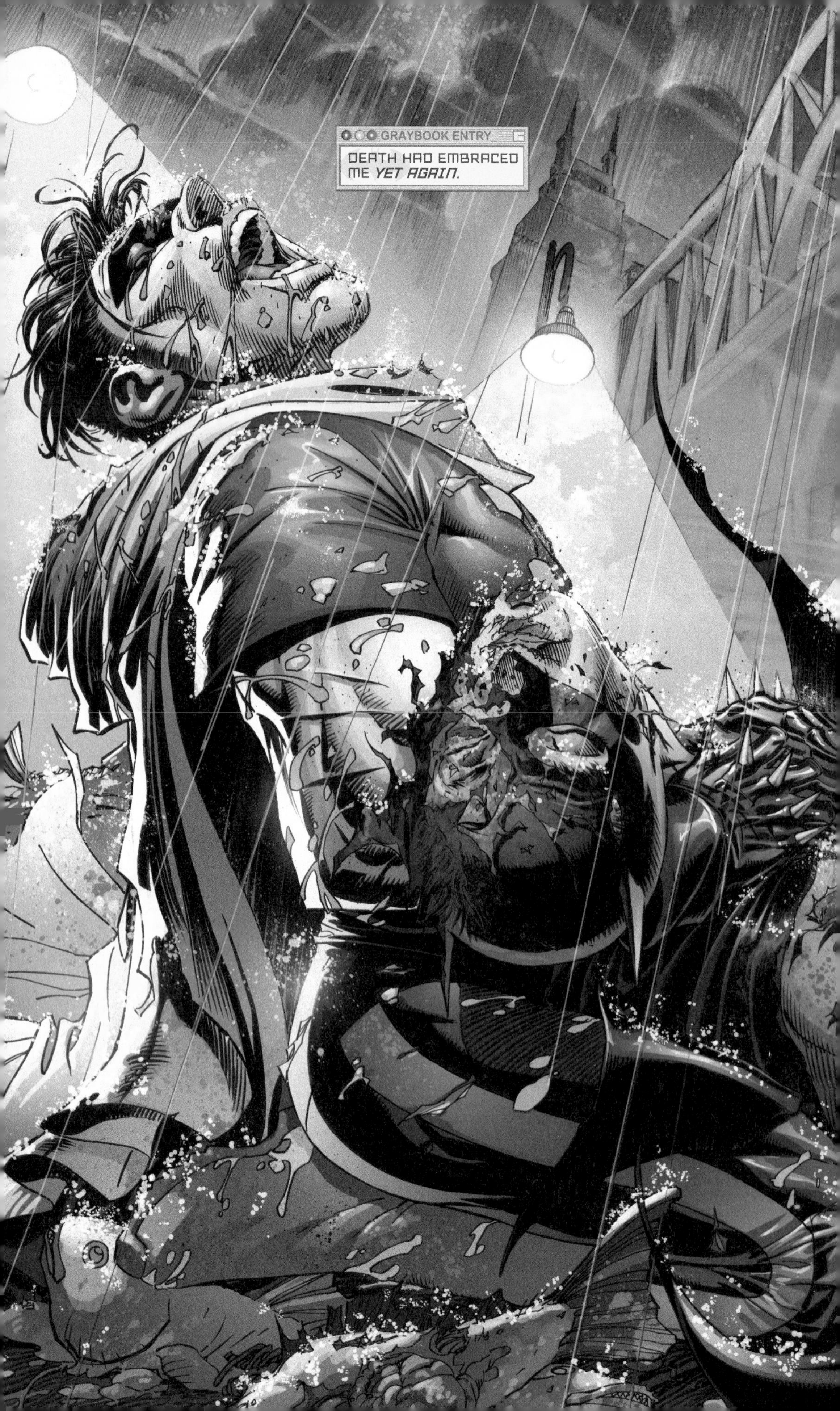
GRAYBOOK ENTRY
DEATH HAD EMBRACED ME YET AGAIN.

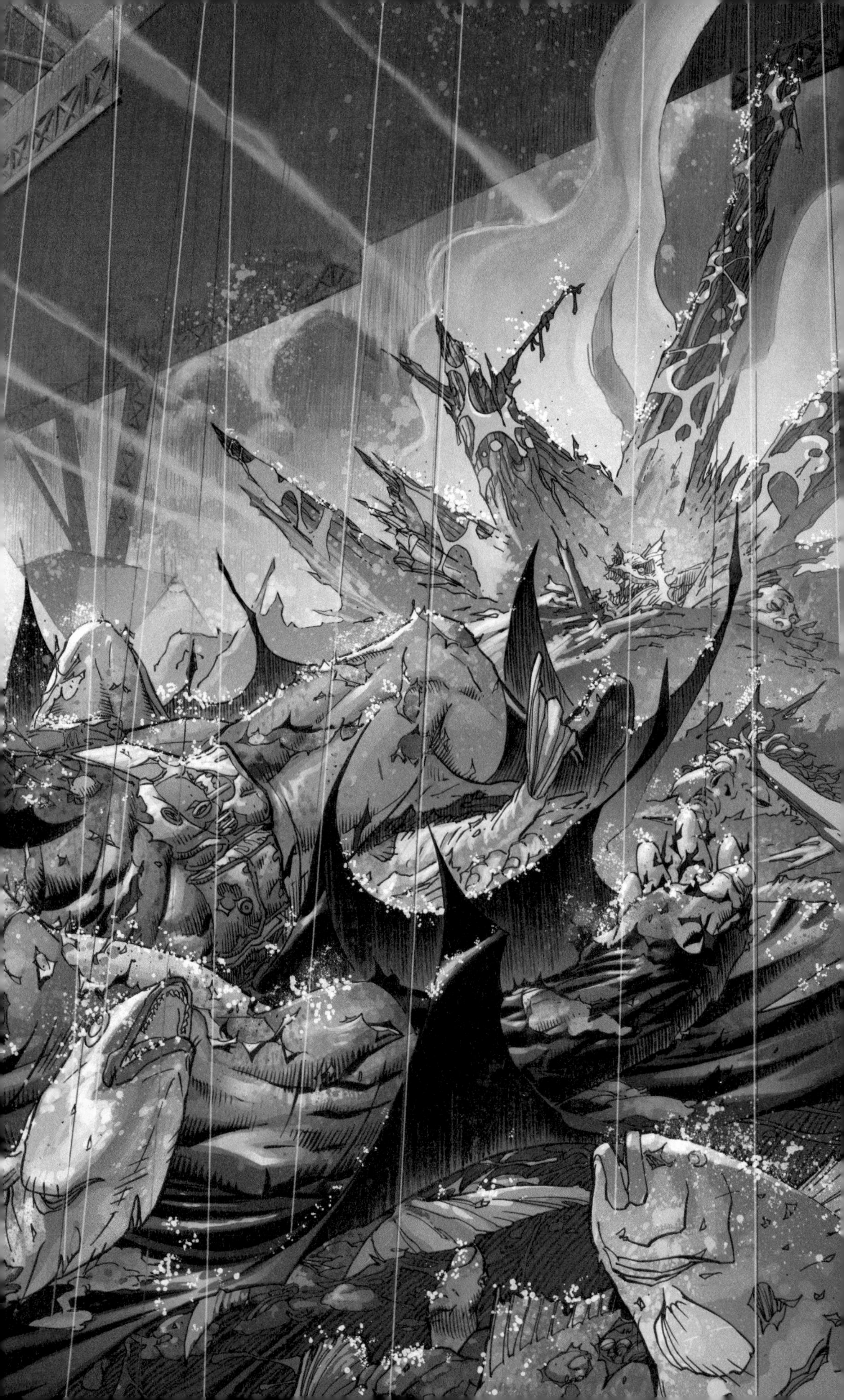

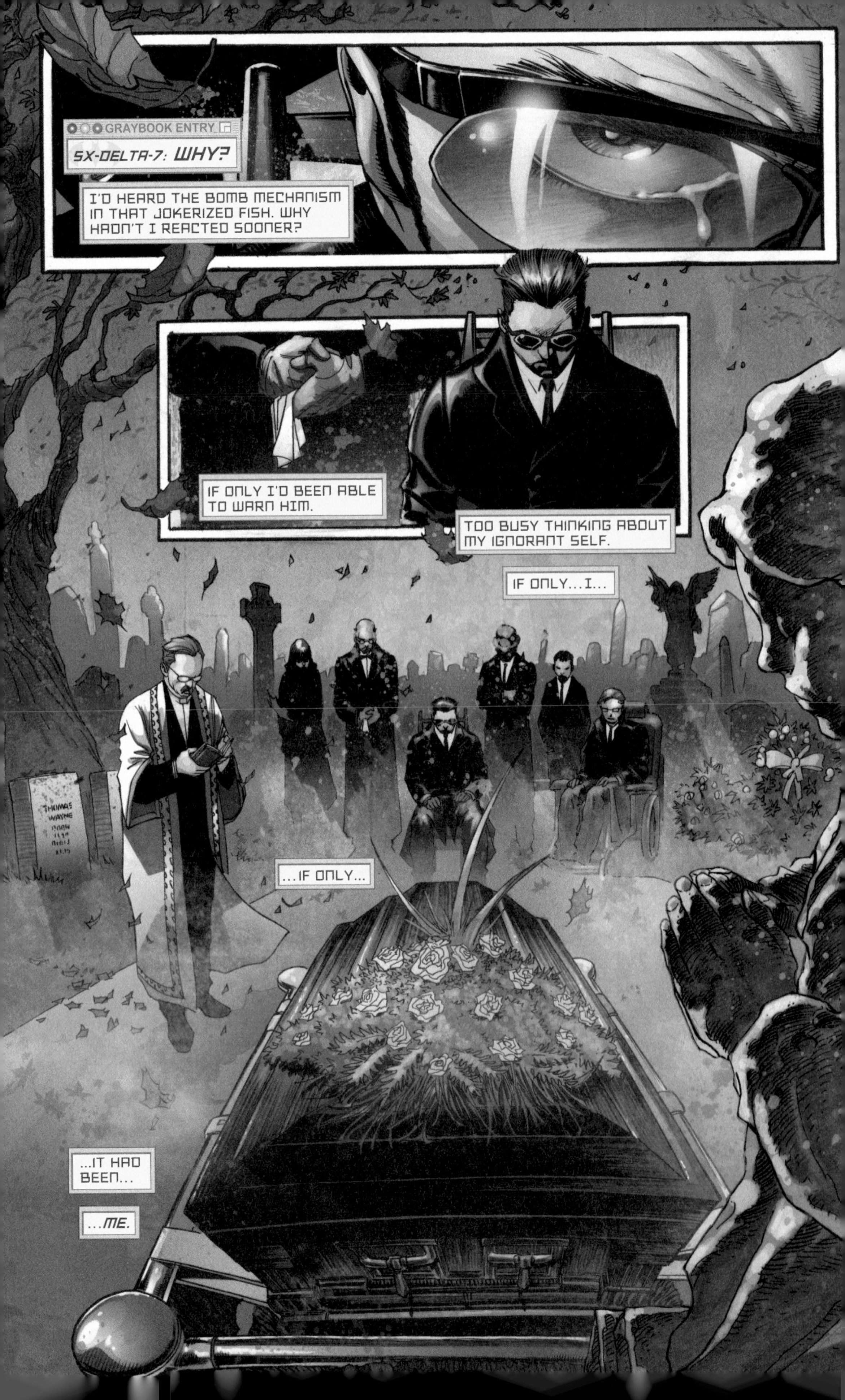
GRAYBOOK ENTRY
SX-DELTA-7: WHY?
I'D HEARD THE BOMB MECHANISM IN THAT JOKERIZED FISH. WHY HADN'T I REACTED SOONER?
IF ONLY I'D BEEN ABLE TO WARN HIM.
TOO BUSY THINKING ABOUT MY IGNORANT SELF.
IF ONLY... I...
THOMAS WAYNE
...IF ONLY...
...IT HAD BEEN...
...ME.

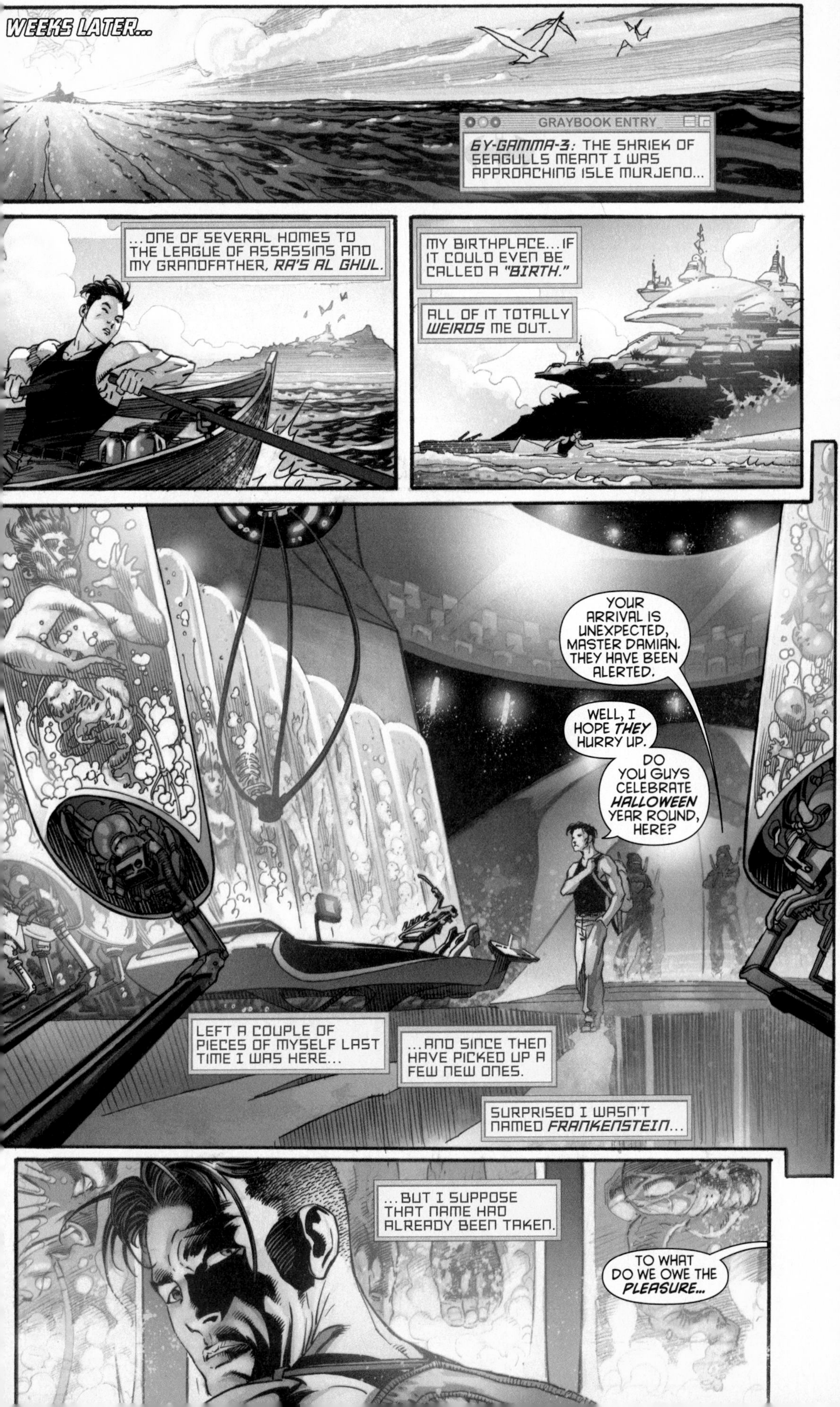
WEEKS LATER...
GRAYBOOK ENTRY
6Y-GAMMA-3: THE SHRIEK OF SEAGULLS MEANT I WAS APPROACHING ISLE MURJENO...
...ONE OF SEVERAL HOMES TO THE LEAGUE OF ASSASSINS AND MY GRANDFATHER, RA'S AL GHUL.
MY BIRTHPLACE...IF IT COULD EVEN BE CALLED A "BIRTH."
ALL OF IT TOTALLY WEIRDS ME OUT.
YOUR ARRIVAL IS UNEXPECTED, MASTER DAMIAN. THEY HAVE BEEN ALERTED.
WELL, I HOPE THEY HURRY UP.
DO YOU GUYS CELEBRATE HALLOWEEN YEAR ROUND, HERE?
LEFT A COUPLE OF PIECES OF MYSELF LAST TIME I WAS HERE...
...AND SINCE THEN HAVE PICKED UP A FEW NEW ONES.
SURPRISED I WASN'T NAMED FRANKENSTEIN...
...BUT I SUPPOSE THAT NAME HAD ALREADY BEEN TAKEN.
TO WHAT DO WE OWE THE PLEASURE...

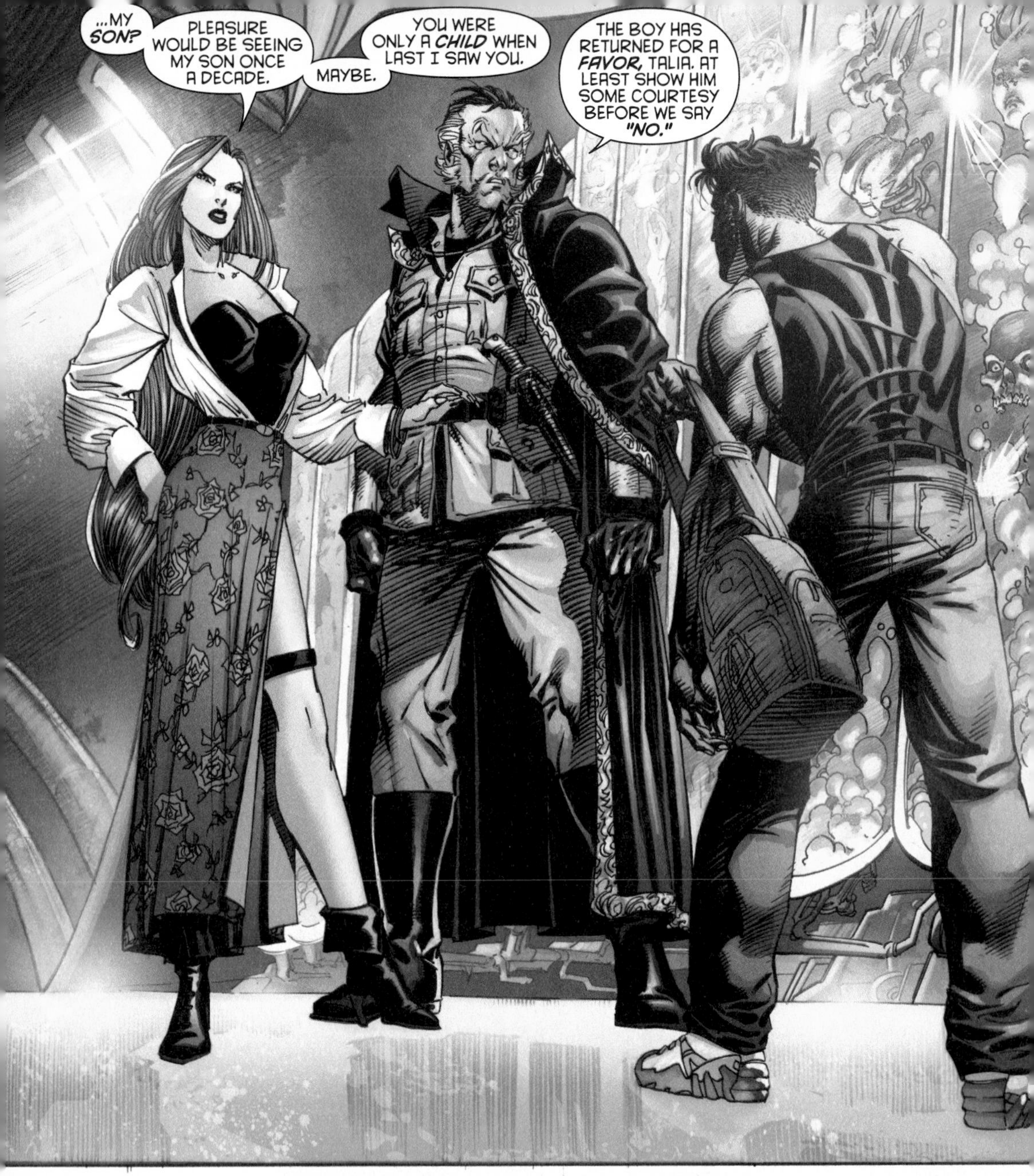
...MY SON?
PLEASURE WOULD BE SEEING MY SON ONCE A DECADE.
MAYBE.
YOU WERE ONLY A CHILD WHEN LAST I SAW YOU.
THE BOY HAS RETURNED FOR A FAVOR, TALIA. AT LEAST SHOW HIM SOME COURTESY BEFORE WE SAY "NO."

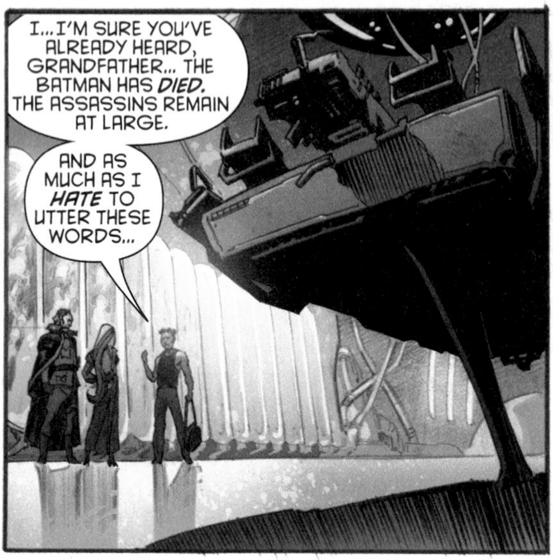
I...I'M SURE YOU'VE ALREADY HEARD, GRANDFATHER... THE BATMAN HAS DIED. THE ASSASSINS REMAIN AT LARGE.
AND AS MUCH AS I HATE TO UTTER THESE WORDS...

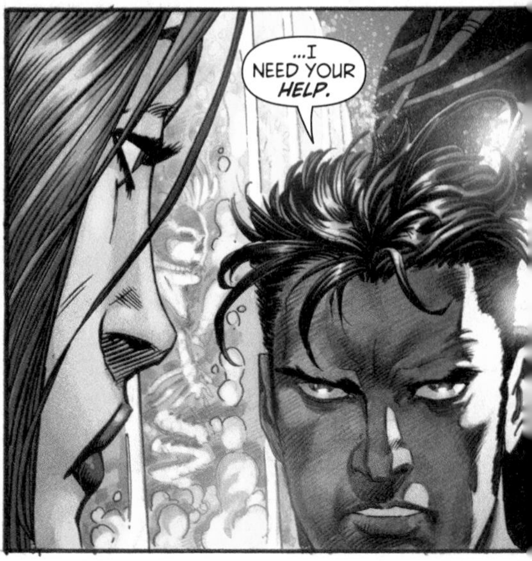
...I NEED YOUR HELP.

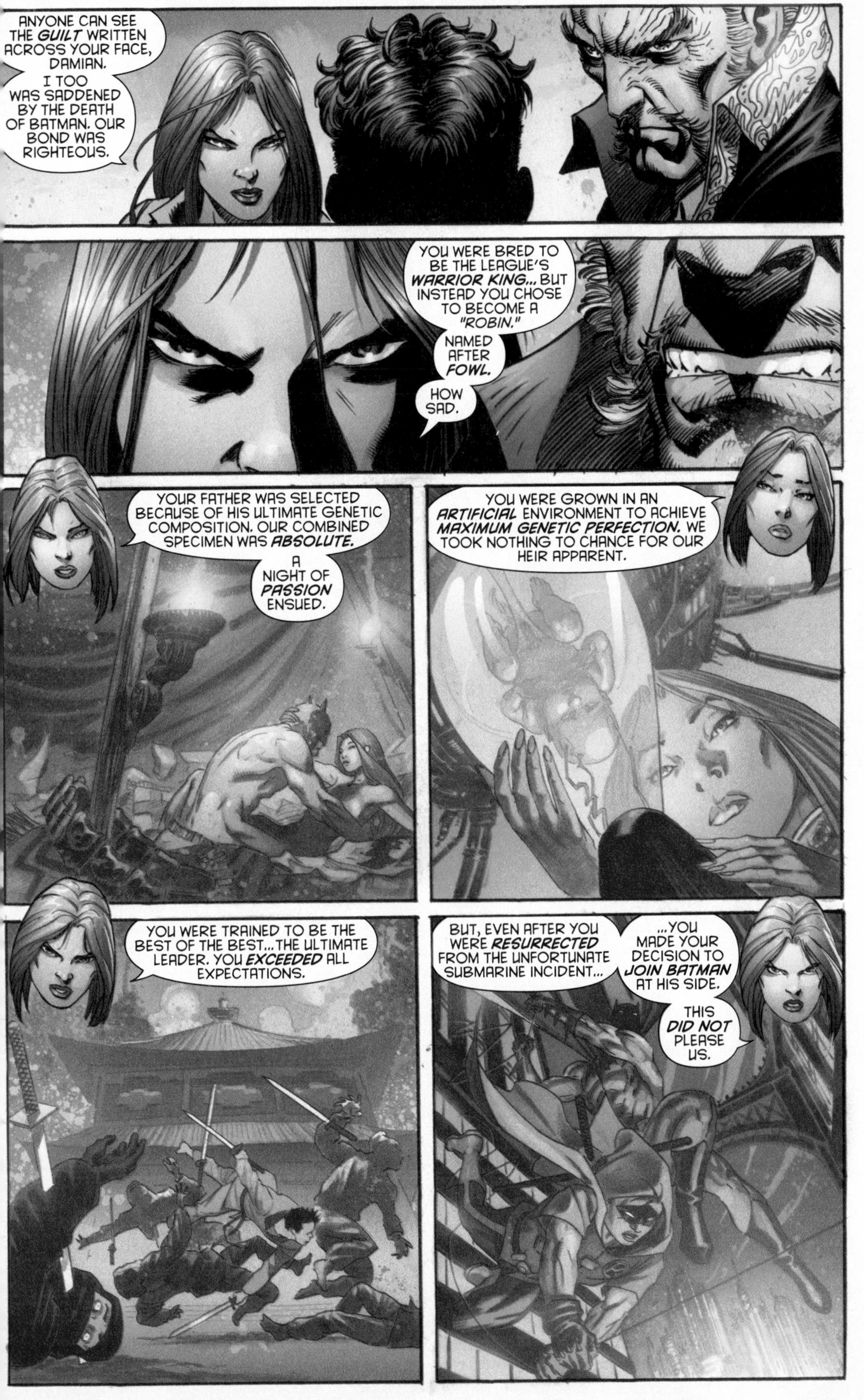
ANYONE CAN SEE THE GUILT WRITTEN ACROSS YOUR FACE, DAMIAN.
I TOO WAS SADDENED BY THE DEATH OF BATMAN. OUR BOND WAS RIGHTEOUS.
YOU WERE BRED TO BE THE LEAGUE'S WARRIOR KING... BUT INSTEAD YOU CHOSE TO BECOME A "ROBIN."
NAMED AFTER FOWL.
HOW SAD.
YOUR FATHER WAS SELECTED BECAUSE OF HIS ULTIMATE GENETIC COMPOSITION. OUR COMBINED SPECIMEN WAS ABSOLUTE.
A NIGHT OF PASSION ENSUED.
YOU WERE GROWN IN AN ARTIFICIAL ENVIRONMENT TO ACHIEVE MAXIMUM GENETIC PERFECTION. WE TOOK NOTHING TO CHANCE FOR OUR HEIR APPARENT.
YOU WERE TRAINED TO BE THE BEST OF THE BEST...THE ULTIMATE LEADER. YOU EXCEEDED ALL EXPECTATIONS.
BUT, EVEN AFTER YOU WERE RESURRECTED FROM THE UNFORTUNATE SUBMARINE INCIDENT...
...YOU MADE YOUR DECISION TO JOIN BATMAN AT HIS SIDE.
THIS DID NOT PLEASE US.

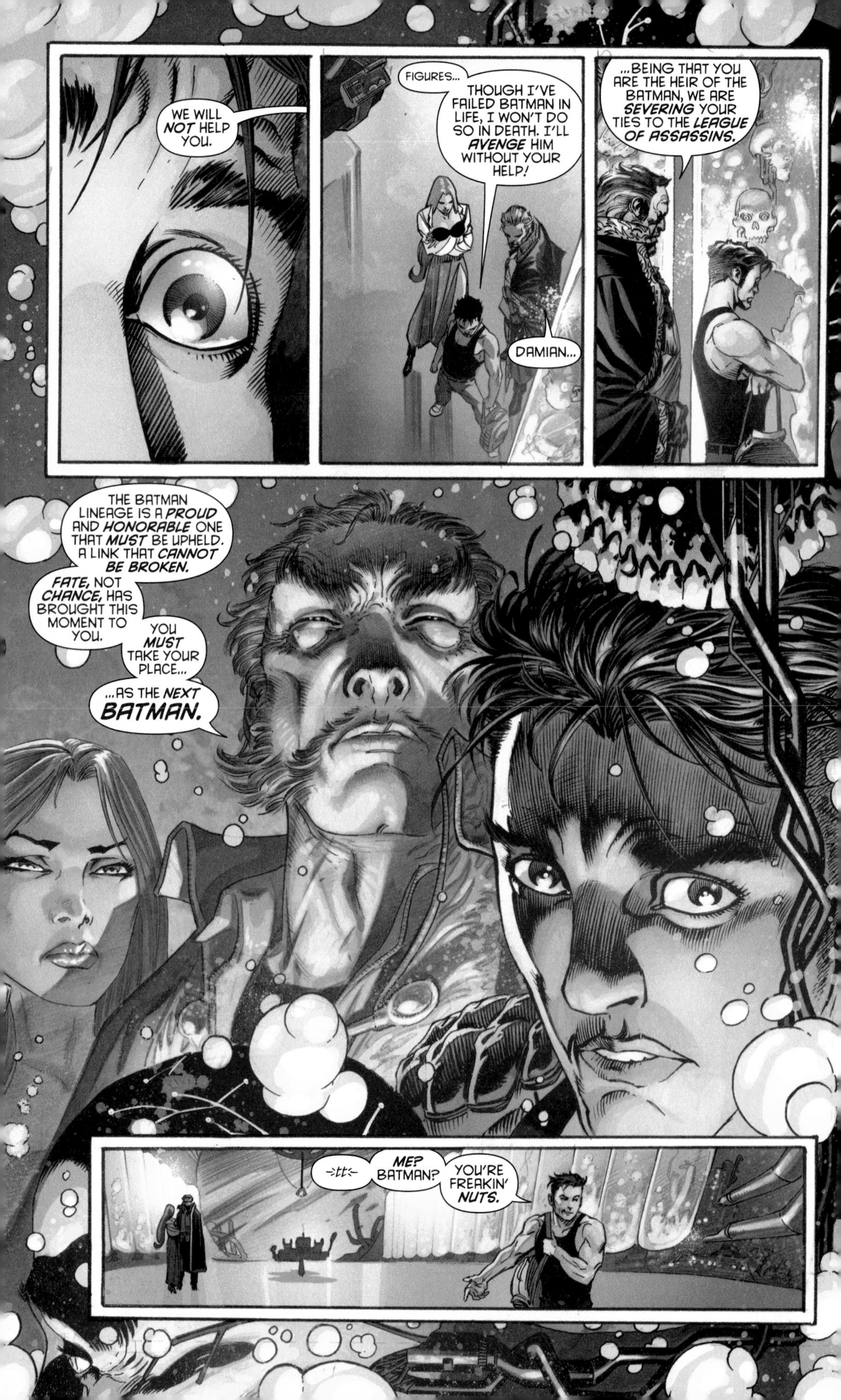

WE WILL NOT HELP YOU.
FIGURES...
THOUGH I'VE FAILED BATMAN IN LIFE, I WON'T DO SO IN DEATH. I'LL AVENGE HIM WITHOUT YOUR HELP!
DAMIAN...
...BEING THAT YOU ARE THE HEIR OF THE BATMAN, WE ARE SEVERING YOUR TIES TO THE LEAGUE OF ASSASSINS.
THE BATMAN LINEAGE IS A PROUD AND HONORABLE ONE THAT MUST BE UPHELD. A LINK THAT CANNOT BE BROKEN.
FATE, NOT CHANCE, HAS BROUGHT THIS MOMENT TO YOU.
YOU MUST TAKE YOUR PLACE...
...AS THE NEXT BATMAN.
-TT-
ME? BATMAN?
YOU'RE FREAKIN' NUTS.

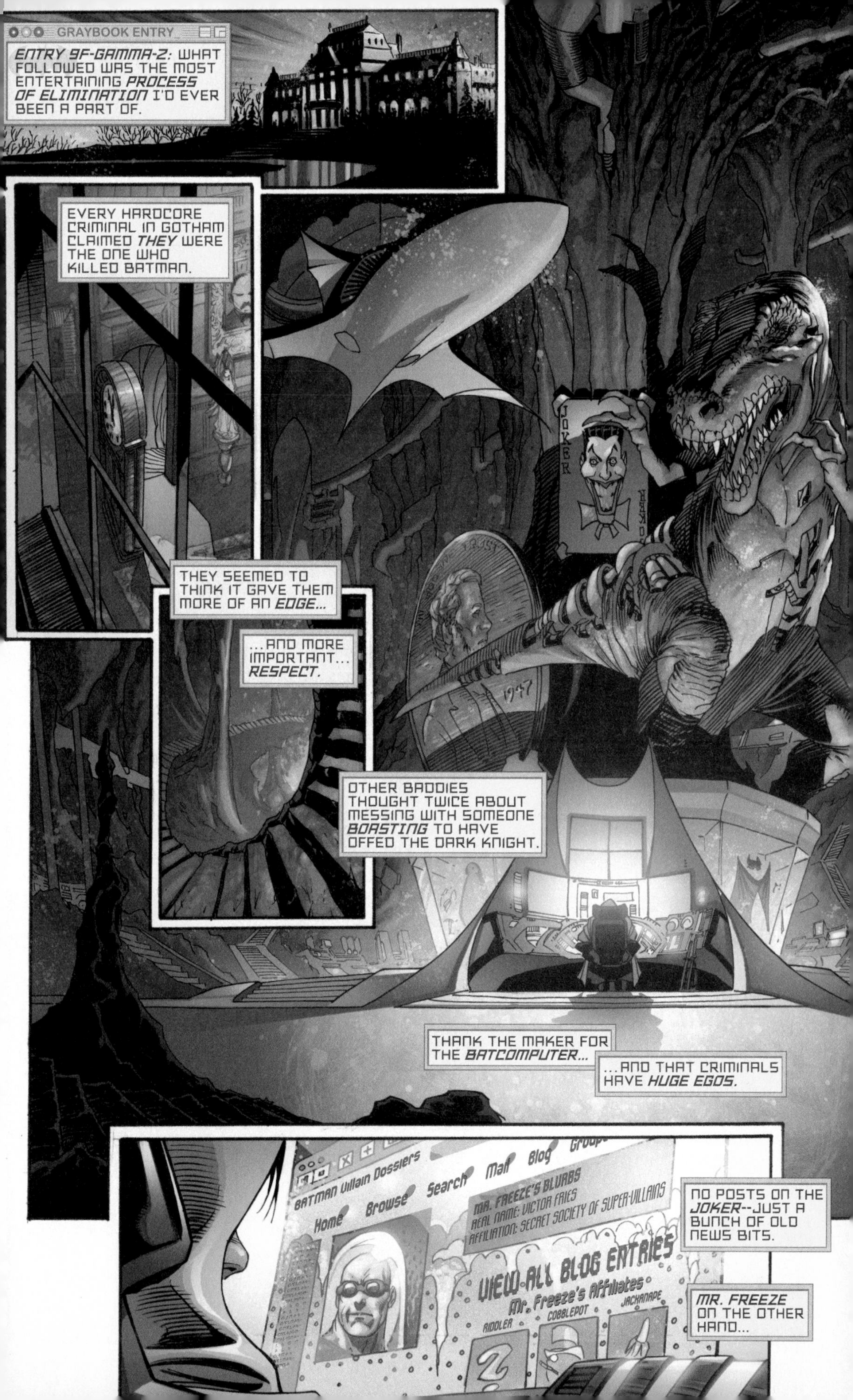
GRAYBOOK ENTRY
ENTRY 9F-GAMMA-Z: WHAT FOLLOWED WAS THE MOST ENTERTAINING PROCESS OF ELIMINATION I'D EVER BEEN A PART OF.
EVERY HARDCORE CRIMINAL IN GOTHAM CLAIMED THEY WERE THE ONE WHO KILLED BATMAN.
JOKER
1947
THEY SEEMED TO THINK IT GAVE THEM MORE OF AN EDGE...
...AND MORE IMPORTANT... RESPECT.
OTHER BADDIES THOUGHT TWICE ABOUT MESSING WITH SOMEONE BOASTING TO HAVE OFFED THE DARK KNIGHT.
THANK THE MAKER FOR THE BATCOMPUTER...
...AND THAT CRIMINALS HAVE HUGE EGOS.
Batman Villain Dossiers
Home
Browse
Search
Mail
Blog
MR. FREEZE'S BLURBS
REAL NAME: VICTOR FRIES
AFFILIATION: SECRET SOCIETY OF SUPER-VILLAINS
VIEW ALL BLOG ENTRIES
Mr. Freeze's Affiliates
RIDDLER
COBBLEPOT
JACKANAPE
NO POSTS ON THE JOKER--JUST A BUNCH OF OLD NEWS BITS.
MR. FREEZE ON THE OTHER HAND...

BATMAN
Villain Dossiers
MR. FREEZE

LIKES 👍 —— SEE ALL ⊗

I ICED THE BATMAN!

THE COLD-HEARTED ONE WINS OUT

ONE...

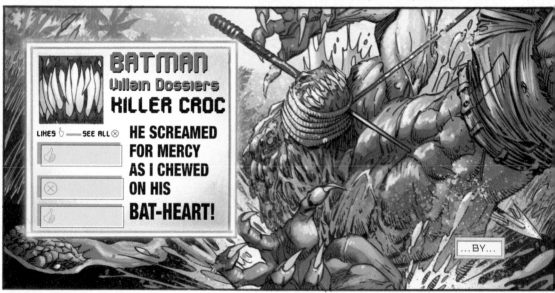

BATMAN
Villain Dossiers
KILLER CROC

LIKES 👍 —— SEE ALL ⊗

HE SCREAMED FOR MERCY AS I CHEWED ON HIS BAT-HEART!

...BY...

50¢ Gotham Gazette OCT

I DID IT!

JACKANAPES CLAIMS RESPONSIBILITY FOR BATMAN'S DEATH

...ONE.

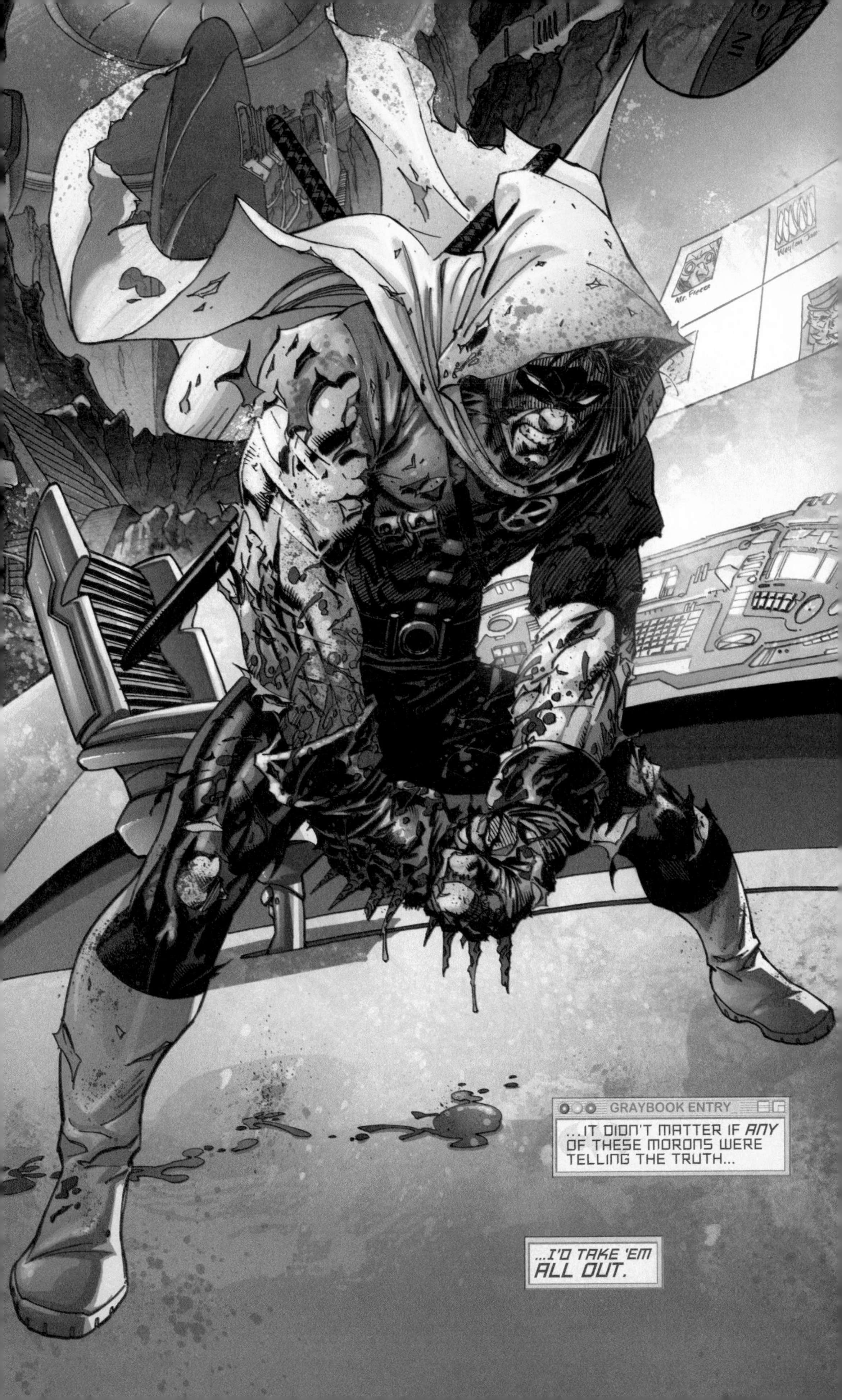
Mr. Freeze
GRAYBOOK ENTRY
...IT DIDN'T MATTER IF ANY OF THESE MORONS WERE TELLING THE TRUTH...
...I'D TAKE 'EM ALL OUT.

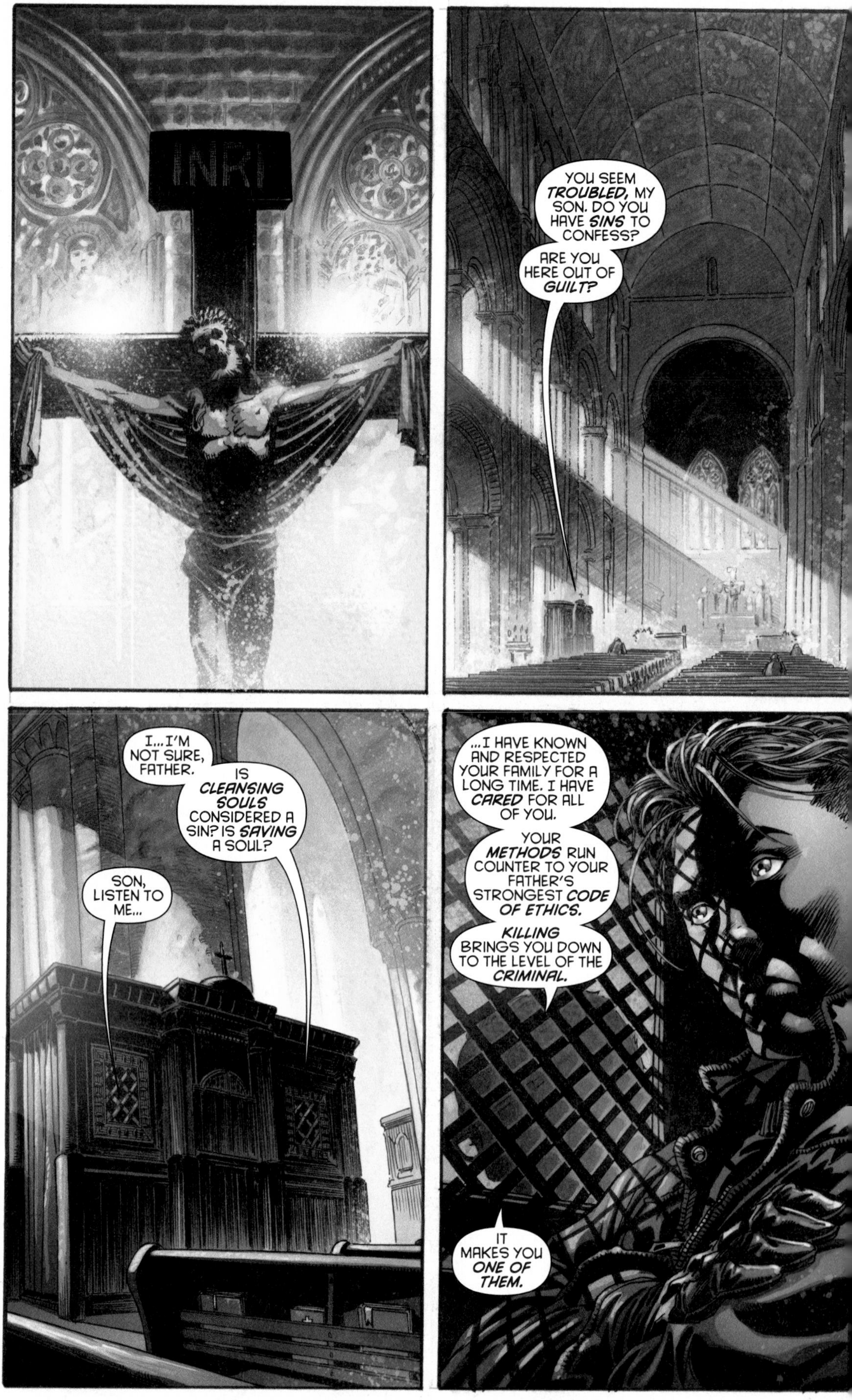

YOU SEEM TROUBLED, MY SON. DO YOU HAVE SINS TO CONFESS?
ARE YOU HERE OUT OF GUILT?
I...I'M NOT SURE, FATHER.
IS CLEANSING SOULS CONSIDERED A SIN? IS SAVING A SOUL?
SON, LISTEN TO ME...
...I HAVE KNOWN AND RESPECTED YOUR FAMILY FOR A LONG TIME. I HAVE CARED FOR ALL OF YOU.
YOUR METHODS RUN COUNTER TO YOUR FATHER'S STRONGEST CODE OF ETHICS.
KILLING BRINGS YOU DOWN TO THE LEVEL OF THE CRIMINAL.
IT MAKES YOU ONE OF THEM.

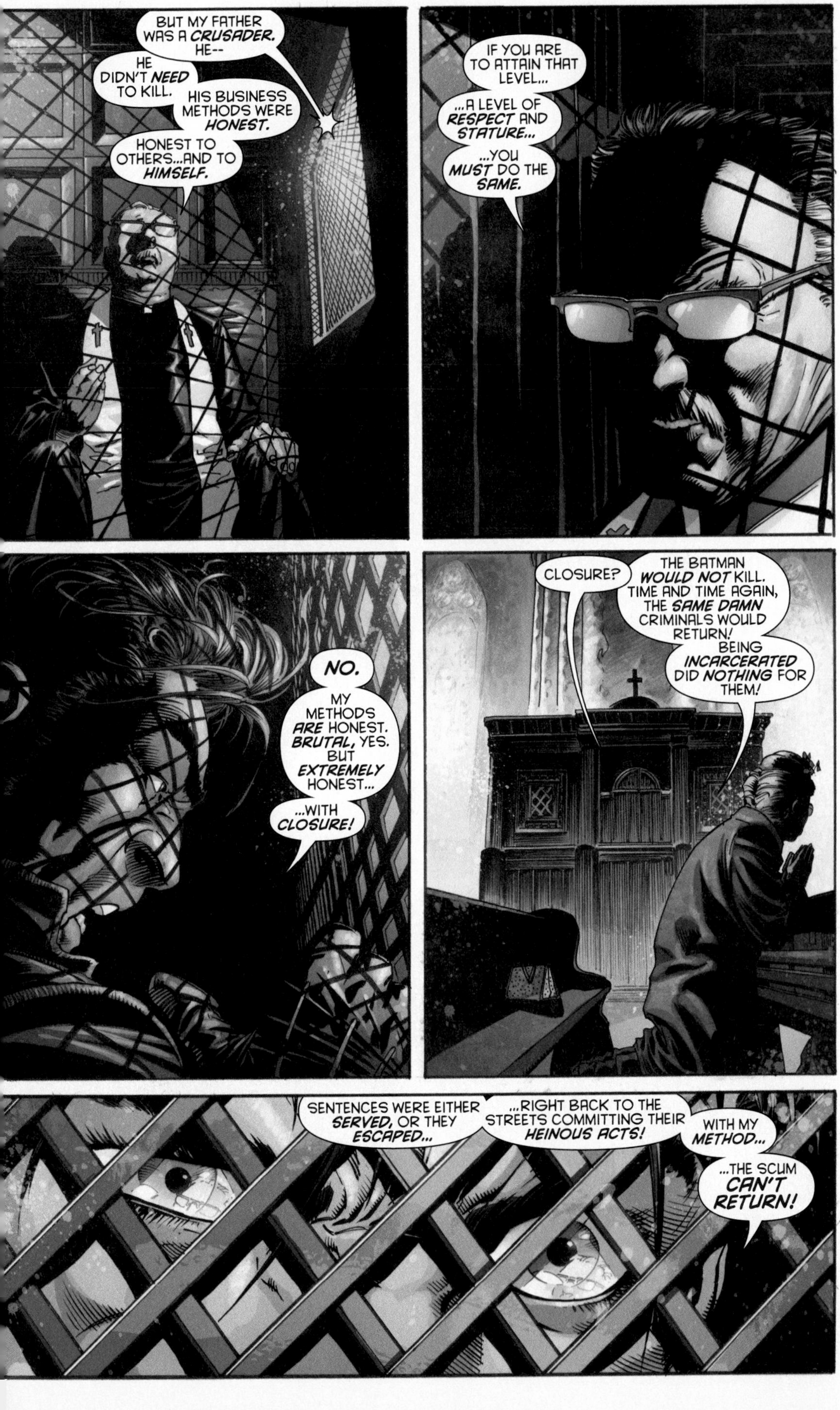
BUT MY FATHER WAS A CRUSADER. HE--
HE DIDN'T NEED TO KILL.
HIS BUSINESS METHODS WERE HONEST.
HONEST TO OTHERS...AND TO HIMSELF.
IF YOU ARE TO ATTAIN THAT LEVEL...
...A LEVEL OF RESPECT AND STATURE...
...YOU MUST DO THE SAME.
NO.
MY METHODS ARE HONEST. BRUTAL, YES. BUT EXTREMELY HONEST...
...WITH CLOSURE!
CLOSURE?
THE BATMAN WOULD NOT KILL. TIME AND TIME AGAIN, THE SAME DAMN CRIMINALS WOULD RETURN!
BEING INCARCERATED DID NOTHING FOR THEM!
SENTENCES WERE EITHER SERVED, OR THEY ESCAPED...
...RIGHT BACK TO THE STREETS COMMITTING THEIR HEINOUS ACTS!
WITH MY METHOD...
...THE SCUM CAN'T RETURN!

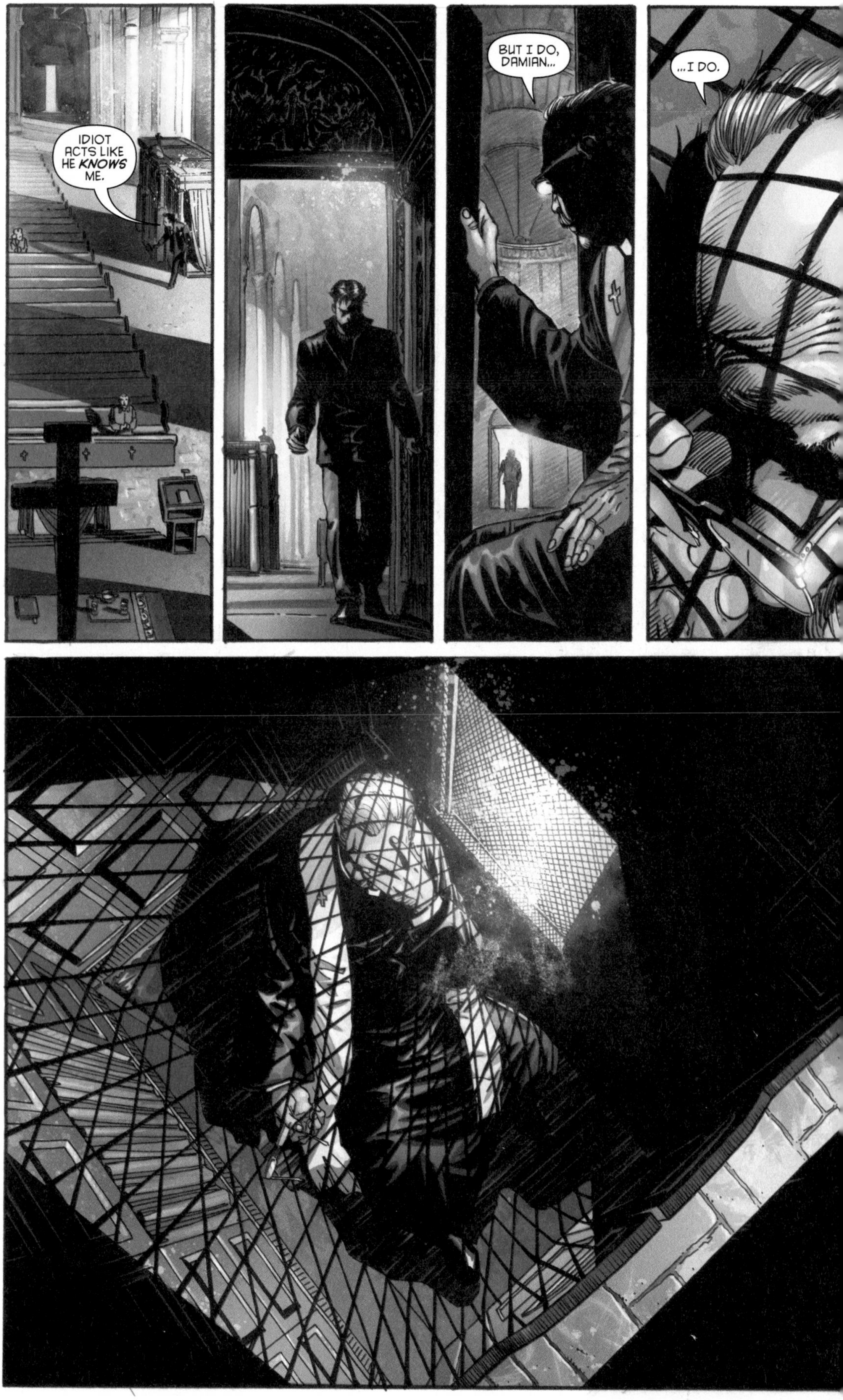
IDIOT ACTS LIKE HE KNOWS ME.
BUT I DO, DAMIAN...
...I DO.

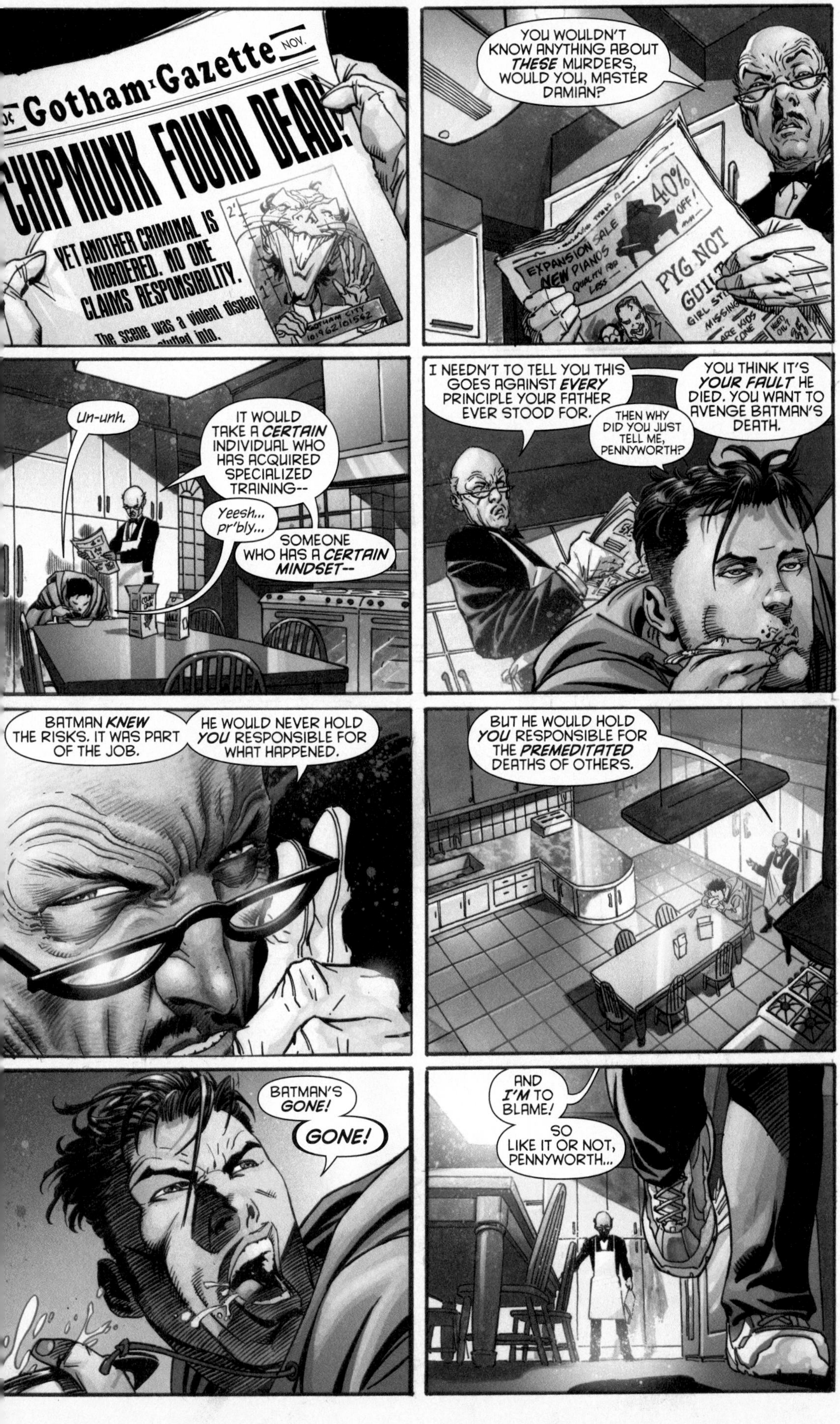

Gotham Gazette
NOV.
CHIPMUNK FOUND DEAD!
YET ANOTHER CRIMINAL IS MURDERED. NO ONE CLAIMS RESPONSIBILITY.
The scene was a violent display
YOU WOULDN'T KNOW ANYTHING ABOUT THESE MURDERS, WOULD YOU, MASTER DAMIAN?
EXPANSION SALE NEW PIANOS QUALITY FOR LESS
40% OFF!
PYG NOT GUILTY
Un-unh.
IT WOULD TAKE A CERTAIN INDIVIDUAL WHO HAS ACQUIRED SPECIALIZED TRAINING--
Yeesh... pr'bly...
SOMEONE WHO HAS A CERTAIN MINDSET--
I NEEDN'T TO TELL YOU THIS GOES AGAINST EVERY PRINCIPLE YOUR FATHER EVER STOOD FOR.
THEN WHY DID YOU JUST TELL ME, PENNYWORTH?
YOU THINK IT'S YOUR FAULT HE DIED. YOU WANT TO AVENGE BATMAN'S DEATH.
BATMAN KNEW THE RISKS. IT WAS PART OF THE JOB.
HE WOULD NEVER HOLD YOU RESPONSIBLE FOR WHAT HAPPENED.
BUT HE WOULD HOLD YOU RESPONSIBLE FOR THE PREMEDITATED DEATHS OF OTHERS.
BATMAN'S GONE!
GONE!
AND I'M TO BLAME!
SO LIKE IT OR NOT, PENNYWORTH...

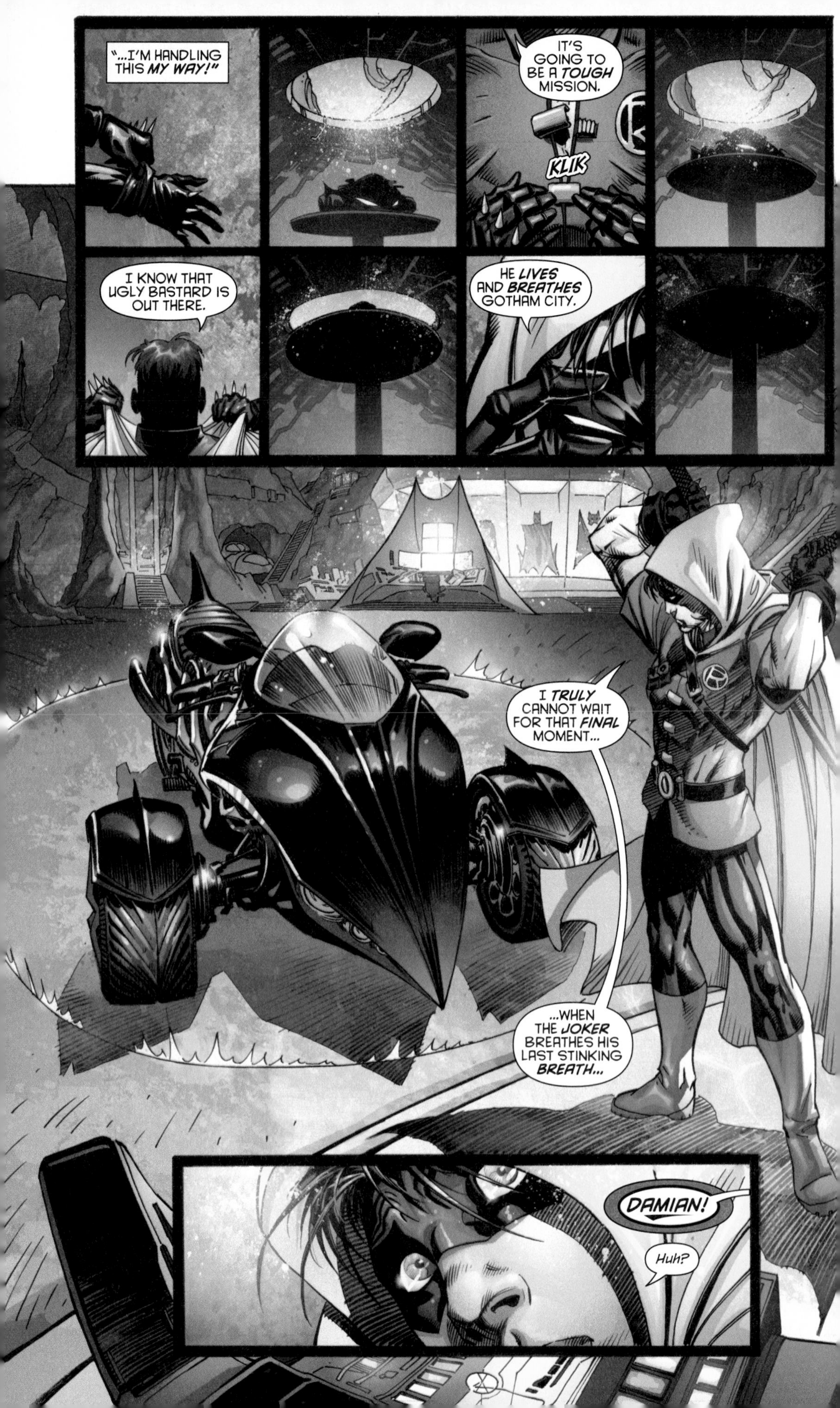

"...I'M HANDLING THIS MY WAY!"
IT'S GOING TO BE A TOUGH MISSION.
KLIK
I KNOW THAT UGLY BASTARD IS OUT THERE.
HE LIVES AND BREATHES GOTHAM CITY.
I TRULY CANNOT WAIT FOR THAT FINAL MOMENT...
...WHEN THE JOKER BREATHES HIS LAST STINKING BREATH...
DAMIAN!
Huh?

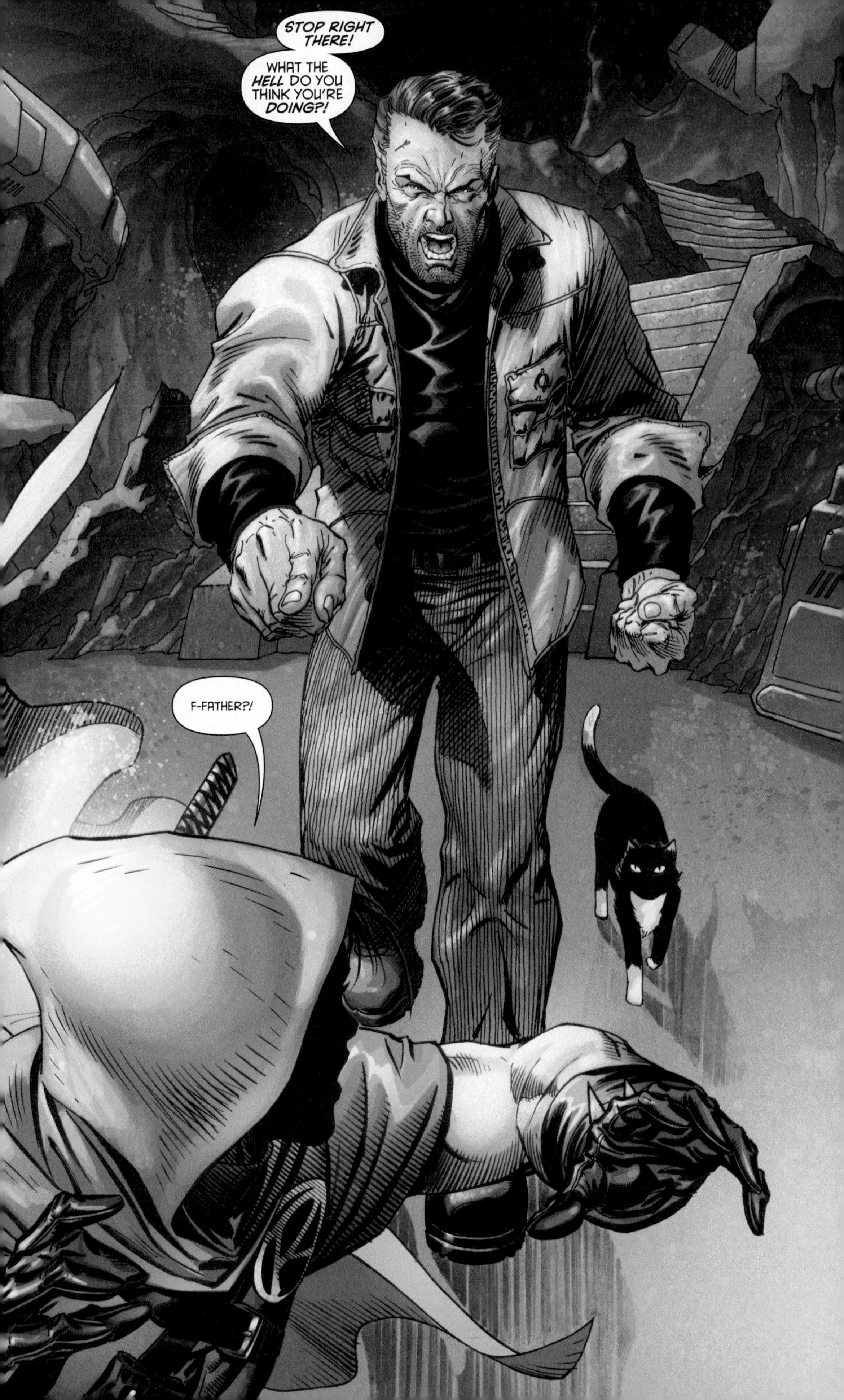
STOP RIGHT THERE!
WHAT THE HELL DO YOU THINK YOU'RE DOING?!
F-FATHER?!

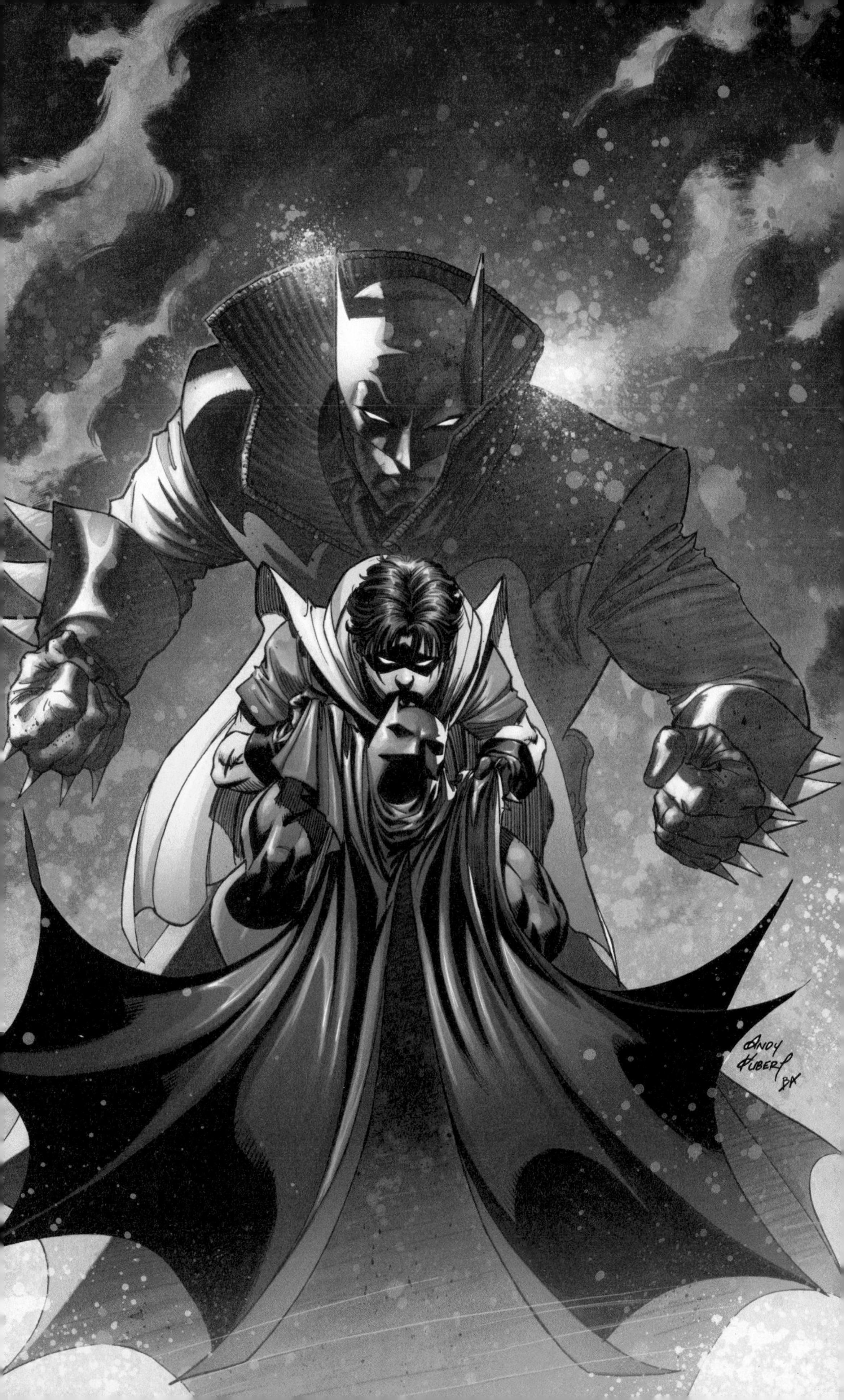
ANDY KUBERT
BA

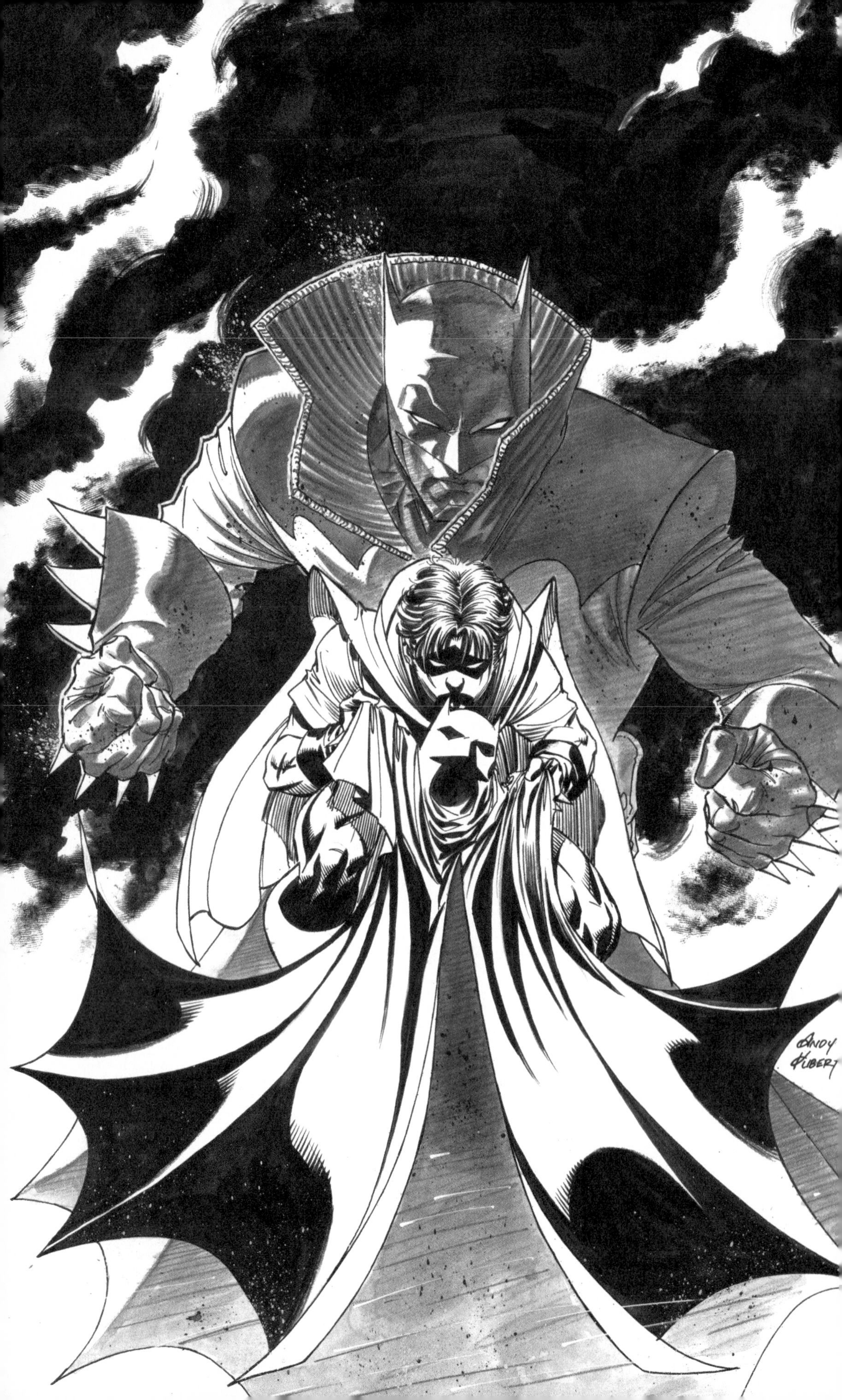
ANDY KUBERT

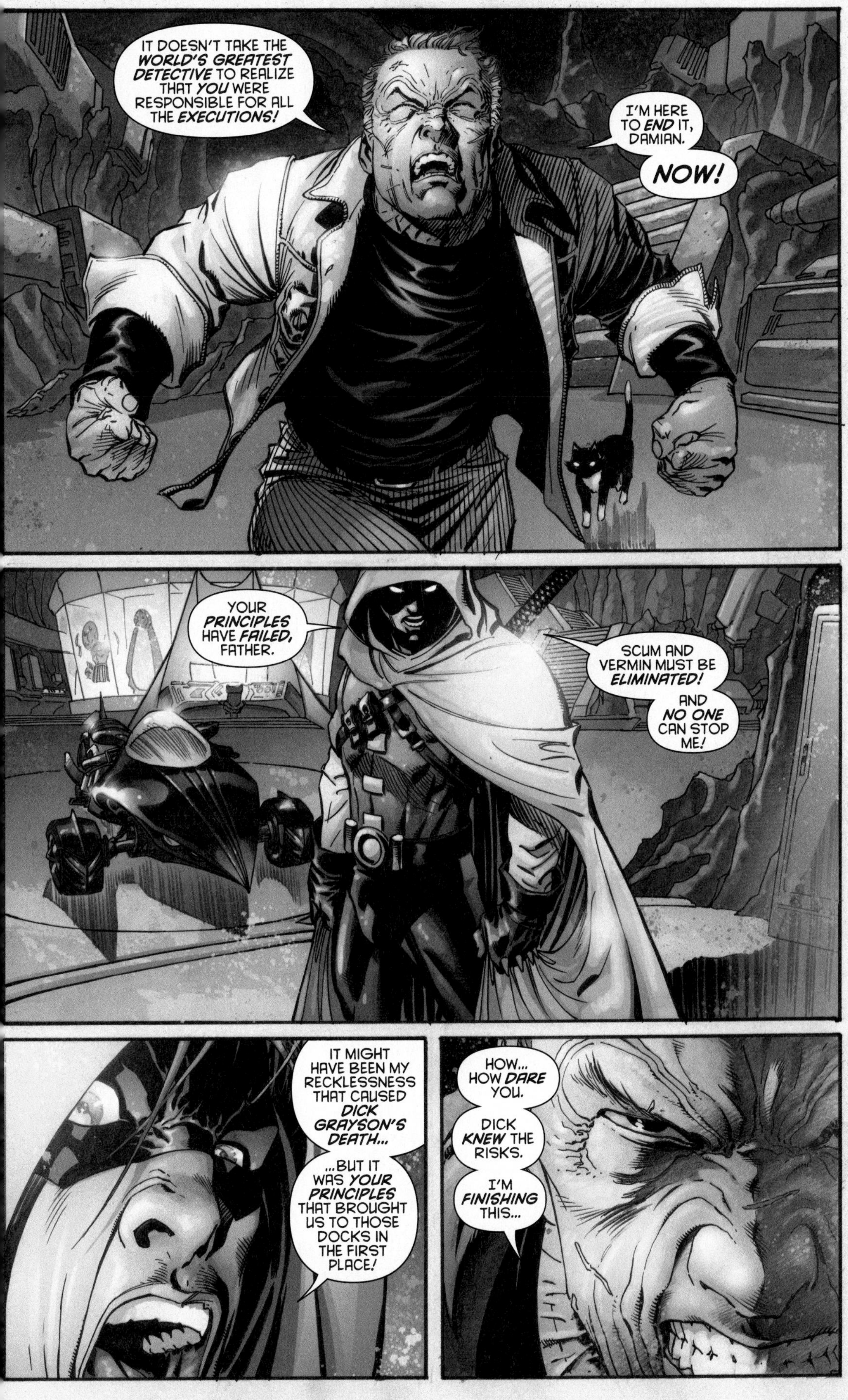
IT DOESN'T TAKE THE WORLD'S GREATEST DETECTIVE TO REALIZE THAT YOU WERE RESPONSIBLE FOR ALL THE EXECUTIONS!
I'M HERE TO END IT, DAMIAN.
NOW!
YOUR PRINCIPLES HAVE FAILED, FATHER.
SCUM AND VERMIN MUST BE ELIMINATED!
AND NO ONE CAN STOP ME!
IT MIGHT HAVE BEEN MY RECKLESSNESS THAT CAUSED DICK GRAYSON'S DEATH...
...BUT IT WAS YOUR PRINCIPLES THAT BROUGHT US TO THOSE DOCKS IN THE FIRST PLACE!
HOW... HOW DARE YOU.
DICK KNEW THE RISKS.
I'M FINISHING THIS...

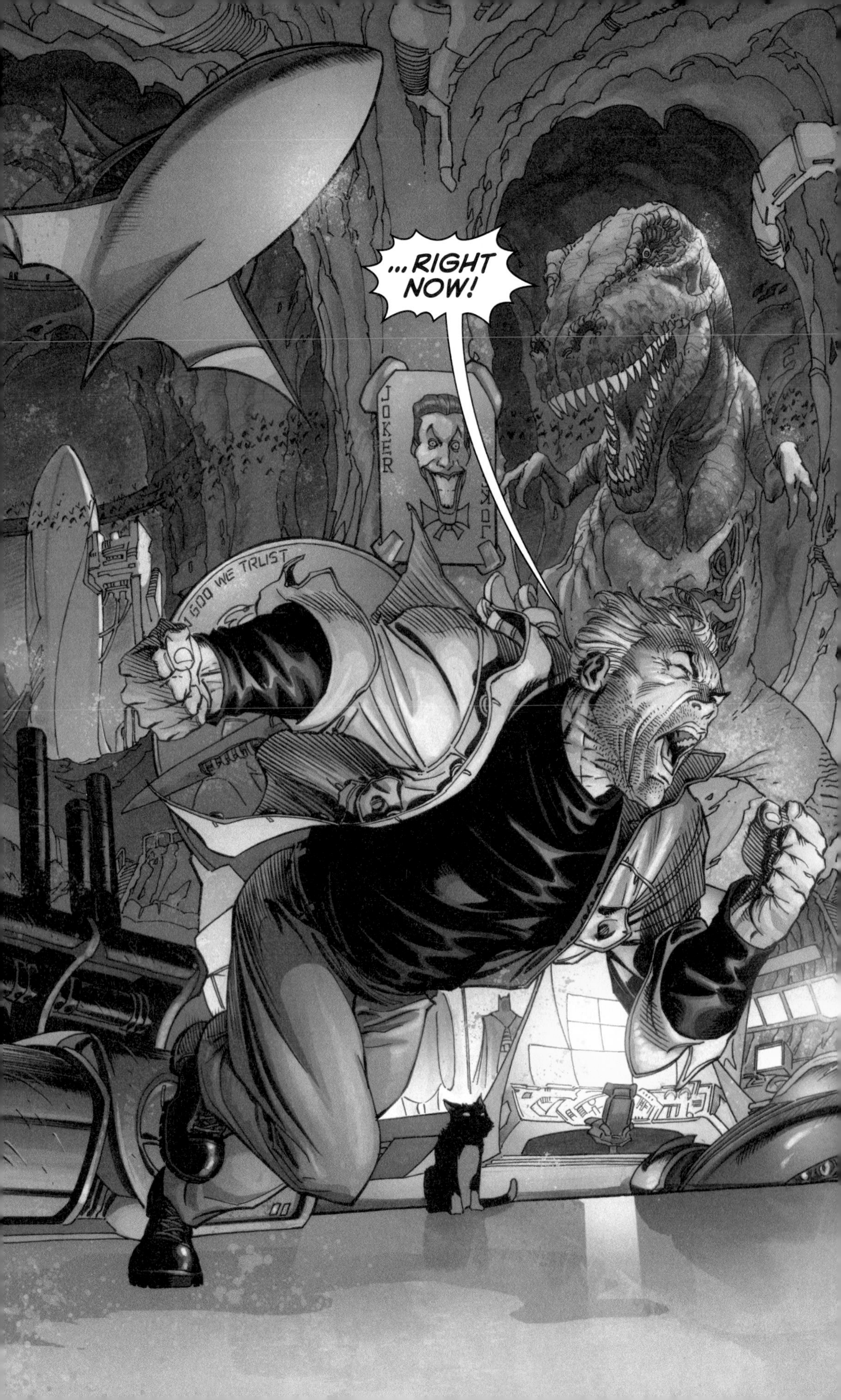
...RIGHT NOW!
JOKER
GOD WE TRUST

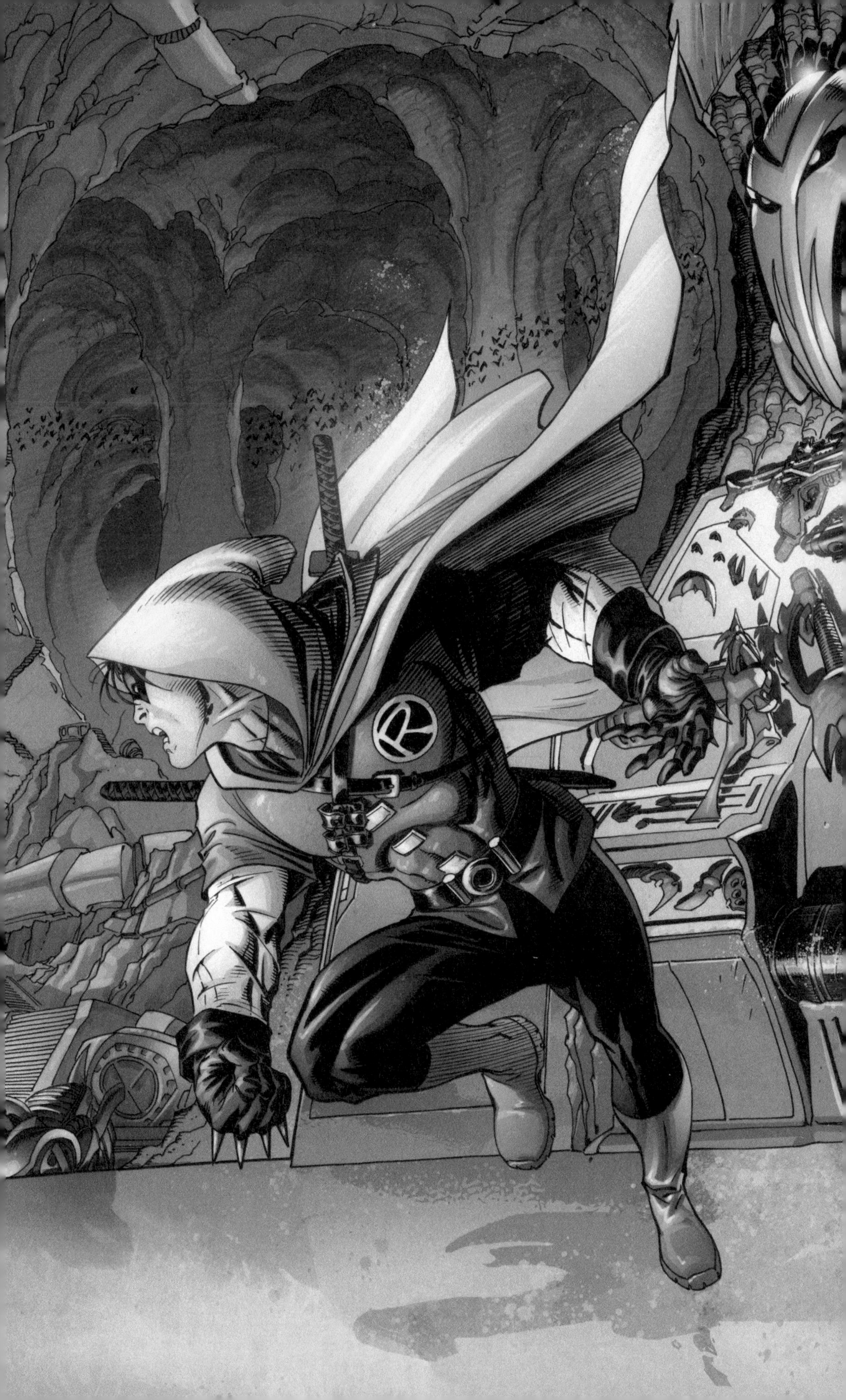

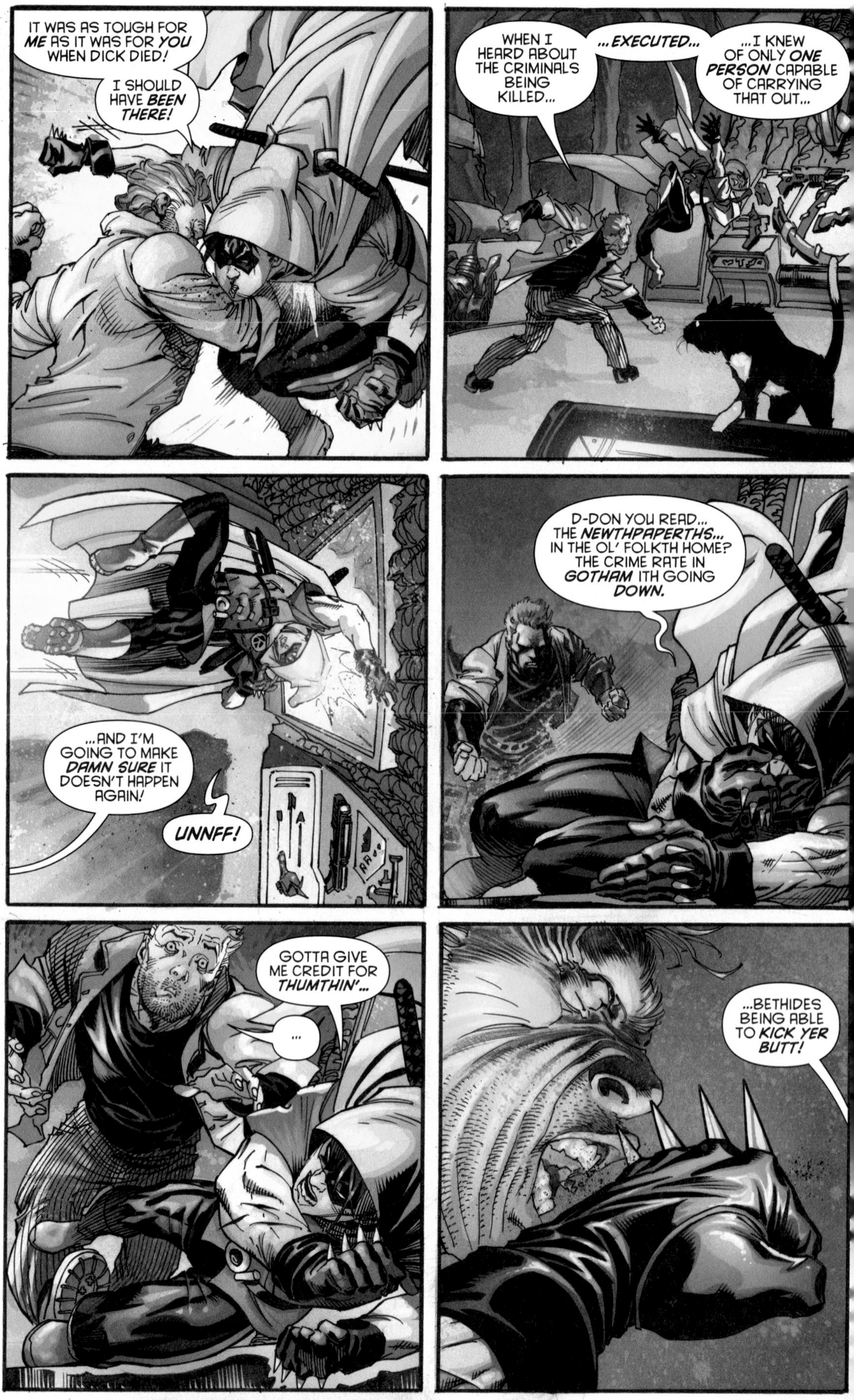
IT WAS AS TOUGH FOR ME AS IT WAS FOR YOU WHEN DICK DIED!
I SHOULD HAVE BEEN THERE!
WHEN I HEARD ABOUT THE CRIMINALS BEING KILLED...
...EXECUTED...
...I KNEW OF ONLY ONE PERSON CAPABLE OF CARRYING THAT OUT...
...AND I'M GOING TO MAKE DAMN SURE IT DOESN'T HAPPEN AGAIN!
UNNFF!
D-DON YOU READ... THE NEWTHPAPERTHS... IN THE OL' FOLKTH HOME? THE CRIME RATE IN GOTHAM ITH GOING DOWN.
GOTTA GIVE ME CREDIT FOR THUMTHIN'...
...
...BETHIDES BEING ABLE TO KICK YER BUTT!

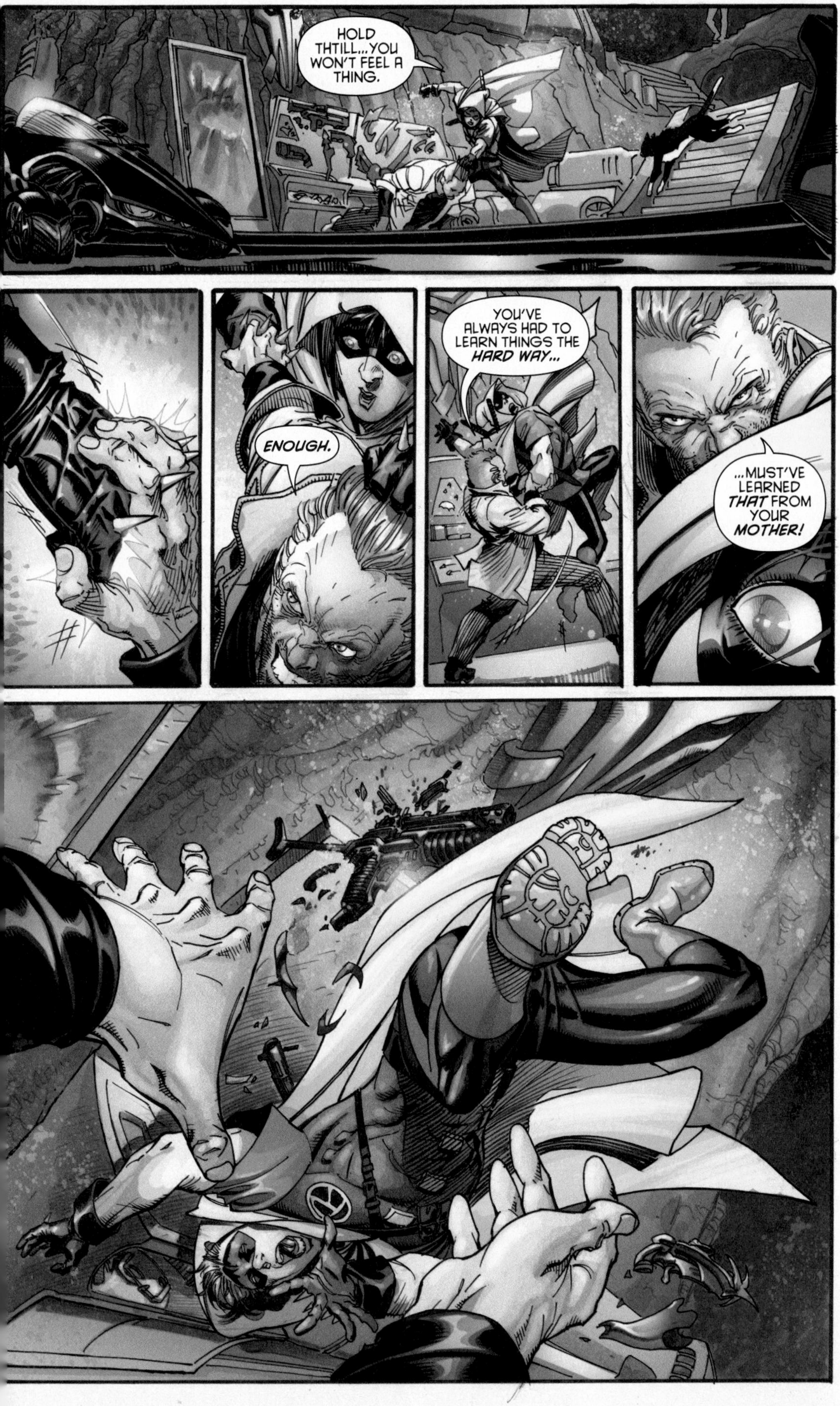
HOLD THTILL...YOU WON'T FEEL A THING.
ENOUGH.
YOU'VE ALWAYS HAD TO LEARN THINGS THE HARD WAY...
...MUST'VE LEARNED THAT FROM YOUR MOTHER!

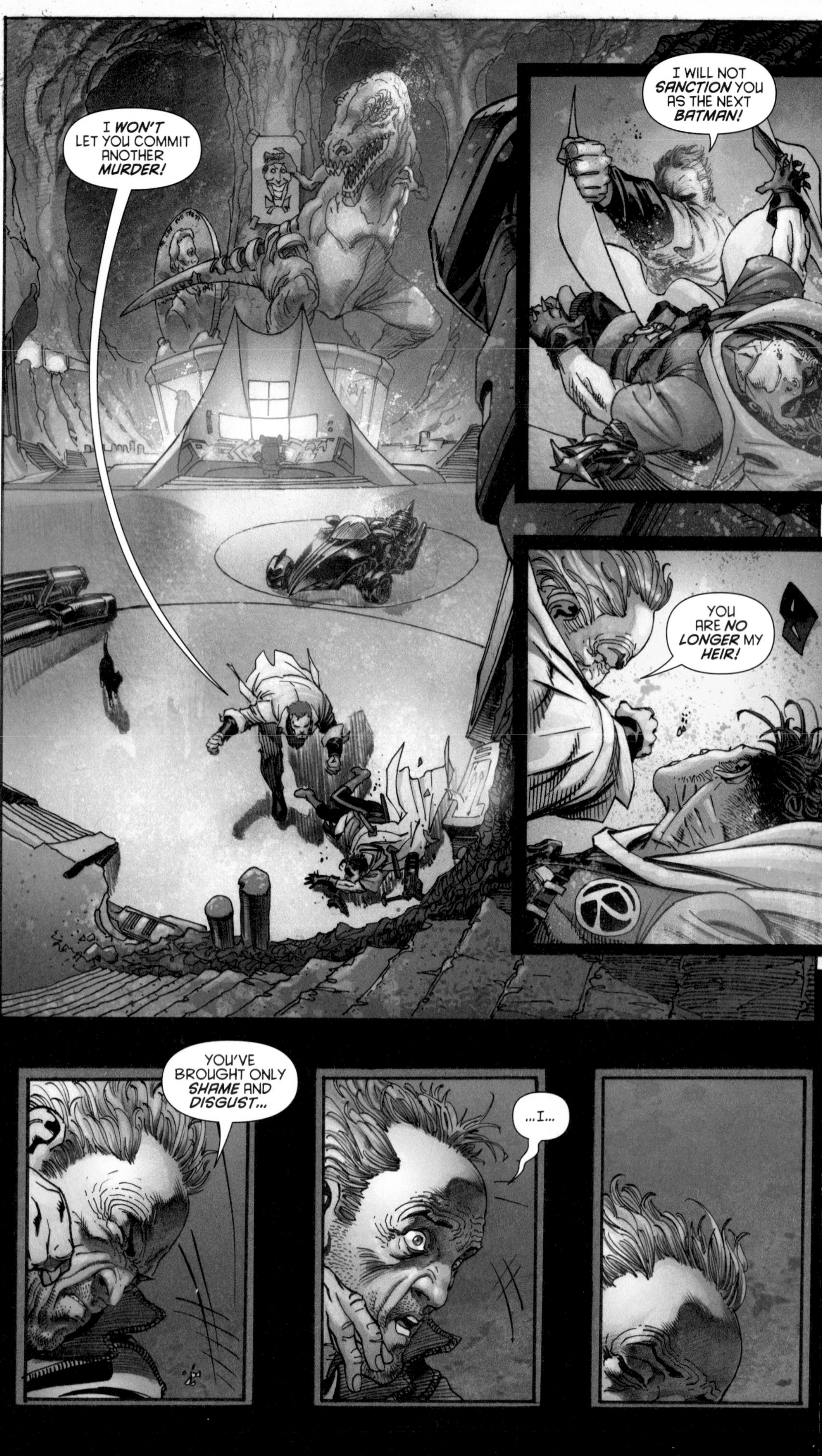

I WON'T LET YOU COMMIT ANOTHER MURDER!
I WILL NOT SANCTION YOU AS THE NEXT BATMAN!
YOU ARE NO LONGER MY HEIR!
YOU'VE BROUGHT ONLY SHAME AND DISGUST...
...I...

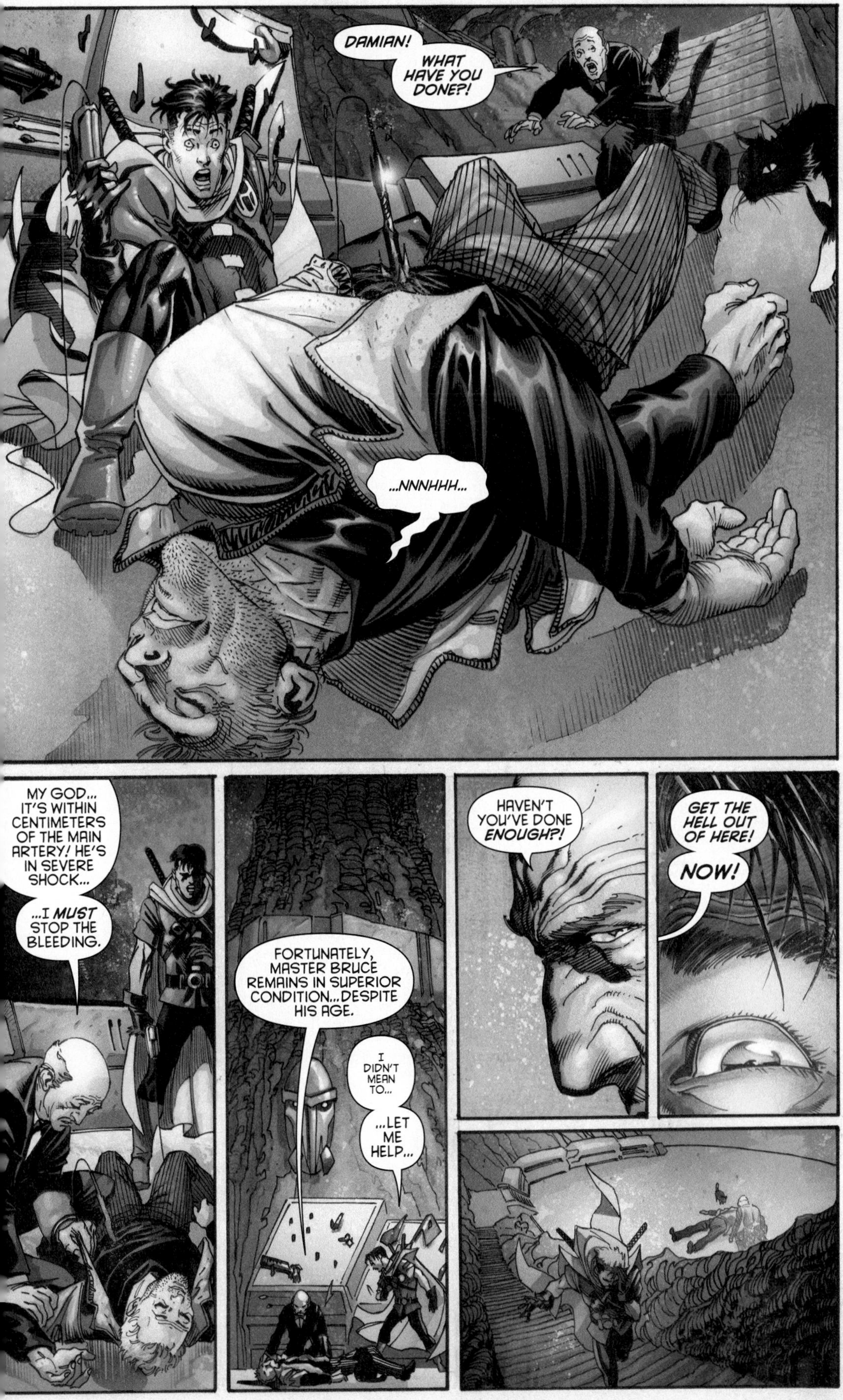
DAMIAN!
WHAT HAVE YOU DONE?!
...NNNHHH...
MY GOD... IT'S WITHIN CENTIMETERS OF THE MAIN ARTERY! HE'S IN SEVERE SHOCK...
...I MUST STOP THE BLEEDING.
FORTUNATELY, MASTER BRUCE REMAINS IN SUPERIOR CONDITION...DESPITE HIS AGE.
I DIDN'T MEAN TO...
...LET ME HELP...
HAVEN'T YOU'VE DONE ENOUGH?!
GET THE HELL OUT OF HERE!
NOW!

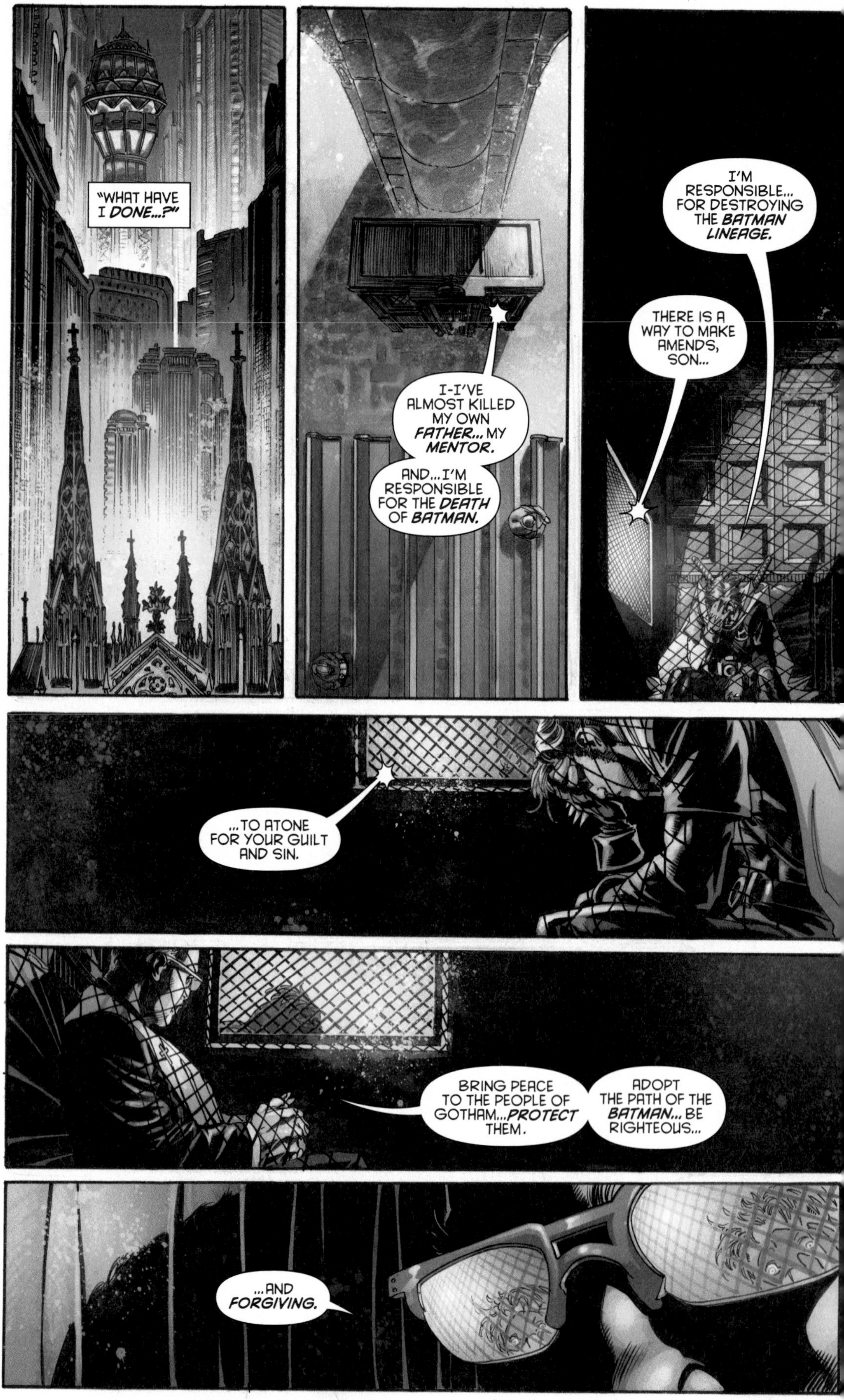
"WHAT HAVE I DONE...?"
I-I'VE ALMOST KILLED MY OWN FATHER... MY MENTOR.
AND... I'M RESPONSIBLE FOR THE DEATH OF BATMAN.
I'M RESPONSIBLE... FOR DESTROYING THE BATMAN LINEAGE.
THERE IS A WAY TO MAKE AMENDS, SON...
...TO ATONE FOR YOUR GUILT AND SIN.
ADOPT THE PATH OF THE BATMAN... BE RIGHTEOUS...
BRING PEACE TO THE PEOPLE OF GOTHAM...PROTECT THEM.
...AND FORGIVING.

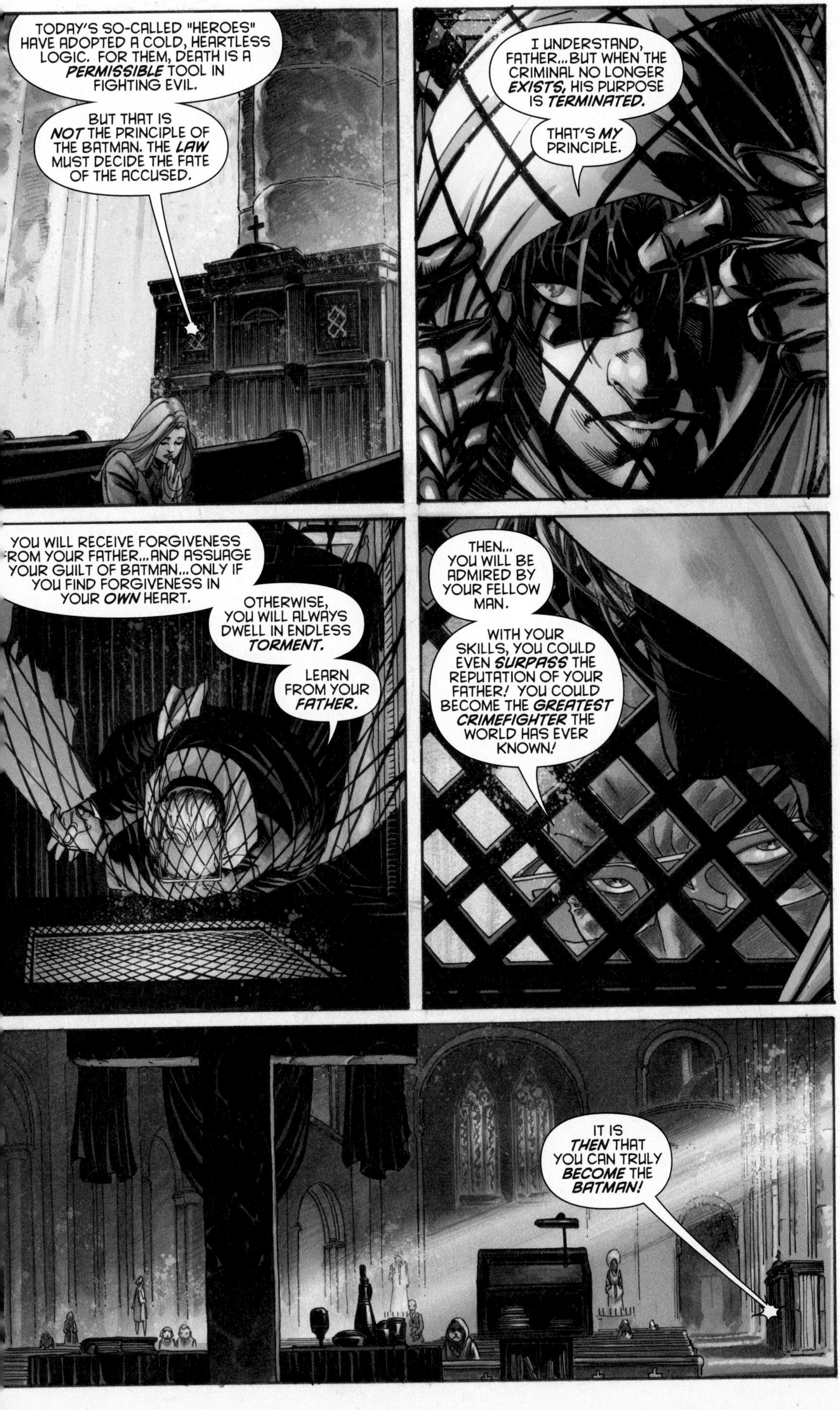

TODAY'S SO-CALLED "HEROES" HAVE ADOPTED A COLD, HEARTLESS LOGIC. FOR THEM, DEATH IS A *PERMISSIBLE* TOOL IN FIGHTING EVIL.
BUT THAT IS *NOT* THE PRINCIPLE OF THE BATMAN. THE *LAW* MUST DECIDE THE FATE OF THE ACCUSED.
I UNDERSTAND, FATHER... BUT WHEN THE CRIMINAL NO LONGER *EXISTS,* HIS PURPOSE IS *TERMINATED.*
THAT'S *MY* PRINCIPLE.
YOU WILL RECEIVE FORGIVENESS FROM YOUR FATHER... AND ASSUAGE YOUR GUILT OF BATMAN... ONLY IF YOU FIND FORGIVENESS IN YOUR *OWN* HEART.
OTHERWISE, YOU WILL ALWAYS DWELL IN ENDLESS *TORMENT.*
LEARN FROM YOUR *FATHER.*
THEN... YOU WILL BE ADMIRED BY YOUR FELLOW MAN.
WITH YOUR SKILLS, YOU COULD EVEN *SURPASS* THE REPUTATION OF YOUR FATHER! YOU COULD BECOME THE *GREATEST CRIMEFIGHTER* THE WORLD HAS EVER KNOWN!
IT IS *THEN* THAT YOU CAN TRULY *BECOME* THE *BATMAN!*

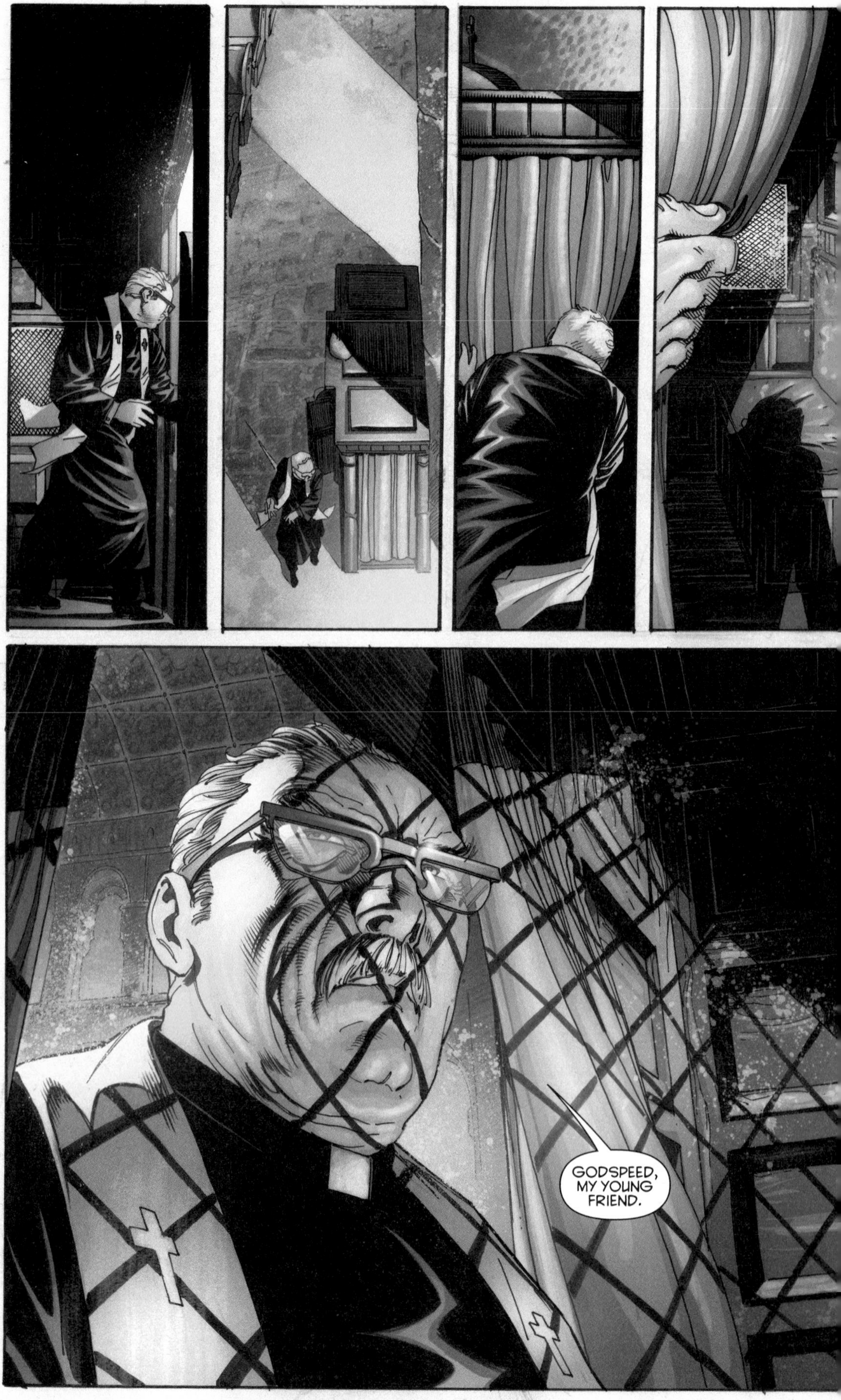
GODSPEED, MY YOUNG FRIEND.

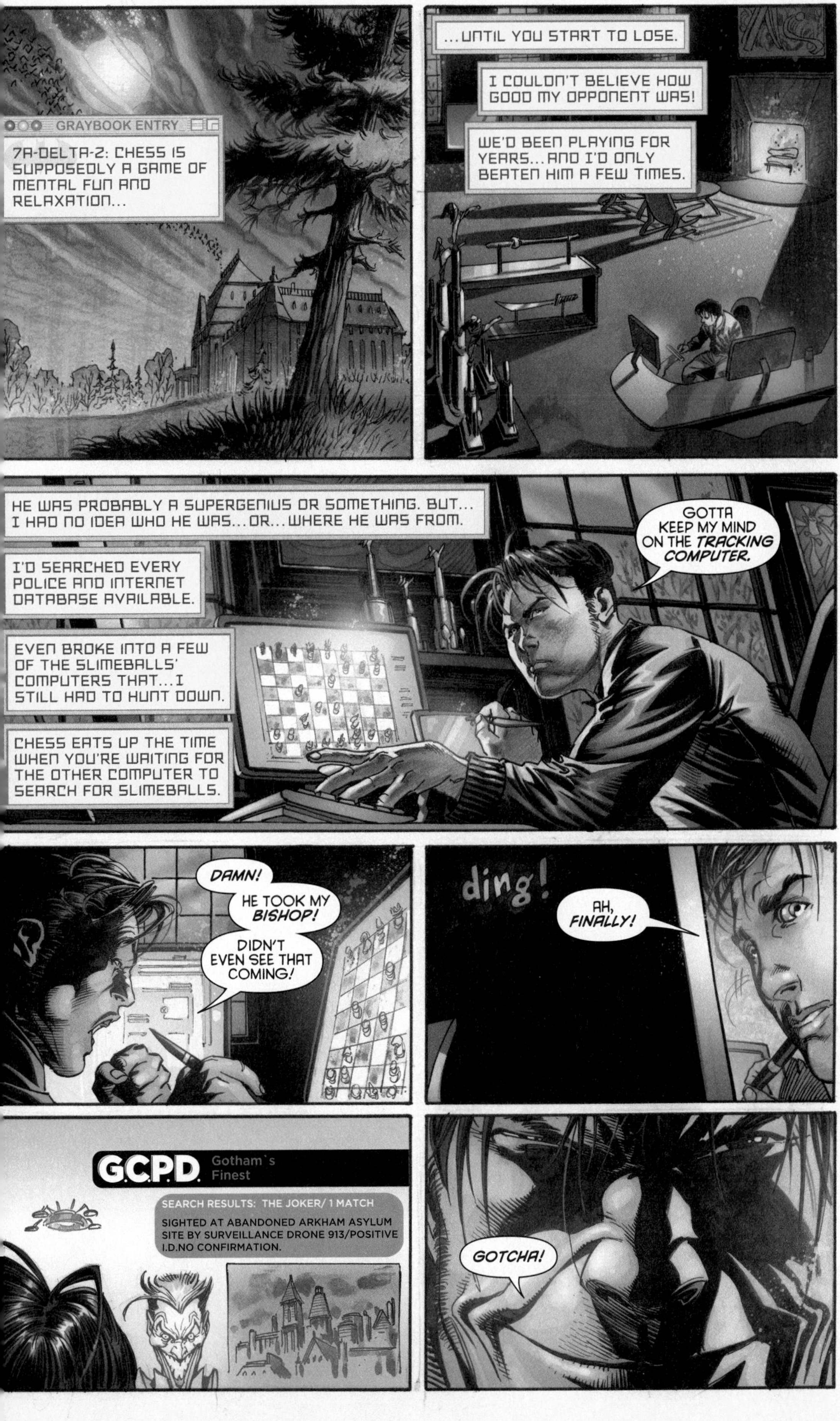
GRAYBOOK ENTRY
7A-DELTA-2: CHESS IS SUPPOSEDLY A GAME OF MENTAL FUN AND RELAXATION...
...UNTIL YOU START TO LOSE.
I COULDN'T BELIEVE HOW GOOD MY OPPONENT WAS!
WE'D BEEN PLAYING FOR YEARS...AND I'D ONLY BEATEN HIM A FEW TIMES.
HE WAS PROBABLY A SUPERGENIUS OR SOMETHING. BUT... I HAD NO IDEA WHO HE WAS...OR...WHERE HE WAS FROM.
I'D SEARCHED EVERY POLICE AND INTERNET DATABASE AVAILABLE.
EVEN BROKE INTO A FEW OF THE SLIMEBALLS' COMPUTERS THAT...I STILL HAD TO HUNT DOWN.
CHESS EATS UP THE TIME WHEN YOU'RE WAITING FOR THE OTHER COMPUTER TO SEARCH FOR SLIMEBALLS.
GOTTA KEEP MY MIND ON THE TRACKING COMPUTER.
DAMN!
HE TOOK MY BISHOP!
DIDN'T EVEN SEE THAT COMING!
ding!
AH, FINALLY!
G.C.P.D. Gotham`s Finest
SEARCH RESULTS: THE JOKER/ 1 MATCH
SIGHTED AT ABANDONED ARKHAM ASYLUM SITE BY SURVEILLANCE DRONE 913/POSITIVE I.D.NO CONFIRMATION.
GOTCHA!

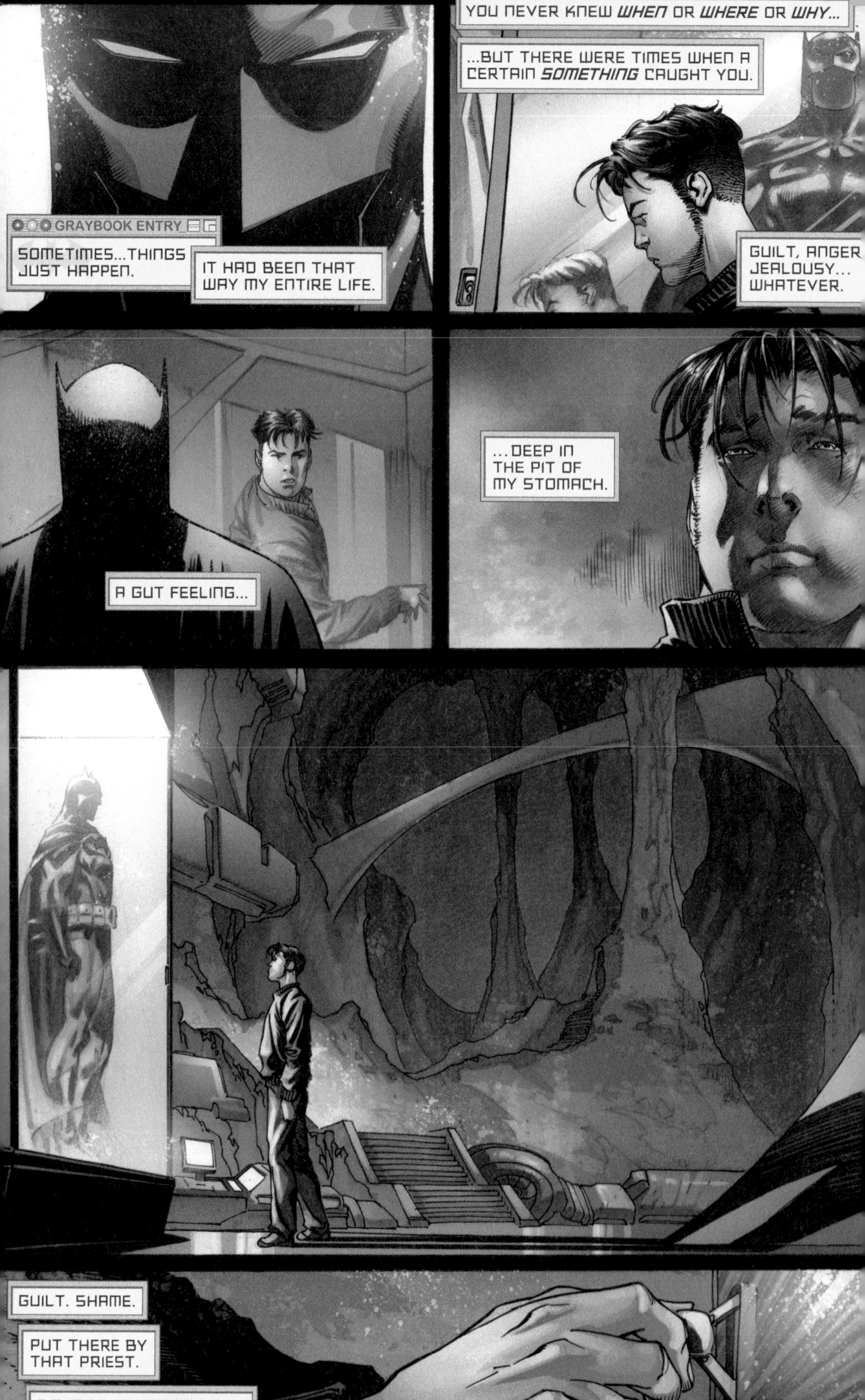
GRAYBOOK ENTRY
SOMETIMES...THINGS JUST HAPPEN.
IT HAD BEEN THAT WAY MY ENTIRE LIFE.
YOU NEVER KNEW *WHEN* OR *WHERE* OR *WHY*...
...BUT THERE WERE TIMES WHEN A CERTAIN *SOMETHING* CAUGHT YOU.
GUILT, ANGER JEALOUSY... WHATEVER.
A GUT FEELING...
...DEEP IN THE PIT OF MY STOMACH.
GUILT. SHAME.
PUT THERE BY THAT PRIEST.
I GUESS IT WAS CALLED... "HAVING A MOMENT."

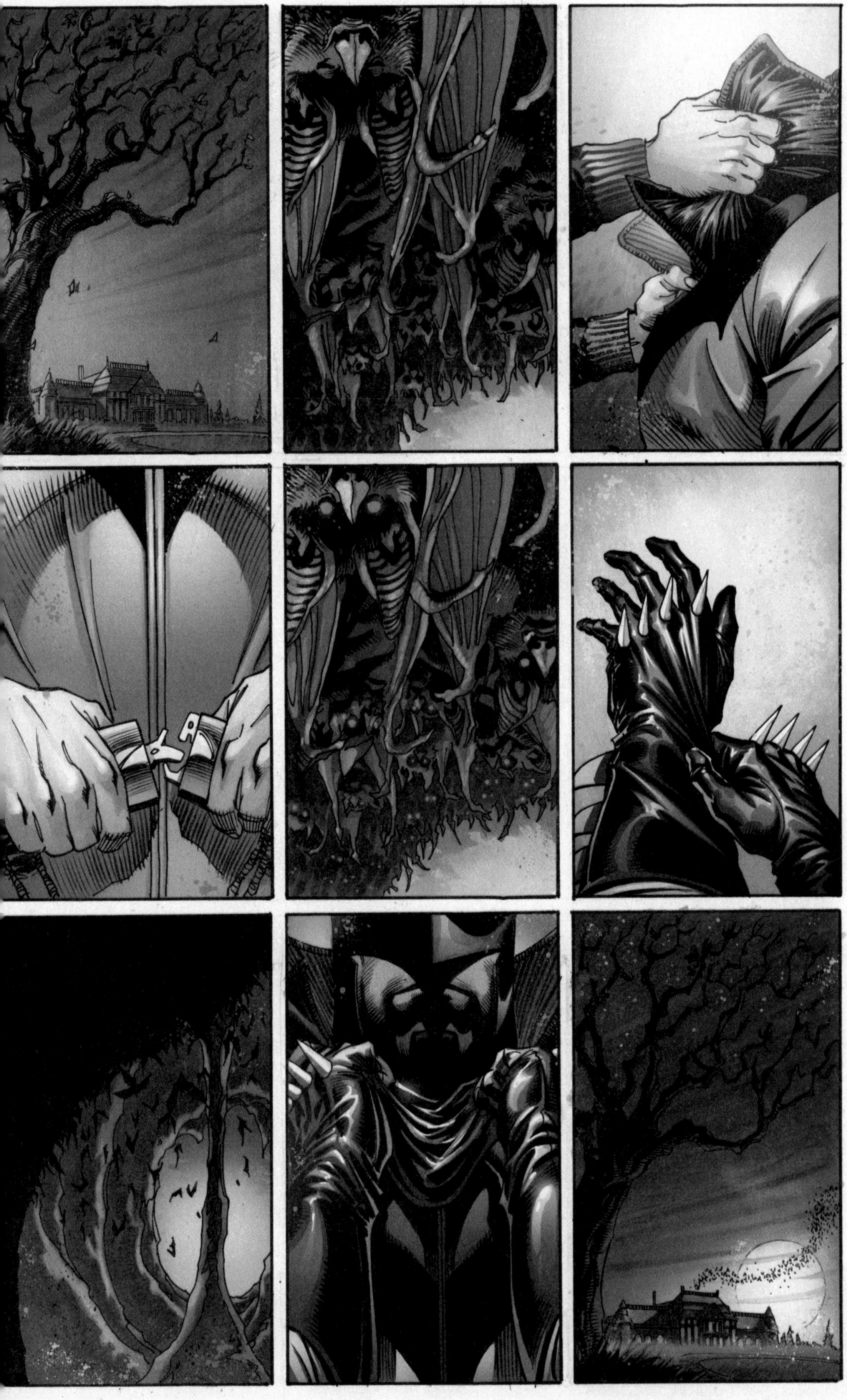

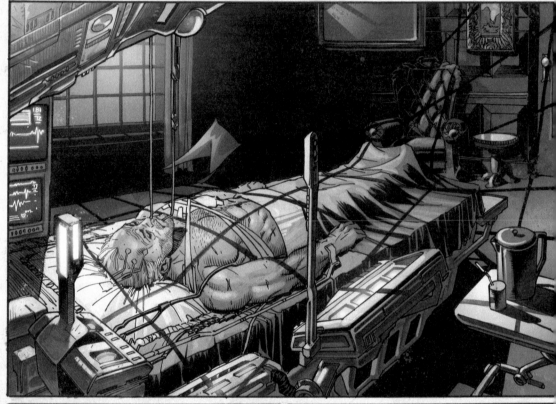

FATHER...

...I....I'M
SORRY.

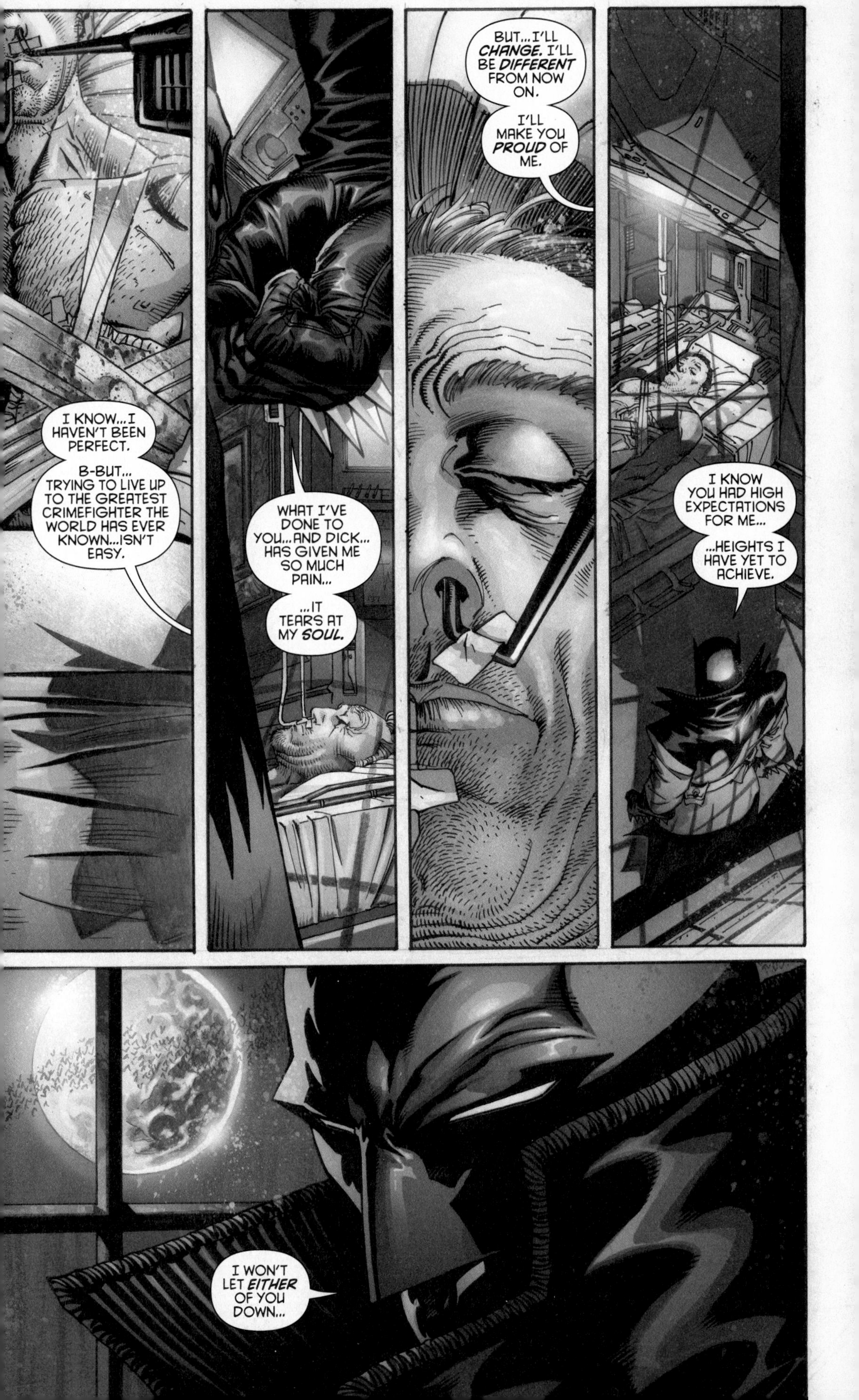
I KNOW...I HAVEN'T BEEN PERFECT.
B-BUT... TRYING TO LIVE UP TO THE GREATEST CRIMEFIGHTER THE WORLD HAS EVER KNOWN...ISN'T EASY.
WHAT I'VE DONE TO YOU...AND DICK... HAS GIVEN ME SO MUCH PAIN...
...IT TEARS AT MY SOUL.
BUT...I'LL CHANGE. I'LL BE DIFFERENT FROM NOW ON.
I'LL MAKE YOU PROUD OF ME.
I KNOW YOU HAD HIGH EXPECTATIONS FOR ME...
...HEIGHTS I HAVE YET TO ACHIEVE.
I WON'T LET EITHER OF YOU DOWN...

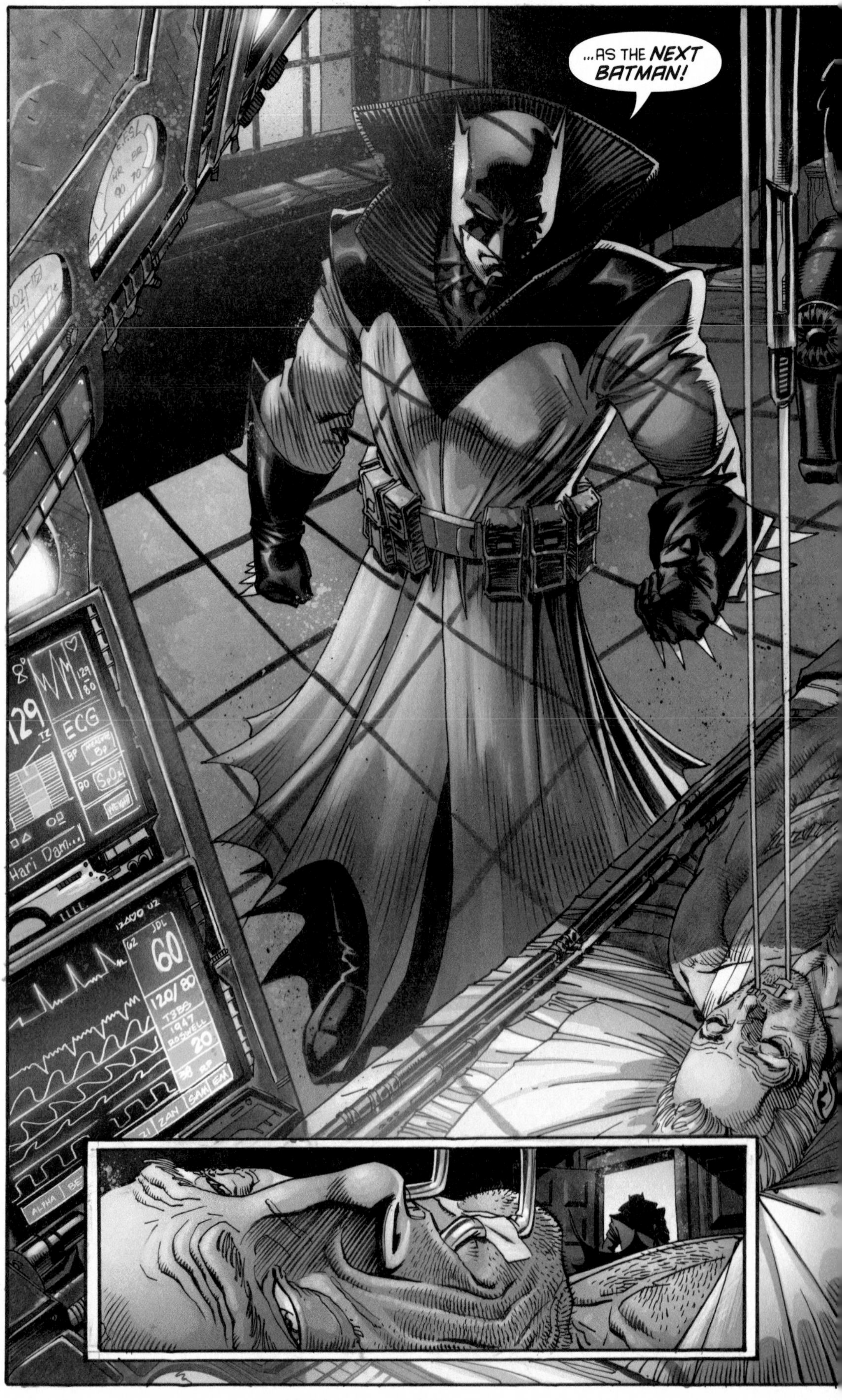
...AS THE NEXT BATMAN!

12C-GAMMA-4: STORIES THAT BRUCE AND DICK TOLD ME ABOUT THIS PLACE USED TO KEEP ME AWAKE AT NIGHT.

I CAN ONLY *IMAGINE* THE HORROR OF BEING INCARCERATED THERE.

IT WAS THE ULTIMATE *LOONY BIN...*

...*ARKHAM ASYLUM.*

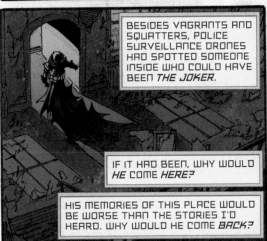

BESIDES VAGRANTS AND SQUATTERS, POLICE SURVEILLANCE DRONES HAD SPOTTED SOMEONE INSIDE WHO COULD HAVE BEEN *THE JOKER.*

IF IT HAD BEEN, WHY WOULD *HE* COME *HERE?*

HIS MEMORIES OF THIS PLACE WOULD BE WORSE THAN THE STORIES I'D HEARD. WHY WOULD HE COME *BACK?*

MR. FREEZE'S CELL.

ALL AT THE TAXPAYERS' EXPENSE.

A WASTE. ESPECIALLY SINCE HE DIDN'T NEED THE CELL FOR LONG.

DITTO FOR *KILLER CROC.*

GENTLEMAN GHOST WAS ONE OF THE ORIGINAL OCCUPANTS.

HE COULD HAVE BEEN IN THERE THE WHOLE TIME AND I WOULD NEVER HAVE KNOWN.

Hmm.

I WAS GETTING WARMER...

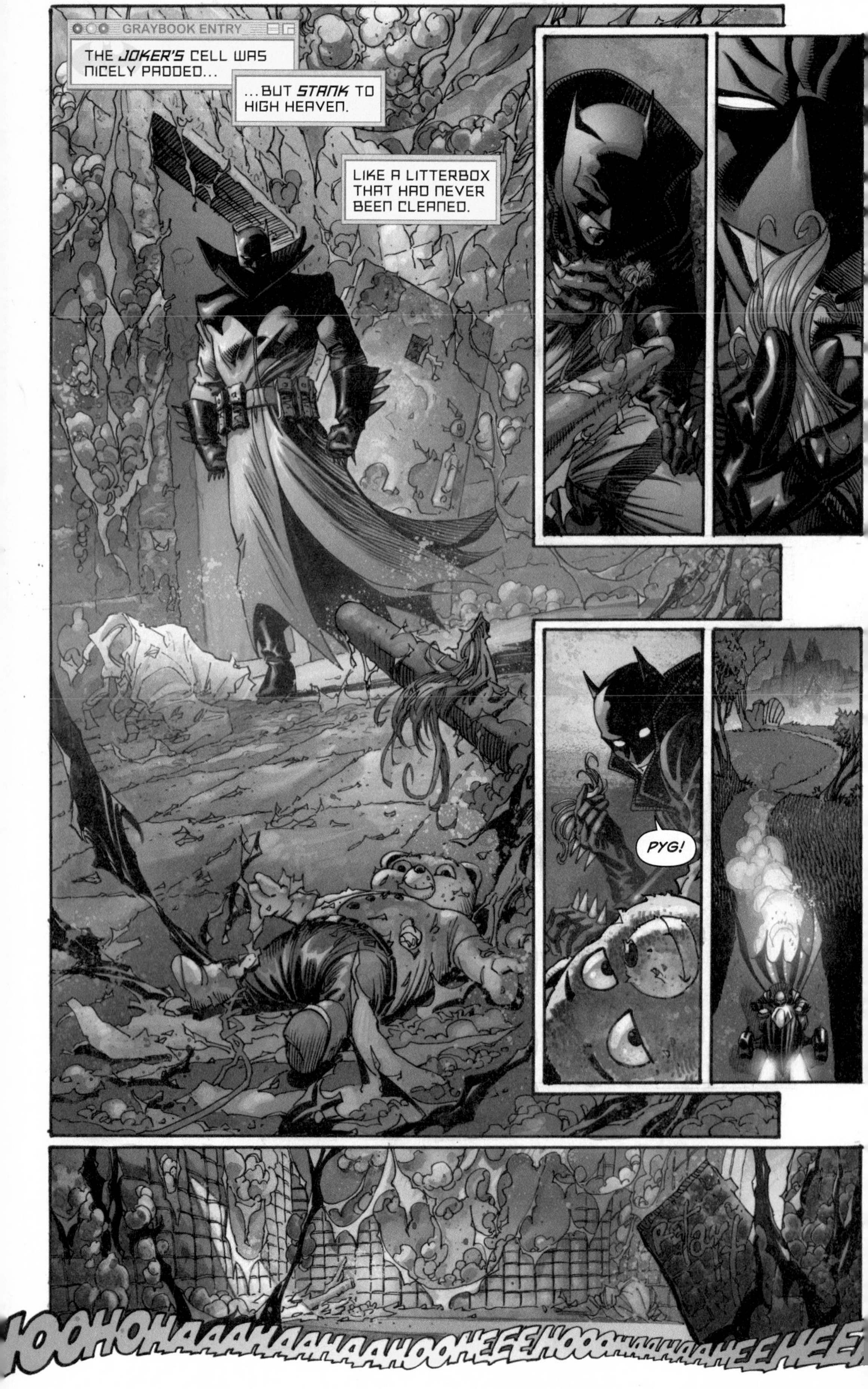
GRAYBOOK ENTRY
THE JOKER'S CELL WAS NICELY PADDED...
...BUT STANK TO HIGH HEAVEN.
LIKE A LITTERBOX THAT HAD NEVER BEEN CLEANED.
PYG!
HOOHOHAAAAHAAAAHOOHEEEHOOOHAAAAAHEEEHEE

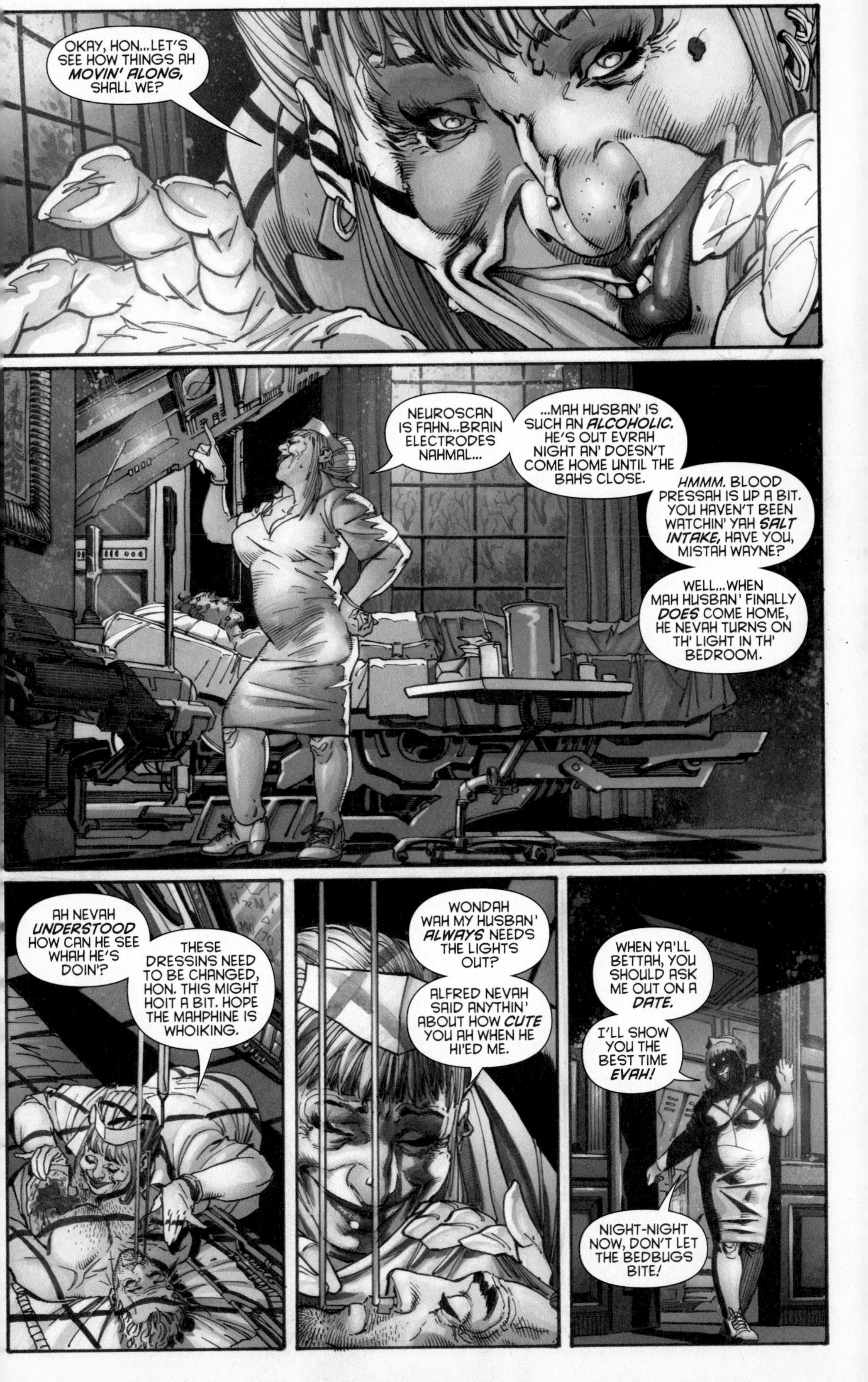
OKAY, HON...LET'S SEE HOW THINGS AH *MOVIN' ALONG,* SHALL WE?
NEUROSCAN IS FAHN...BRAIN ELECTRODES NAHMAL...
...MAH HUSBAN' IS SUCH AN *ALCOHOLIC.* HE'S OUT EVRAH NIGHT AN' DOESN'T COME HOME UNTIL THE BAHS CLOSE.
HMMM. BLOOD PRESSAH IS UP A BIT. YOU HAVEN'T BEEN WATCHIN' YAH *SALT INTAKE,* HAVE YOU, MISTAH WAYNE?
WELL...WHEN MAH HUSBAN' FINALLY *DOES* COME HOME, HE NEVAH TURNS ON TH' LIGHT IN TH' BEDROOM.
AH NEVAH *UNDERSTOOD* HOW CAN HE SEE WHAH HE'S DOIN'?
THESE DRESSINS NEED TO BE CHANGED, HON. THIS MIGHT HOIT A BIT. HOPE THE MAHPHINE IS WHOIKING.
WONDAH WAH MY HUSBAN' *ALWAYS* NEEDS THE LIGHTS OUT?
ALFRED NEVAH SAID ANYTHIN' ABOUT HOW *CUTE* YOU AH WHEN HE HI'ED ME.
WHEN YA'LL BETTAH, YOU SHOULD ASK ME OUT ON A *DATE.*
I'LL SHOW YOU THE BEST TIME *EVAH!*
NIGHT-NIGHT NOW, DON'T LET THE BEDBUGS BITE!

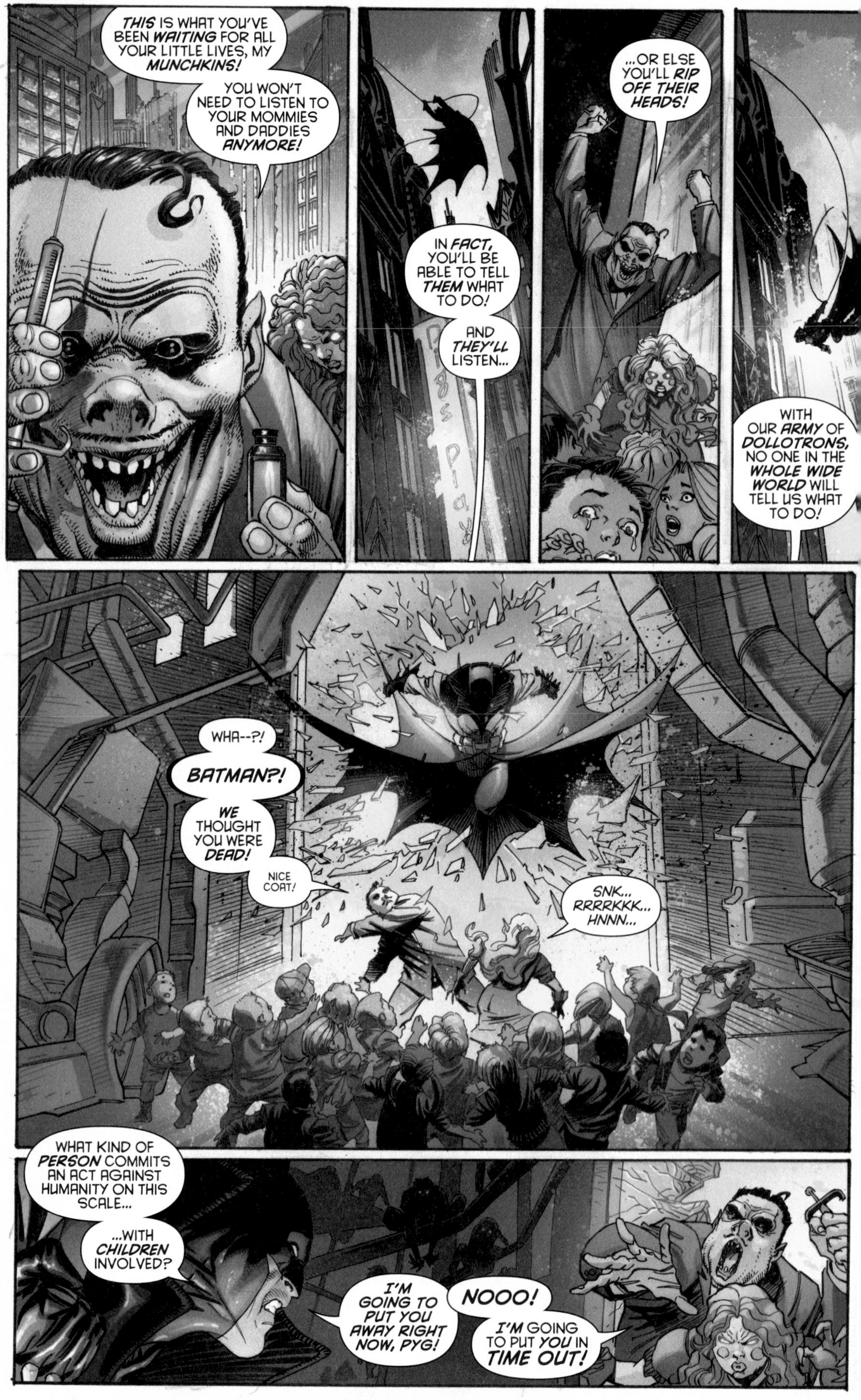
THIS IS WHAT YOU'VE BEEN WAITING FOR ALL YOUR LITTLE LIVES, MY MUNCHKINS!
YOU WON'T NEED TO LISTEN TO YOUR MOMMIES AND DADDIES ANYMORE!
IN FACT, YOU'LL BE ABLE TO TELL THEM WHAT TO DO!
AND THEY'LL LISTEN...
...OR ELSE YOU'LL RIP OFF THEIR HEADS!
WITH OUR ARMY OF DOLLOTRONS, NO ONE IN THE WHOLE WIDE WORLD WILL TELL US WHAT TO DO!
WHA--?!
BATMAN?!
WE THOUGHT YOU WERE DEAD!
NICE COAT!
SNK... RRRRKKK... HNNN...
WHAT KIND OF PERSON COMMITS AN ACT AGAINST HUMANITY ON THIS SCALE...
...WITH CHILDREN INVOLVED?
I'M GOING TO PUT YOU AWAY RIGHT NOW, PYG!
NOOO!
I'M GOING TO PUT YOU IN TIME OUT!

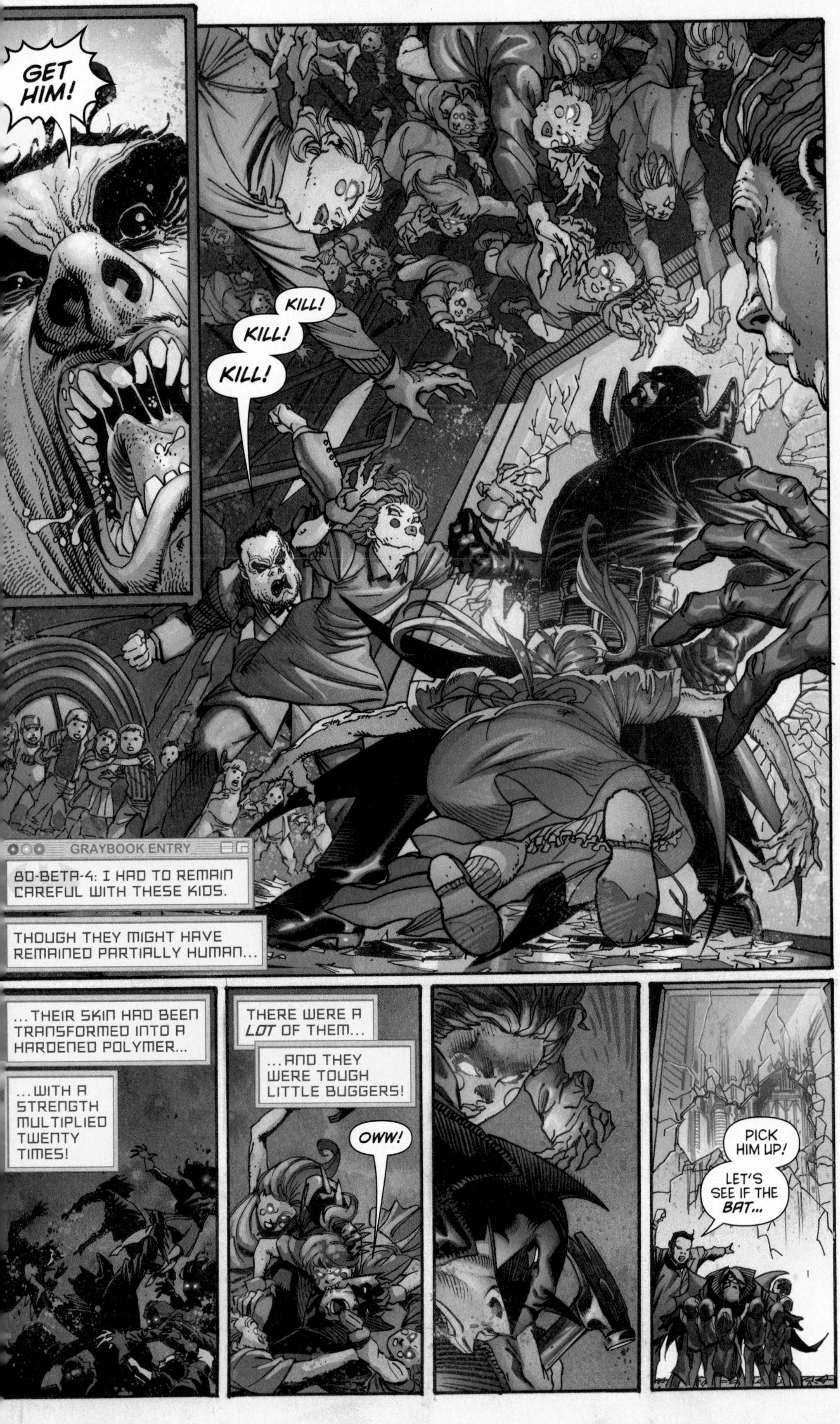
GET HIM!
KILL!
KILL!
KILL!
GRAYBOOK ENTRY
8D-BETA-4: I HAD TO REMAIN CAREFUL WITH THESE KIDS.
THOUGH THEY MIGHT HAVE REMAINED PARTIALLY HUMAN...
...THEIR SKIN HAD BEEN TRANSFORMED INTO A HARDENED POLYMER...
...WITH A STRENGTH MULTIPLIED TWENTY TIMES!
THERE WERE A LOT OF THEM...
...AND THEY WERE TOUGH LITTLE BUGGERS!
OWW!
PICK HIM UP!
LET'S SEE IF THE BAT...

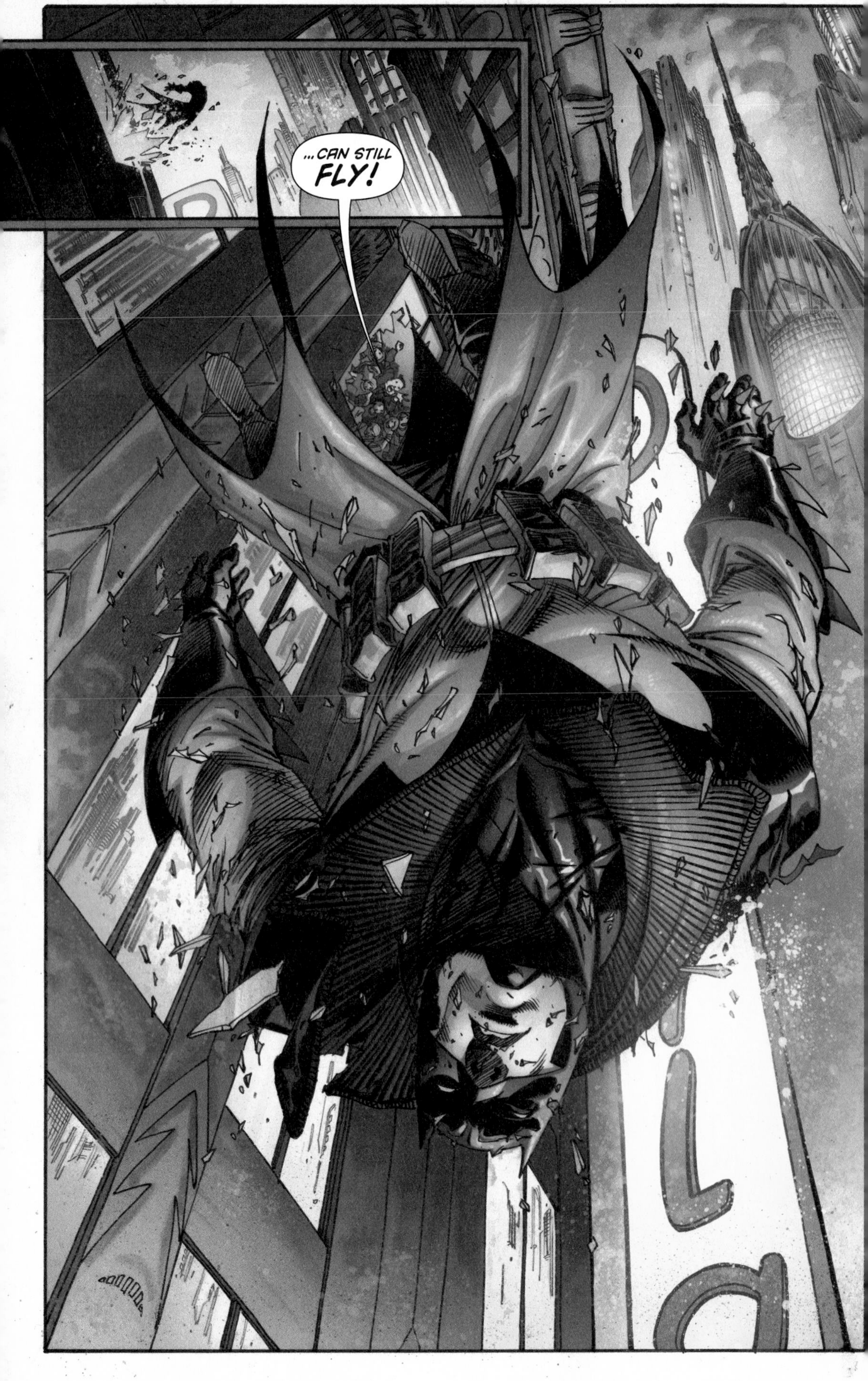
...CAN STILL FLY!

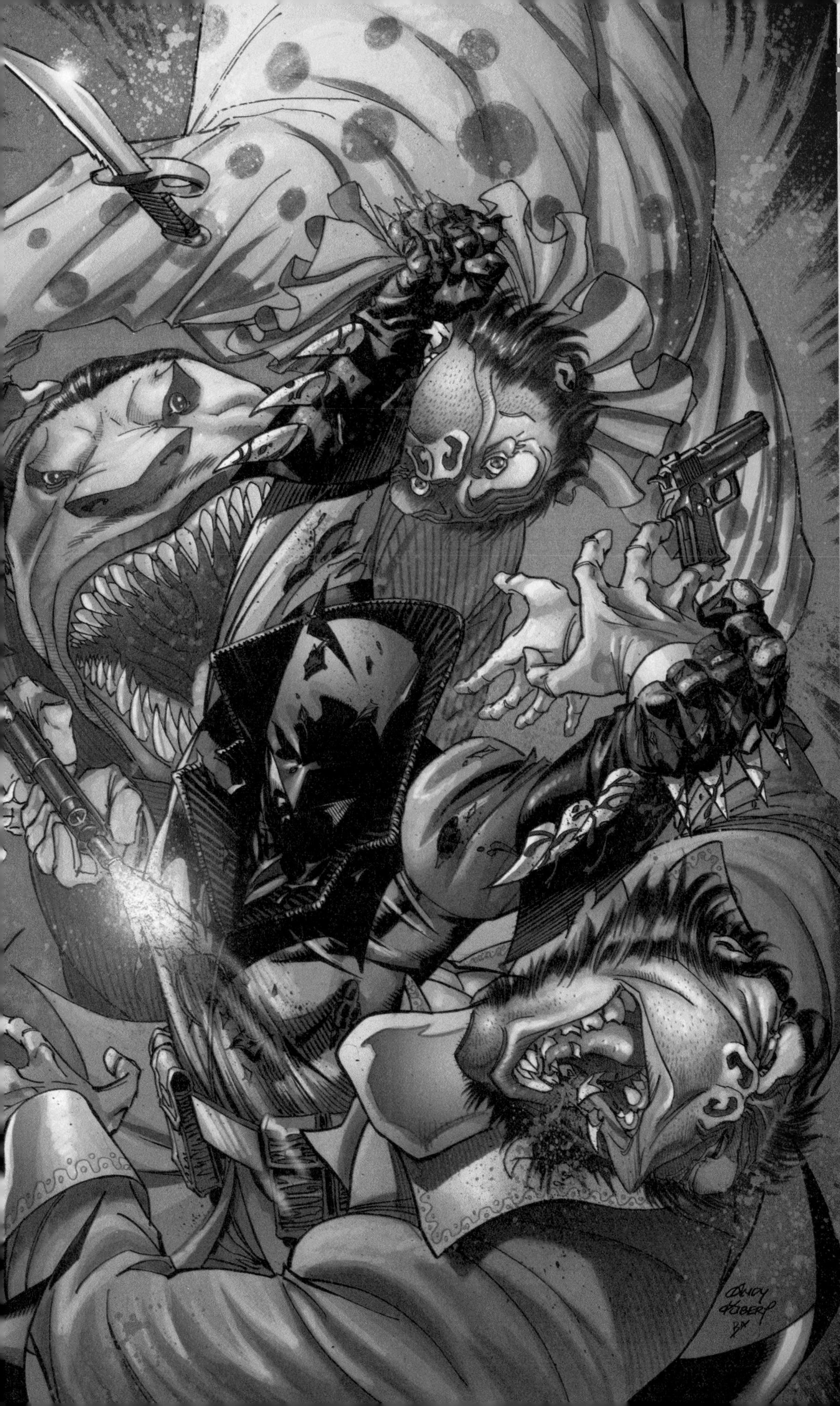

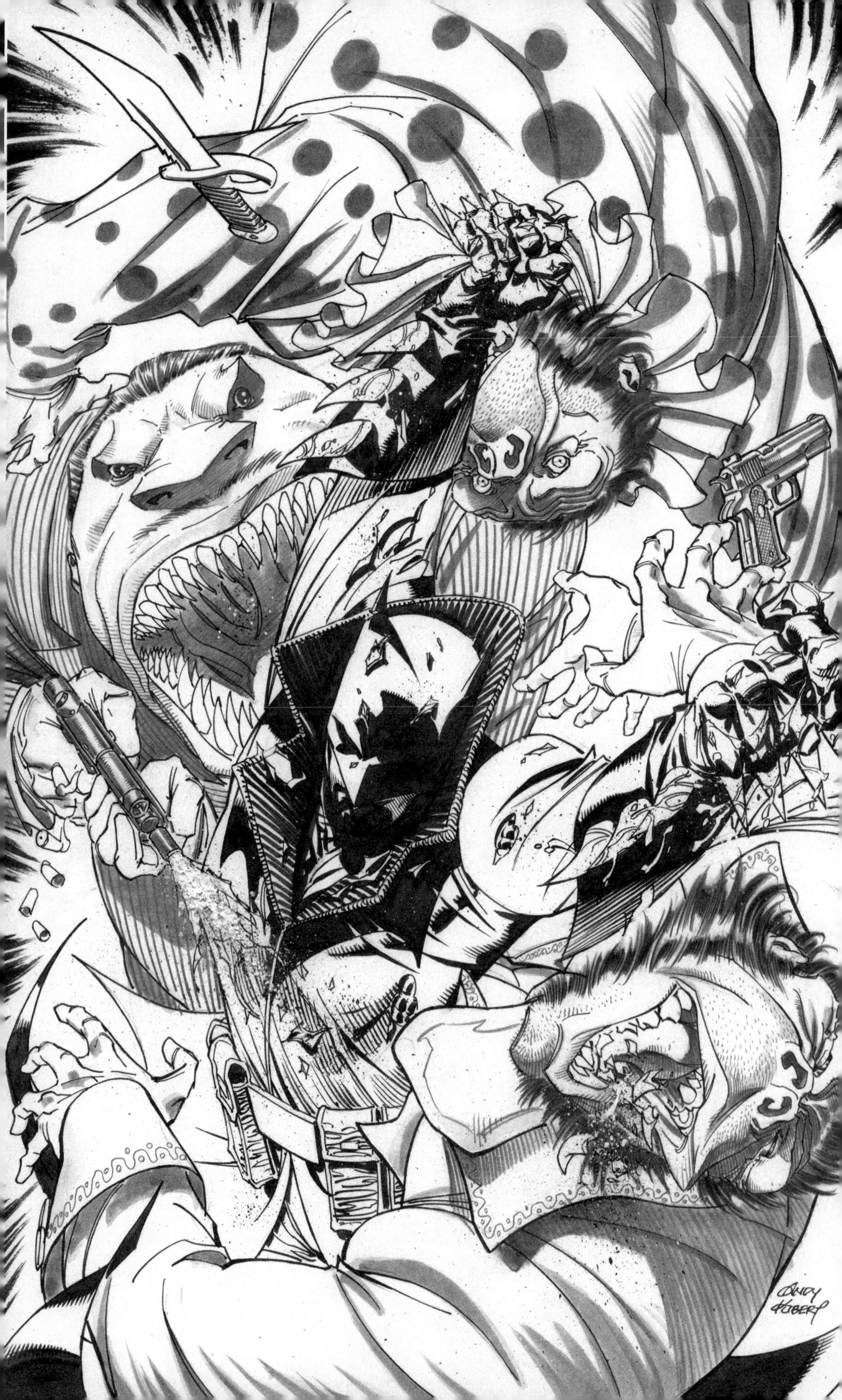
ANDY
KUBERT

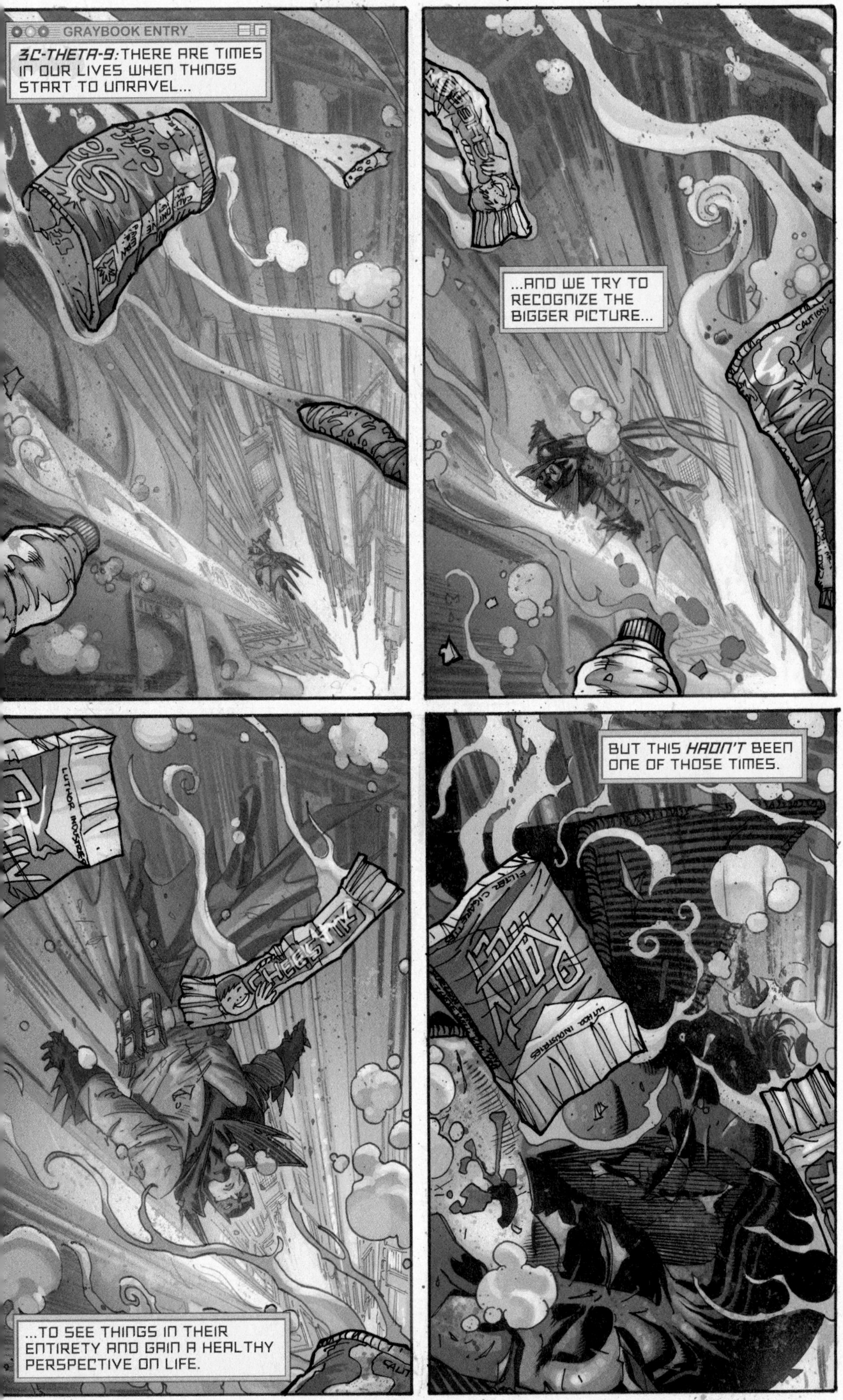
GRAYBOOK ENTRY
3C-THETA-9: THERE ARE TIMES IN OUR LIVES WHEN THINGS START TO UNRAVEL...
...AND WE TRY TO RECOGNIZE THE BIGGER PICTURE...
...TO SEE THINGS IN THEIR ENTIRETY AND GAIN A HEALTHY PERSPECTIVE ON LIFE.
BUT THIS HADN'T BEEN ONE OF THOSE TIMES.

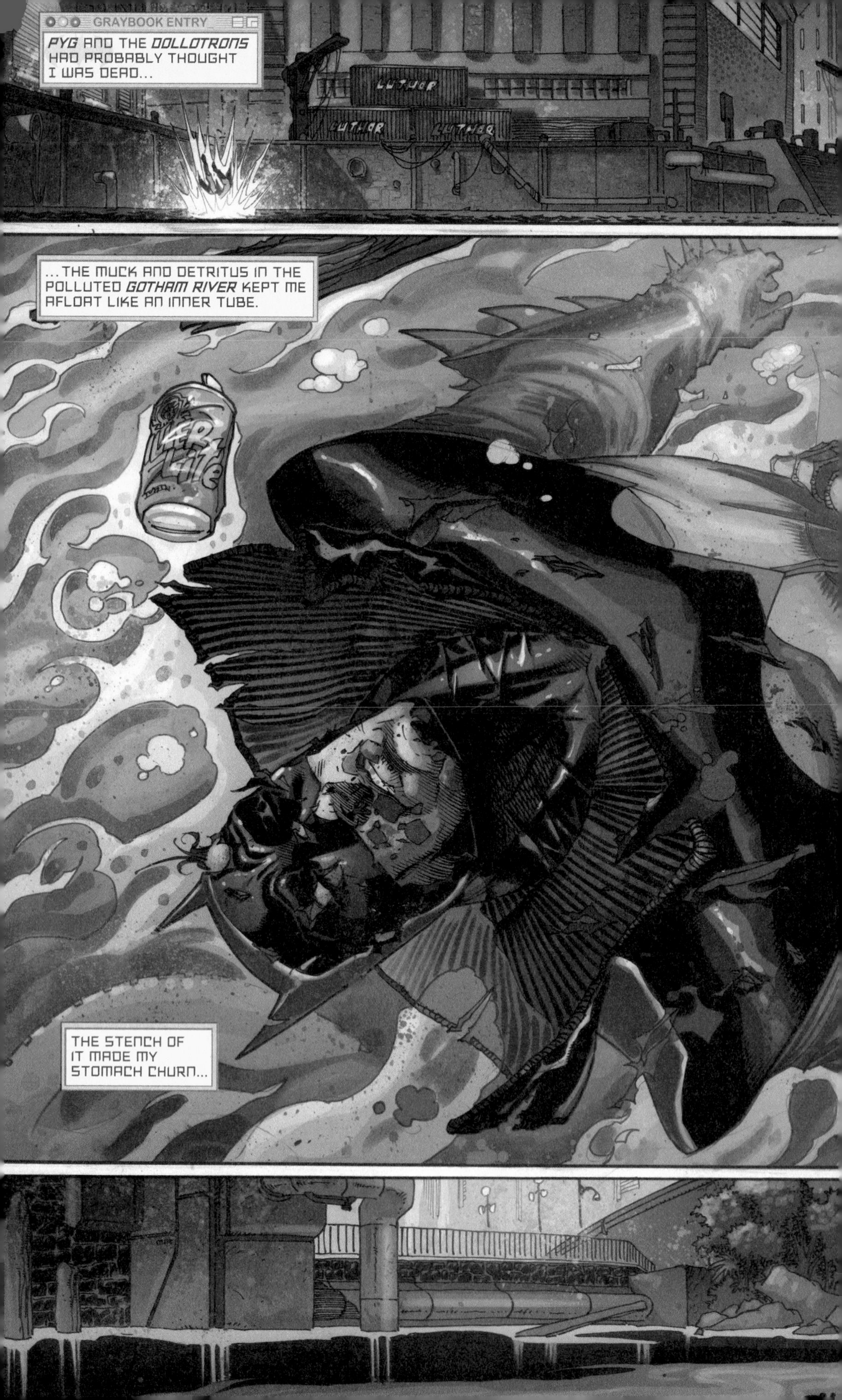
GRAYBOOK ENTRY
PYG AND THE DOLLOTRONS HAD PROBABLY THOUGHT I WAS DEAD...
LUTHOR
LUTHOR
LUTHOR
...THE MUCK AND DETRITUS IN THE POLLUTED GOTHAM RIVER KEPT ME AFLOAT LIKE AN INNER TUBE.
THE STENCH OF IT MADE MY STOMACH CHURN...

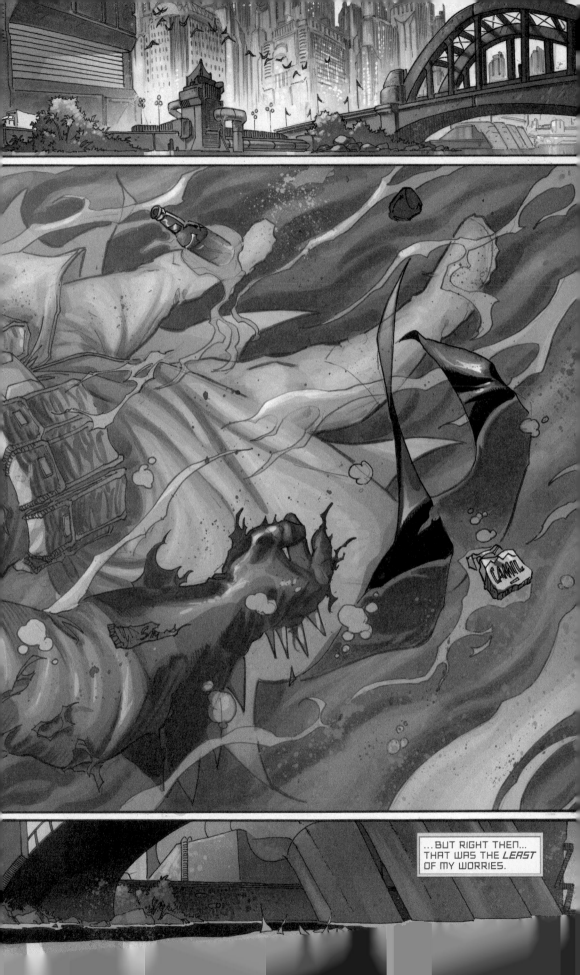

...BUT RIGHT THEN... THAT WAS THE *LEAST* OF MY WORRIES.

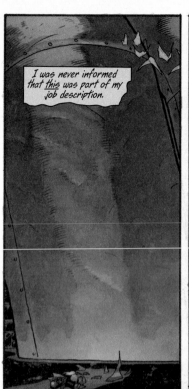
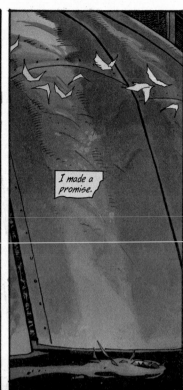

I was never informed that *this* was part of my job description.

I made a promise.

I shall file a grievance.

I tried my best to be on hand at such short notice...

...but...I am getting *too* old for this.

When Master Bruce "retired," I made a promise to look after young Damian.

However...his actions of late made it difficult to fulfill my vow...

...but...a *promise* is a *promise*.

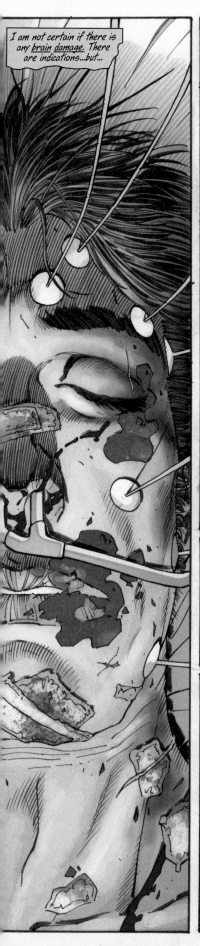

I am not certain if there is any *brain damage*. There are indications...but...

...that is not to say they might have existed previously.

Damian is *extremely* fortunate.

It could have been *much* worse.

I...I'm more exhausted...than... I expected.

Pulling him...out of the river...has depleted me.

I...I feel...very...

...old...

...I must rest...perhaps...

...a cup...

...of tea...

...s-some... rest...

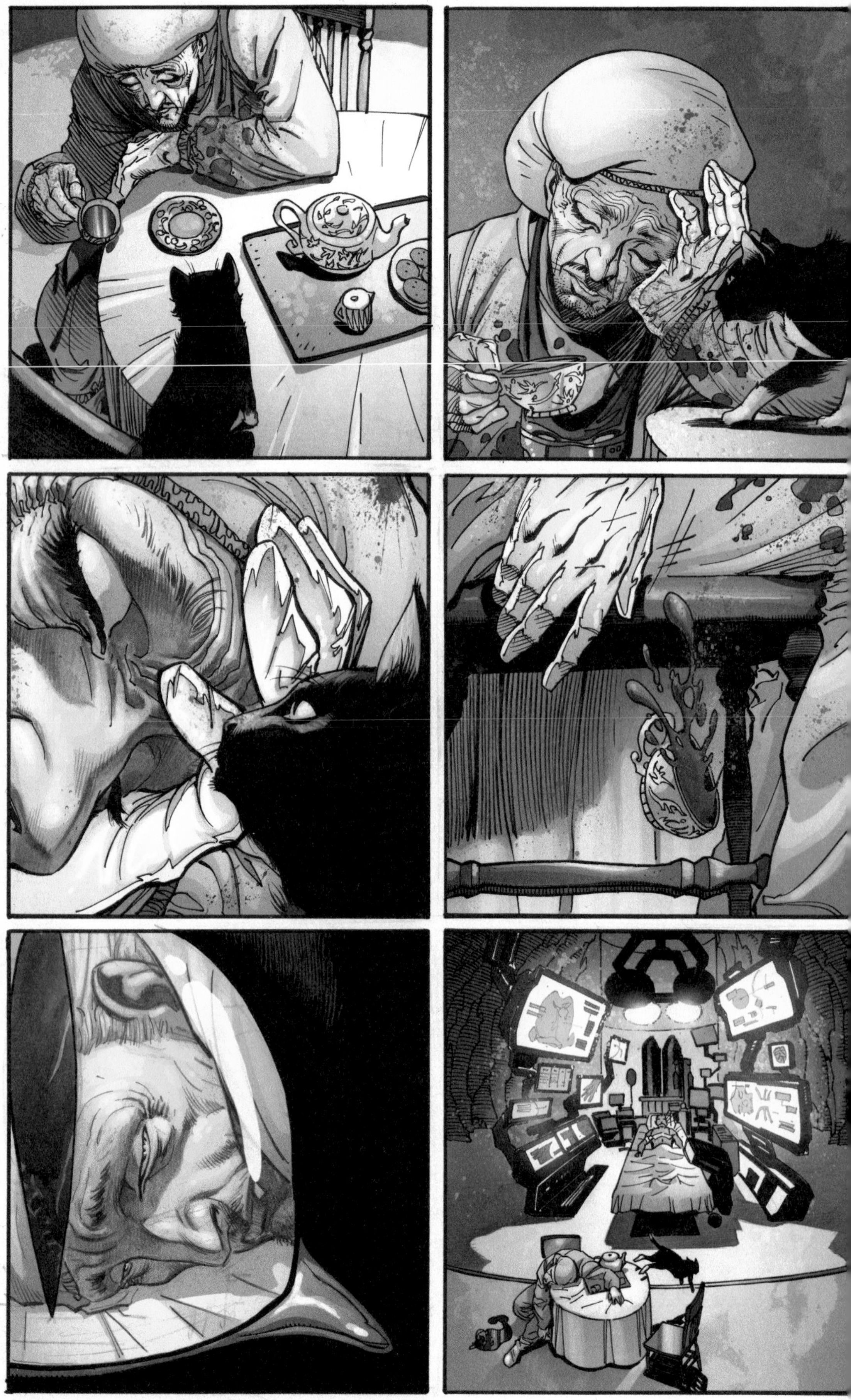

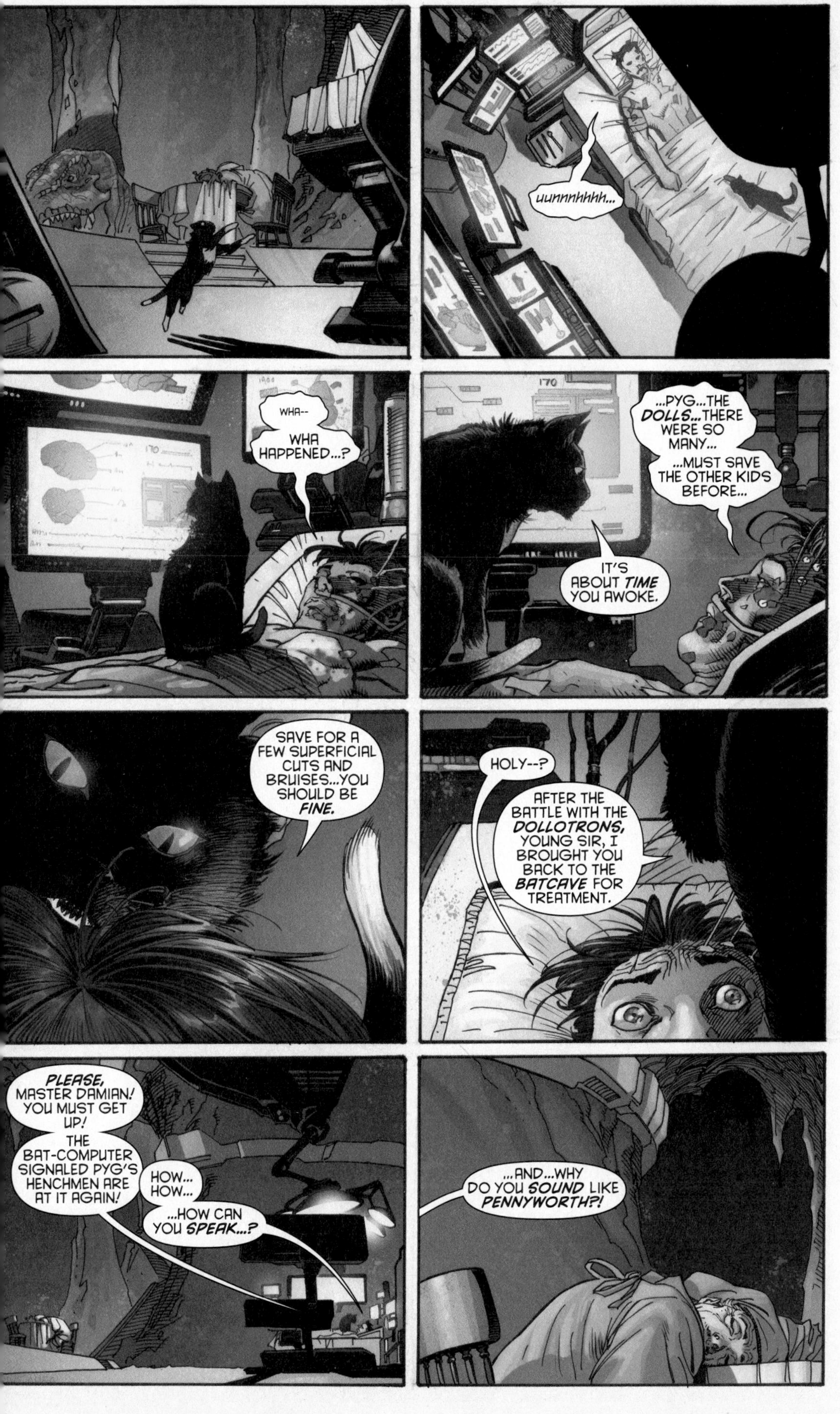
uunnnhhhh...
WHA--
WHA HAPPENED...?
...PYG...THE DOLLS...THERE WERE SO MANY...
...MUST SAVE THE OTHER KIDS BEFORE...
IT'S ABOUT TIME YOU AWOKE.
SAVE FOR A FEW SUPERFICIAL CUTS AND BRUISES...YOU SHOULD BE FINE.
HOLY--?
AFTER THE BATTLE WITH THE DOLLOTRONS, YOUNG SIR, I BROUGHT YOU BACK TO THE BATCAVE FOR TREATMENT.
PLEASE, MASTER DAMIAN! YOU MUST GET UP!
THE BAT-COMPUTER SIGNALED PYG'S HENCHMEN ARE AT IT AGAIN!
HOW... HOW...
...HOW CAN YOU SPEAK...?
...AND...WHY DO YOU SOUND LIKE PENNYWORTH?!

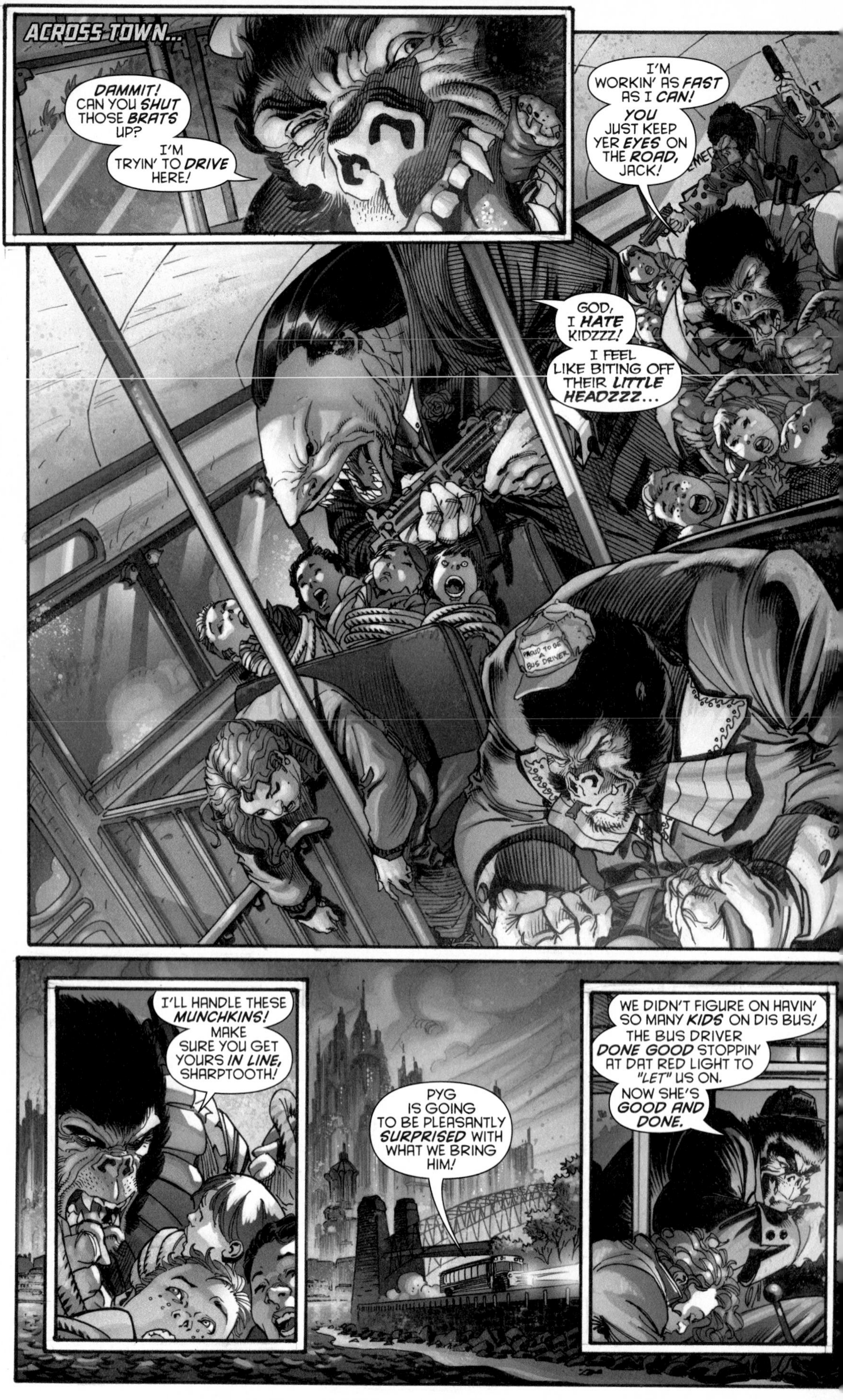
ACROSS TOWN...
DAMMIT! CAN YOU SHUT THOSE BRATS UP?
I'M TRYIN' TO DRIVE HERE!
I'M WORKIN' AS FAST AS I CAN!
YOU JUST KEEP YER EYES ON THE ROAD, JACK!
GOD, I HATE KIDZZZ!
I FEEL LIKE BITING OFF THEIR LITTLE HEADZZZ...
PROUD TO BE A BUS DRIVER
I'LL HANDLE THESE MUNCHKINS! MAKE SURE YOU GET YOURS IN LINE, SHARPTOOTH!
PYG IS GOING TO BE PLEASANTLY SURPRISED WITH WHAT WE BRING HIM!
WE DIDN'T FIGURE ON HAVIN' SO MANY KIDS ON DIS BUS!
THE BUS DRIVER DONE GOOD STOPPIN' AT DAT RED LIGHT TO "LET" US ON.
NOW SHE'S GOOD AND DONE.

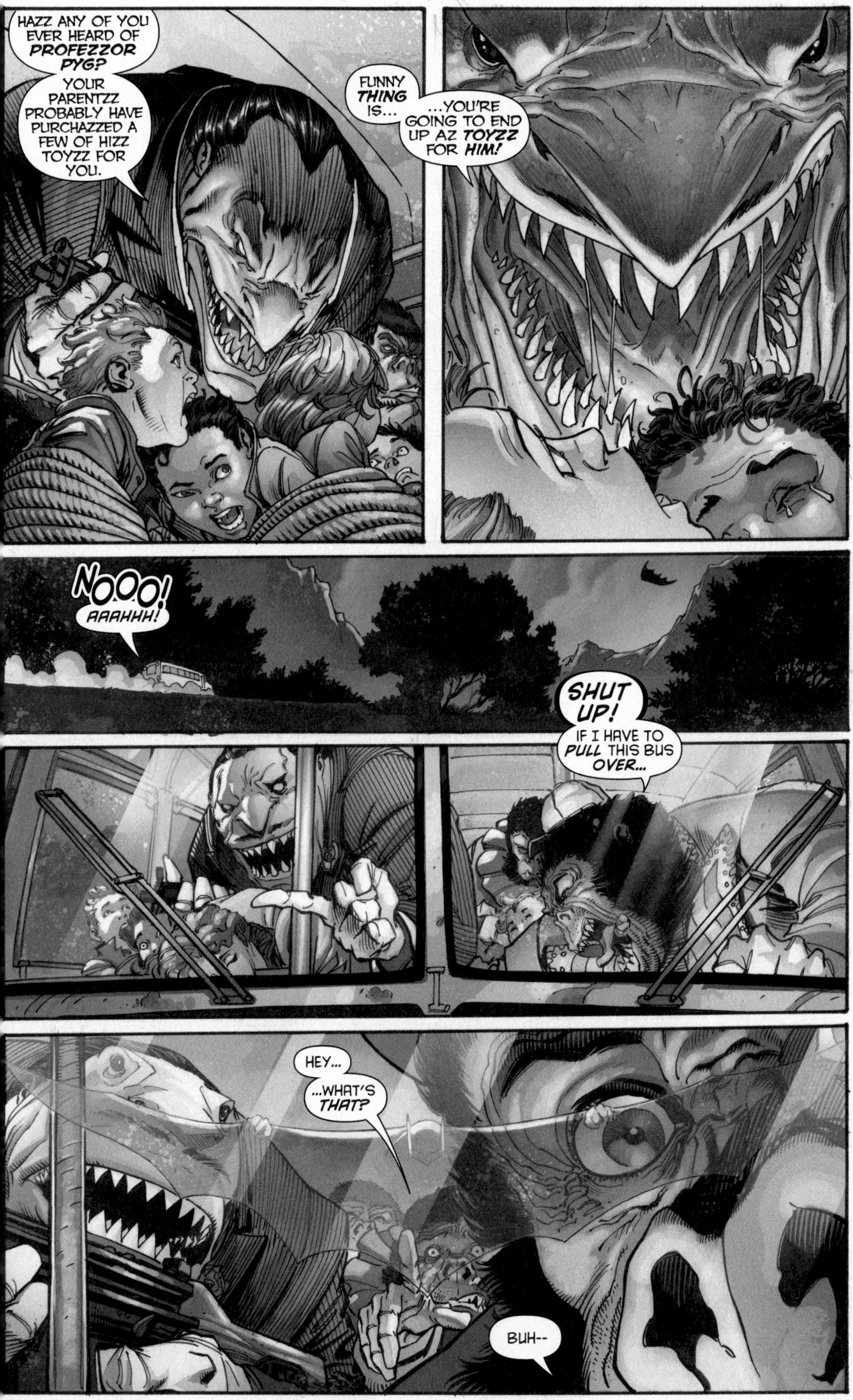
HAZZ ANY OF YOU EVER HEARD OF PROFEZZOR PYG?
YOUR PARENTZZ PROBABLY HAVE PURCHAZZED A FEW OF HIZZ TOYZZ FOR YOU.
FUNNY THING IS...
...YOU'RE GOING TO END UP AZ TOYZZ FOR HIM!
NOOO! AAAHHH!
SHUT UP!
IF I HAVE TO PULL THIS BUS OVER...
HEY...
...WHAT'S THAT?
BUH--

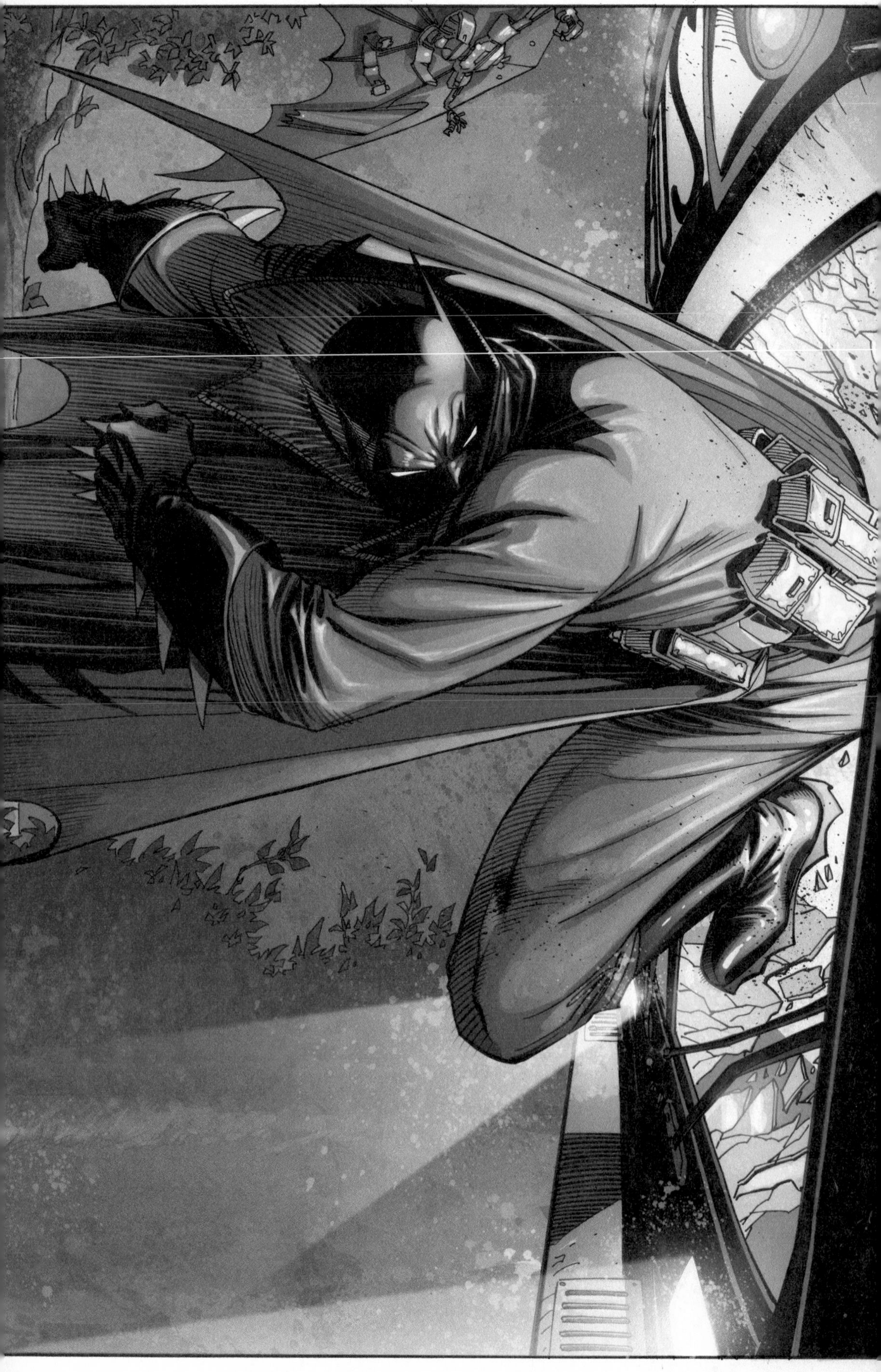

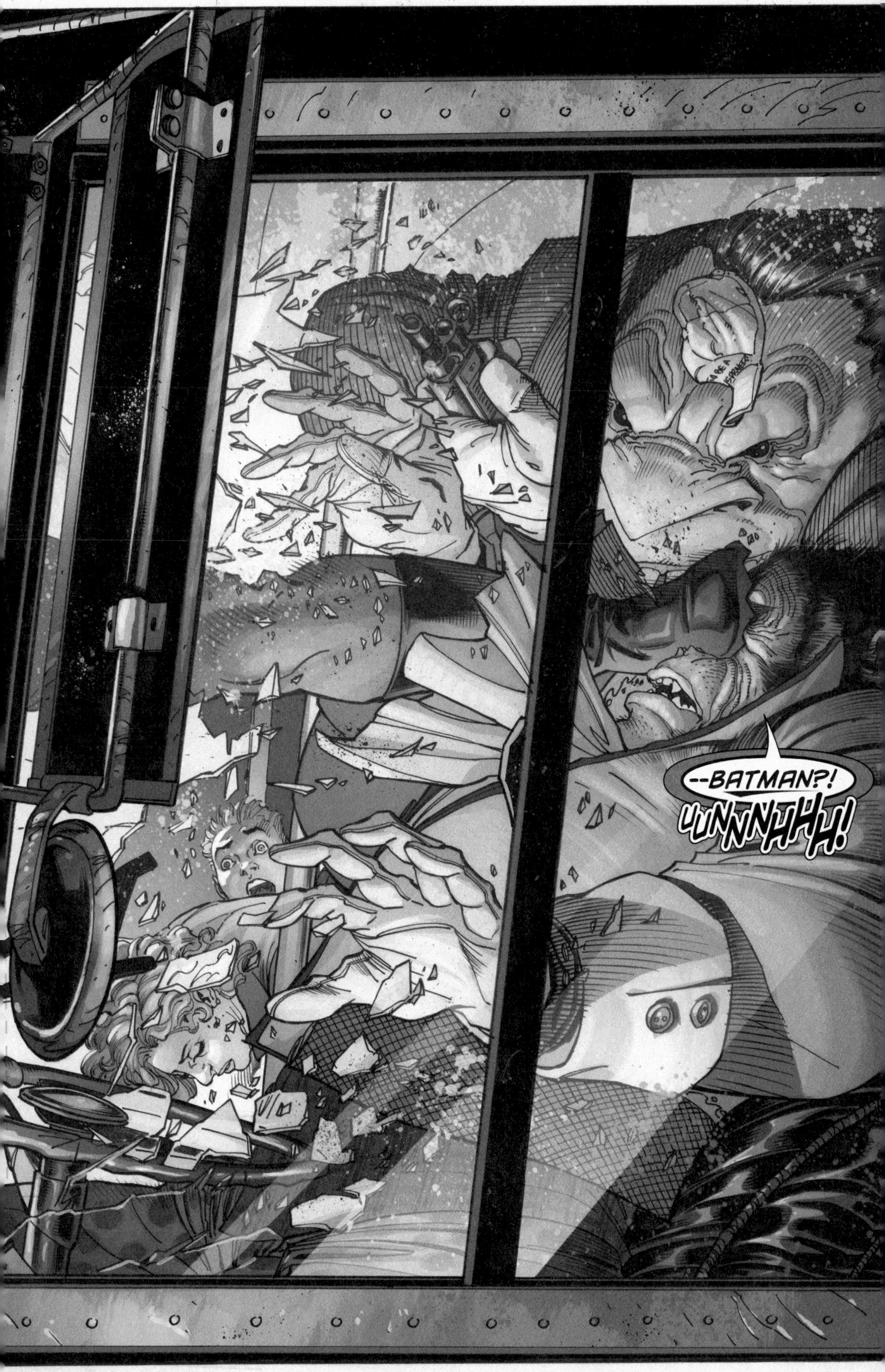
--BATMAN?!
UUNNHHH!

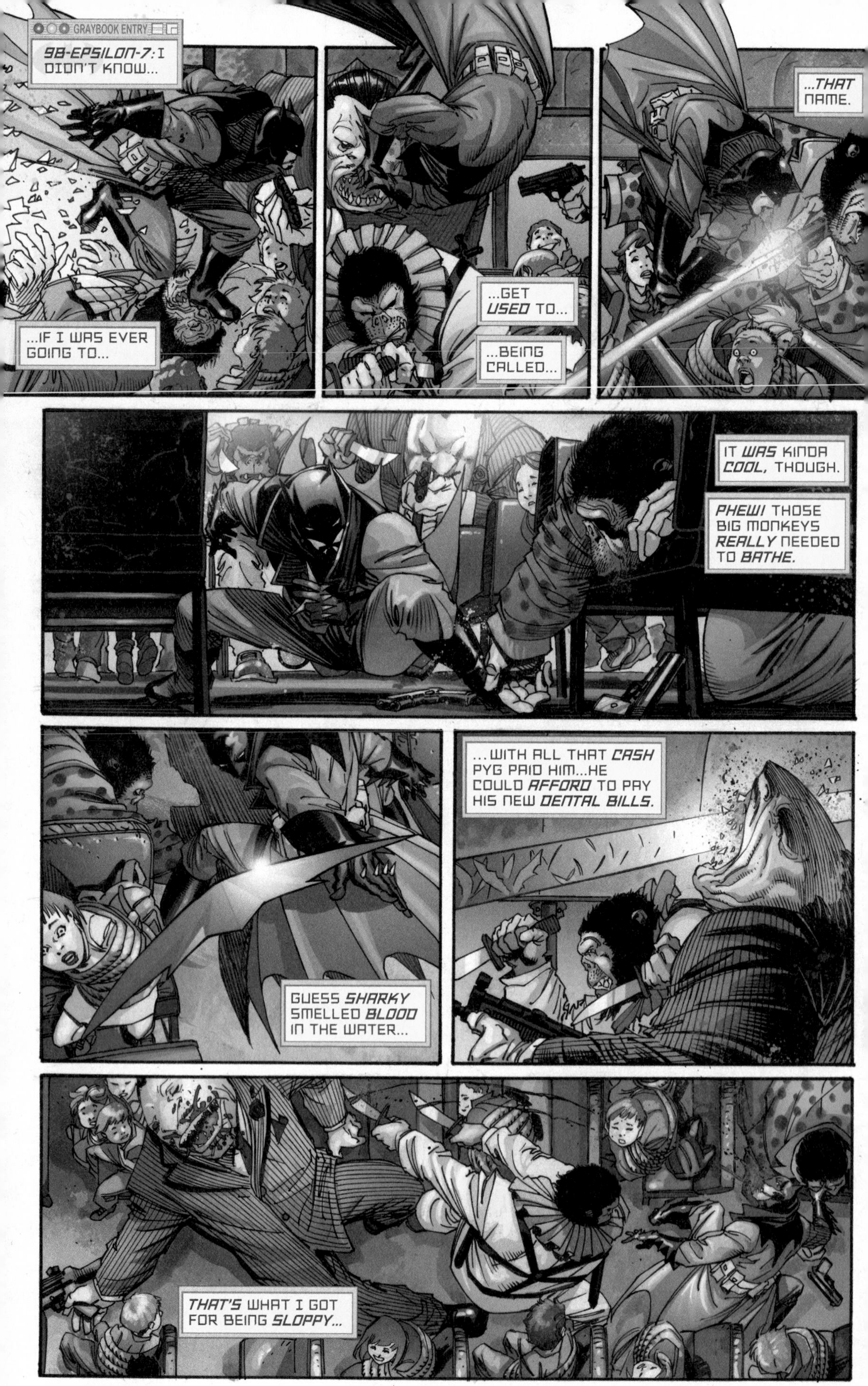
GRAYBOOK ENTRY
98-EPSILON-7: I DIDN'T KNOW...
...IF I WAS EVER GOING TO...
...GET USED TO...
...BEING CALLED...
...THAT NAME.
IT WAS KINDA COOL, THOUGH.
PHEW! THOSE BIG MONKEYS REALLY NEEDED TO BATHE.
GUESS SHARKY SMELLED BLOOD IN THE WATER...
...WITH ALL THAT CASH PYG PAID HIM...HE COULD AFFORD TO PAY HIS NEW DENTAL BILLS.
THAT'S WHAT I GOT FOR BEING SLOPPY...

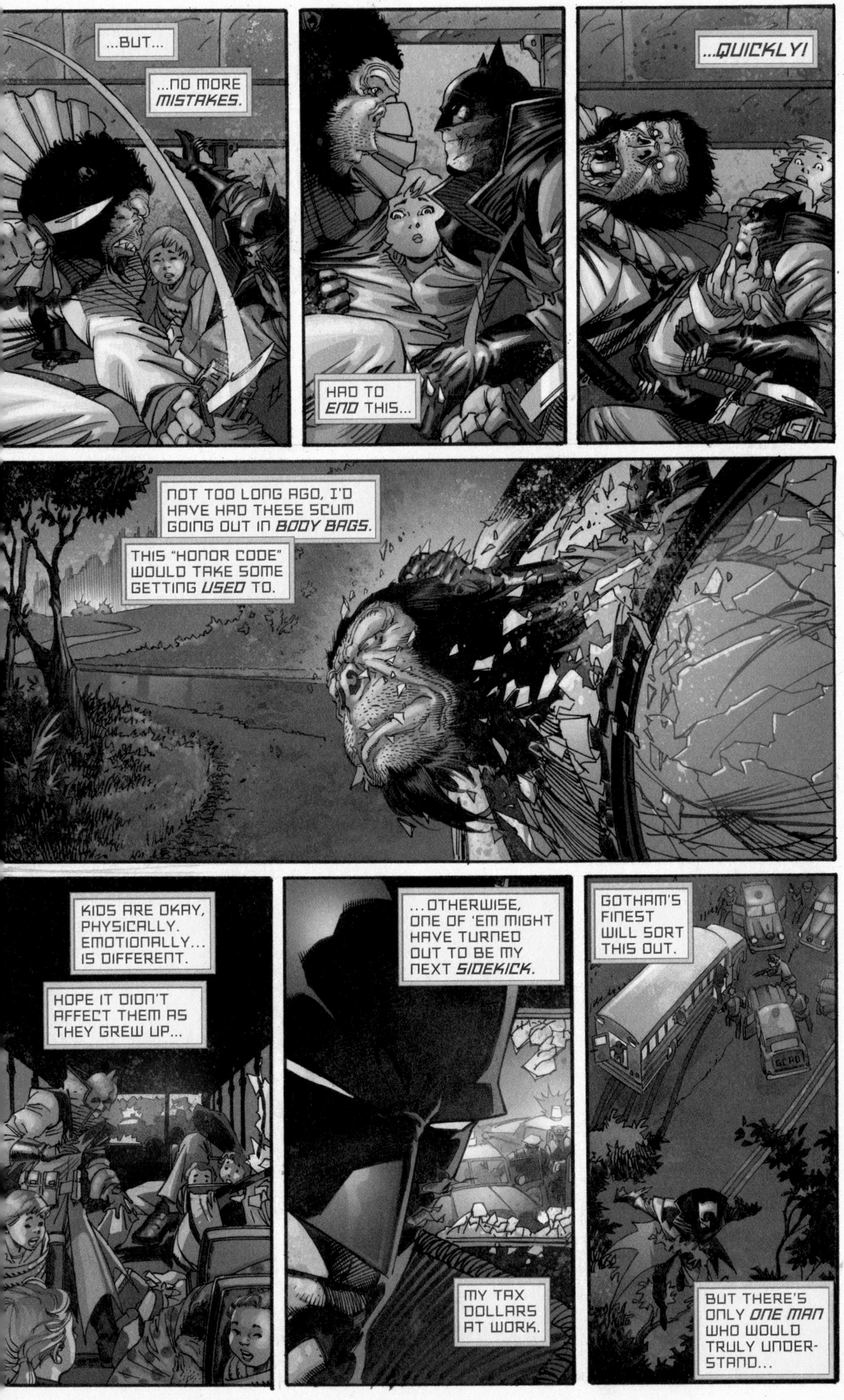
...BUT...
...NO MORE MISTAKES.
HAD TO END THIS...
...QUICKLY!
NOT TOO LONG AGO, I'D HAVE HAD THESE SCUM GOING OUT IN BODY BAGS.
THIS "HONOR CODE" WOULD TAKE SOME GETTING USED TO.
KIDS ARE OKAY, PHYSICALLY. EMOTIONALLY... IS DIFFERENT.
HOPE IT DIDN'T AFFECT THEM AS THEY GREW UP...
...OTHERWISE, ONE OF 'EM MIGHT HAVE TURNED OUT TO BE MY NEXT SIDEKICK.
MY TAX DOLLARS AT WORK.
GOTHAM'S FINEST WILL SORT THIS OUT.
BUT THERE'S ONLY ONE MAN WHO WOULD TRULY UNDER-STAND...

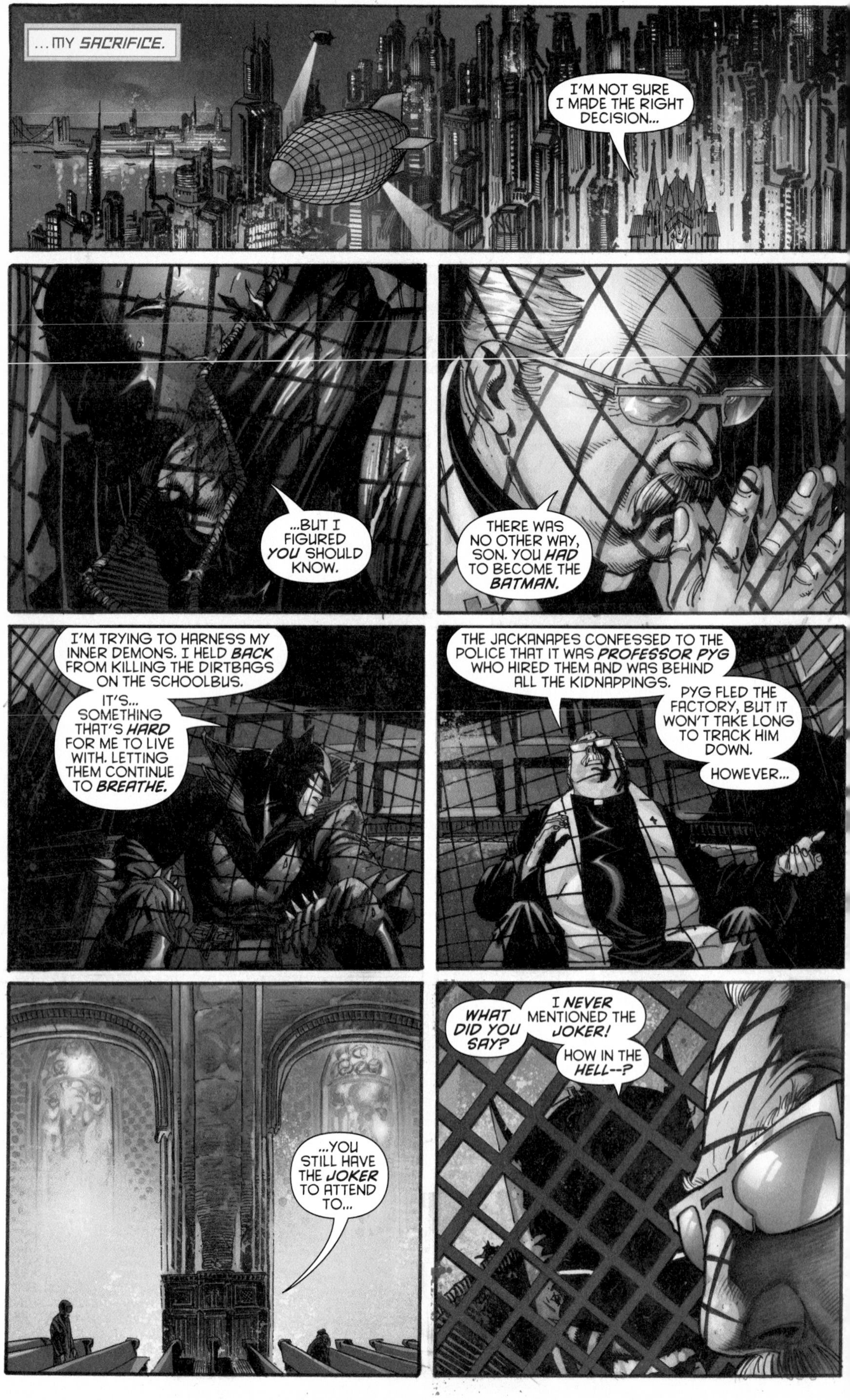
...MY SACRIFICE.
I'M NOT SURE I MADE THE RIGHT DECISION...
...BUT I FIGURED YOU SHOULD KNOW.
THERE WAS NO OTHER WAY, SON. YOU HAD TO BECOME THE BATMAN.
I'M TRYING TO HARNESS MY INNER DEMONS. I HELD BACK FROM KILLING THE DIRTBAGS ON THE SCHOOLBUS.
IT'S... SOMETHING THAT'S HARD FOR ME TO LIVE WITH. LETTING THEM CONTINUE TO BREATHE.
THE JACKANAPES CONFESSED TO THE POLICE THAT IT WAS PROFESSOR PYG WHO HIRED THEM AND WAS BEHIND ALL THE KIDNAPPINGS.
PYG FLED THE FACTORY, BUT IT WON'T TAKE LONG TO TRACK HIM DOWN.
HOWEVER...
...YOU STILL HAVE THE JOKER TO ATTEND TO...
WHAT DID YOU SAY?
I NEVER MENTIONED THE JOKER!
HOW IN THE HELL--?

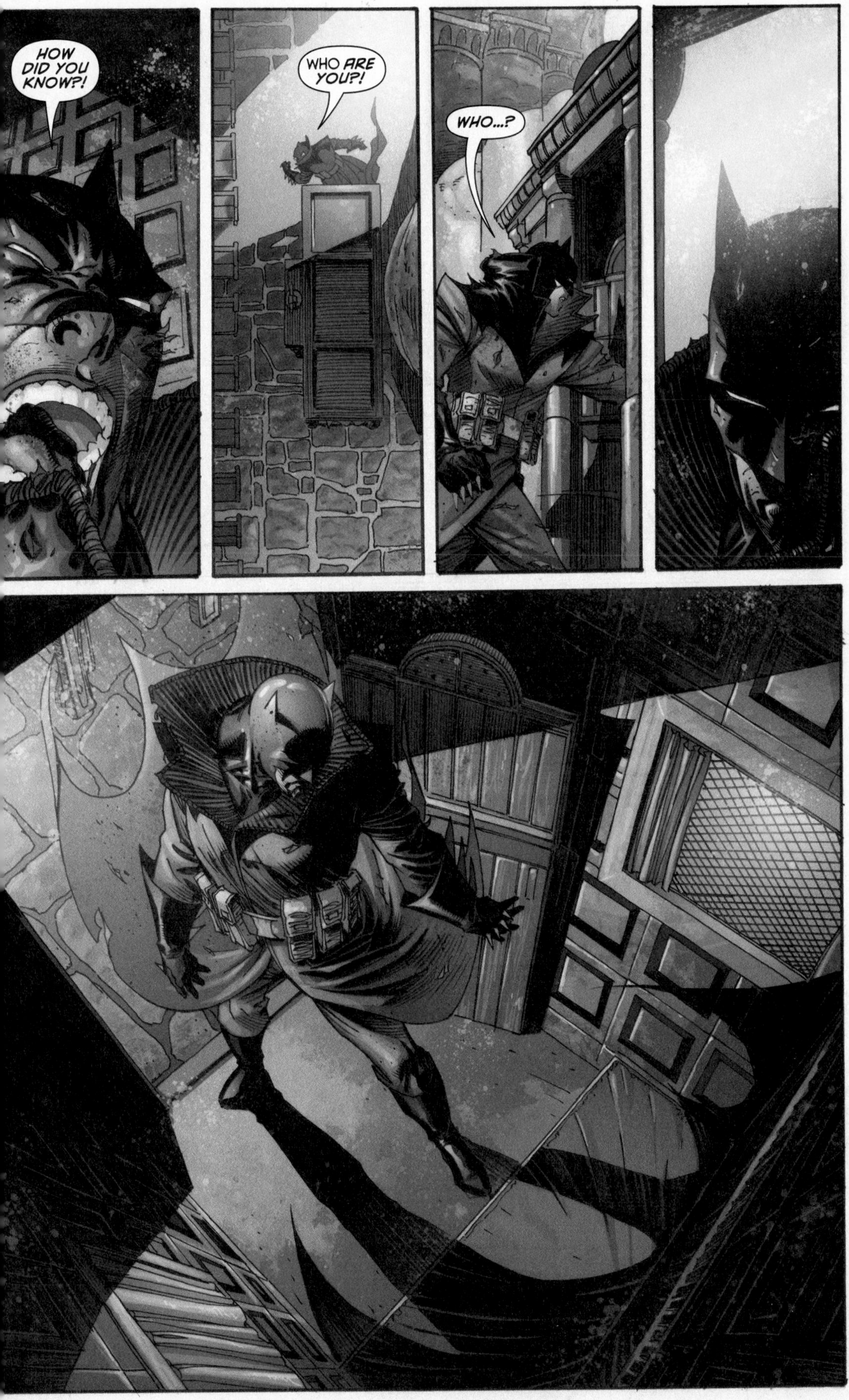
HOW DID YOU KNOW?!
WHO ARE YOU?!
WHO...?

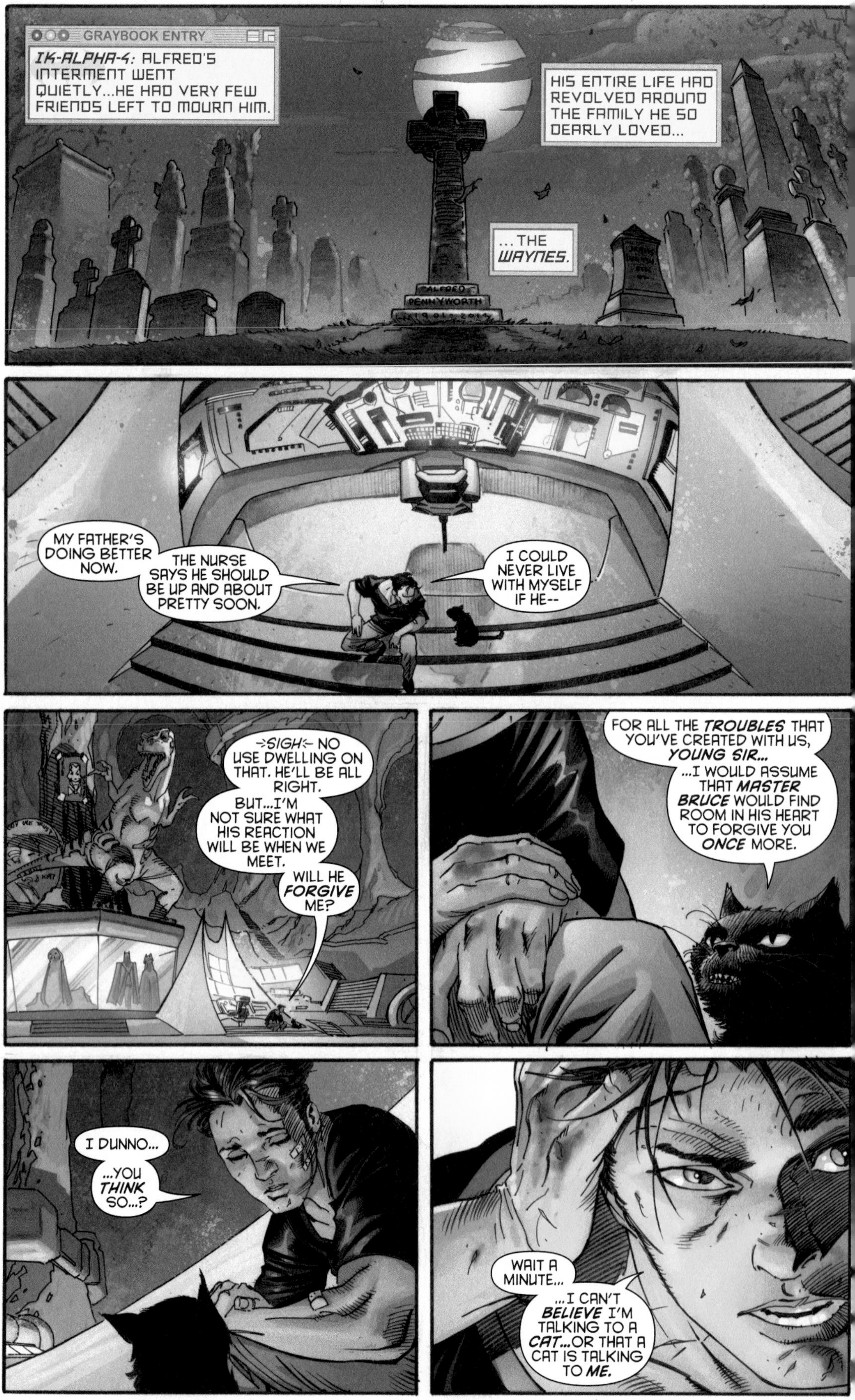

GRAYBOOK ENTRY
IK-ALPHA-4: ALFRED'S INTERMENT WENT QUIETLY...HE HAD VERY FEW FRIENDS LEFT TO MOURN HIM.
HIS ENTIRE LIFE HAD REVOLVED AROUND THE FAMILY HE SO DEARLY LOVED...
...THE WAYNES.
ALFRED PENNYWORTH
MY FATHER'S DOING BETTER NOW.
THE NURSE SAYS HE SHOULD BE UP AND ABOUT PRETTY SOON.
I COULD NEVER LIVE WITH MYSELF IF HE--
SIGH NO USE DWELLING ON THAT. HE'LL BE ALL RIGHT.
BUT...I'M NOT SURE WHAT HIS REACTION WILL BE WHEN WE MEET.
WILL HE FORGIVE ME?
FOR ALL THE TROUBLES THAT YOU'VE CREATED WITH US, YOUNG SIR...
...I WOULD ASSUME THAT MASTER BRUCE WOULD FIND ROOM IN HIS HEART TO FORGIVE YOU ONCE MORE.
I DUNNO...
...YOU THINK SO...?
WAIT A MINUTE...
...I CAN'T BELIEVE I'M TALKING TO A CAT...OR THAT A CAT IS TALKING TO ME.

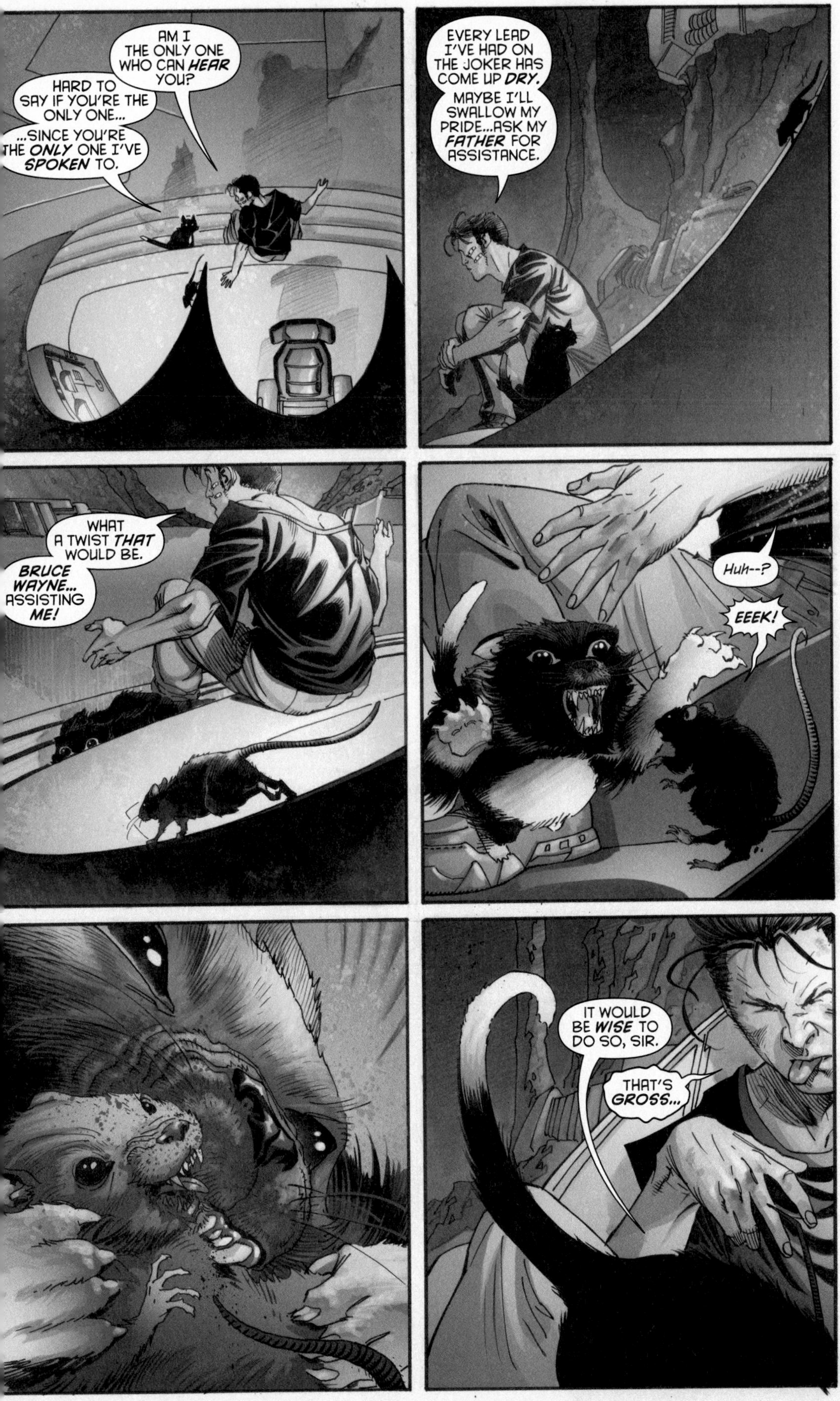
AM I THE ONLY ONE WHO CAN *HEAR* YOU?
HARD TO SAY IF YOU'RE THE ONLY ONE...
...SINCE YOU'RE THE *ONLY* ONE I'VE *SPOKEN* TO.
EVERY LEAD I'VE HAD ON THE JOKER HAS COME UP *DRY.*
MAYBE I'LL SWALLOW MY PRIDE...ASK MY *FATHER* FOR ASSISTANCE.
WHAT A TWIST *THAT* WOULD BE.
BRUCE WAYNE... ASSISTING *ME!*
Huh--?
EEEK!
IT WOULD BE *WISE* TO DO SO, SIR.
THAT'S *GROSS...*

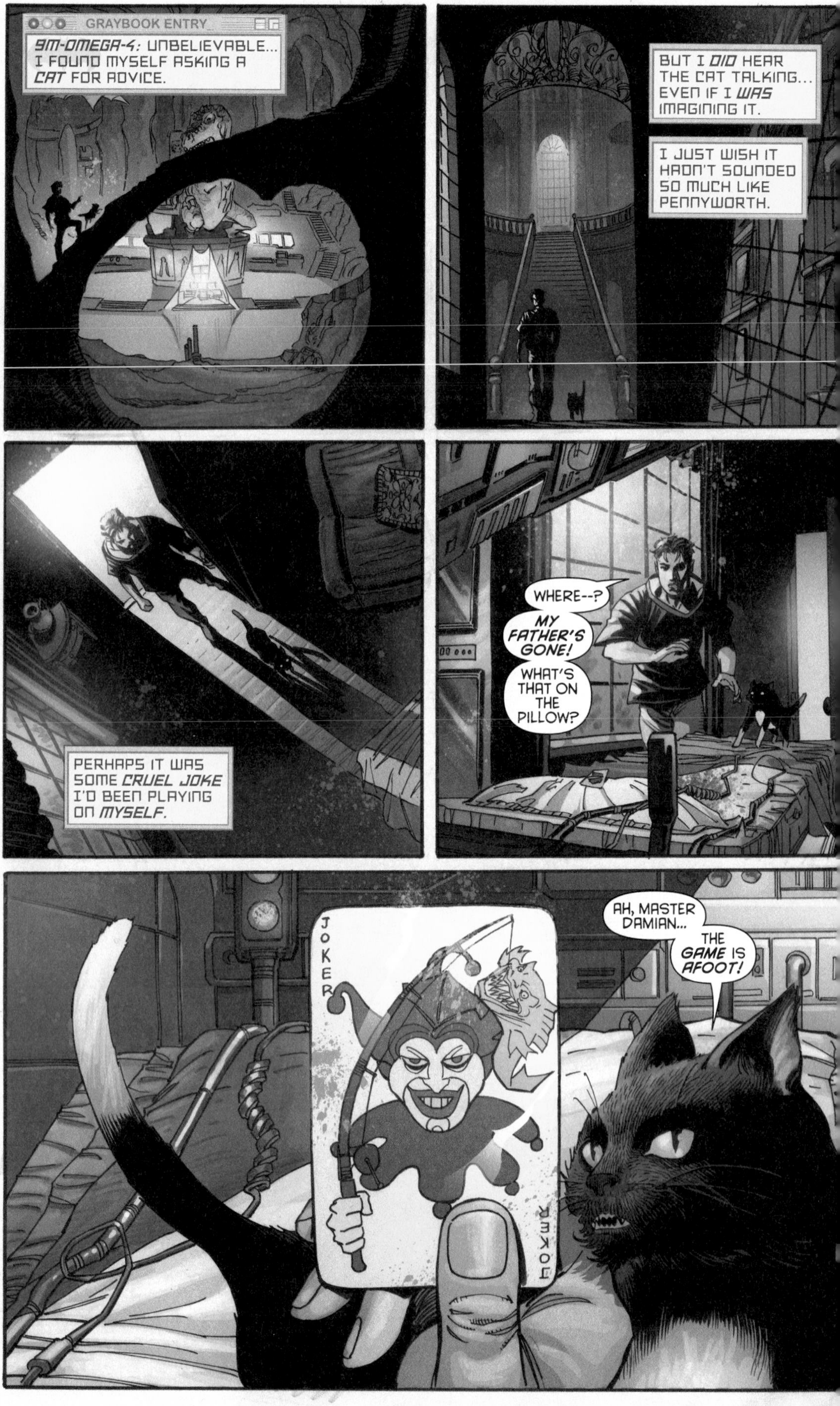
GRAYBOOK ENTRY
9M-OMEGA-4: UNBELIEVABLE... I FOUND MYSELF ASKING A CAT FOR ADVICE.
BUT I DID HEAR THE CAT TALKING... EVEN IF I WAS IMAGINING IT.
I JUST WISH IT HADN'T SOUNDED SO MUCH LIKE PENNYWORTH.
PERHAPS IT WAS SOME CRUEL JOKE I'D BEEN PLAYING ON MYSELF.
WHERE--?
MY FATHER'S GONE!
WHAT'S THAT ON THE PILLOW?
JOKER
AH, MASTER DAMIAN...
THE GAME IS AFOOT!

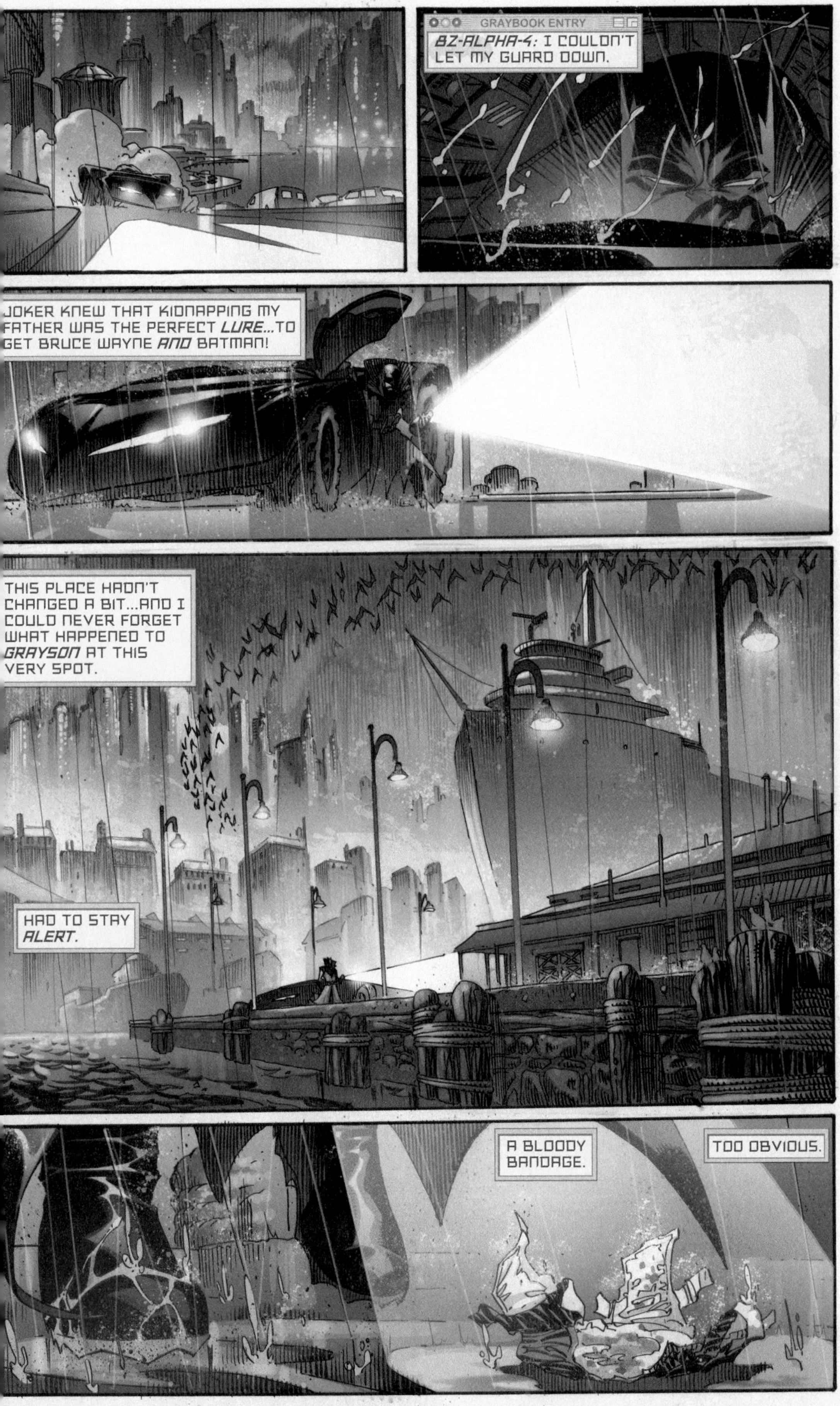
GRAYBOOK ENTRY
BZ-ALPHA-4: I COULDN'T LET MY GUARD DOWN.
JOKER KNEW THAT KIDNAPPING MY FATHER WAS THE PERFECT LURE...TO GET BRUCE WAYNE AND BATMAN!
THIS PLACE HADN'T CHANGED A BIT...AND I COULD NEVER FORGET WHAT HAPPENED TO GRAYSON AT THIS VERY SPOT.
HAD TO STAY ALERT.
A BLOODY BANDAGE.
TOO OBVIOUS.

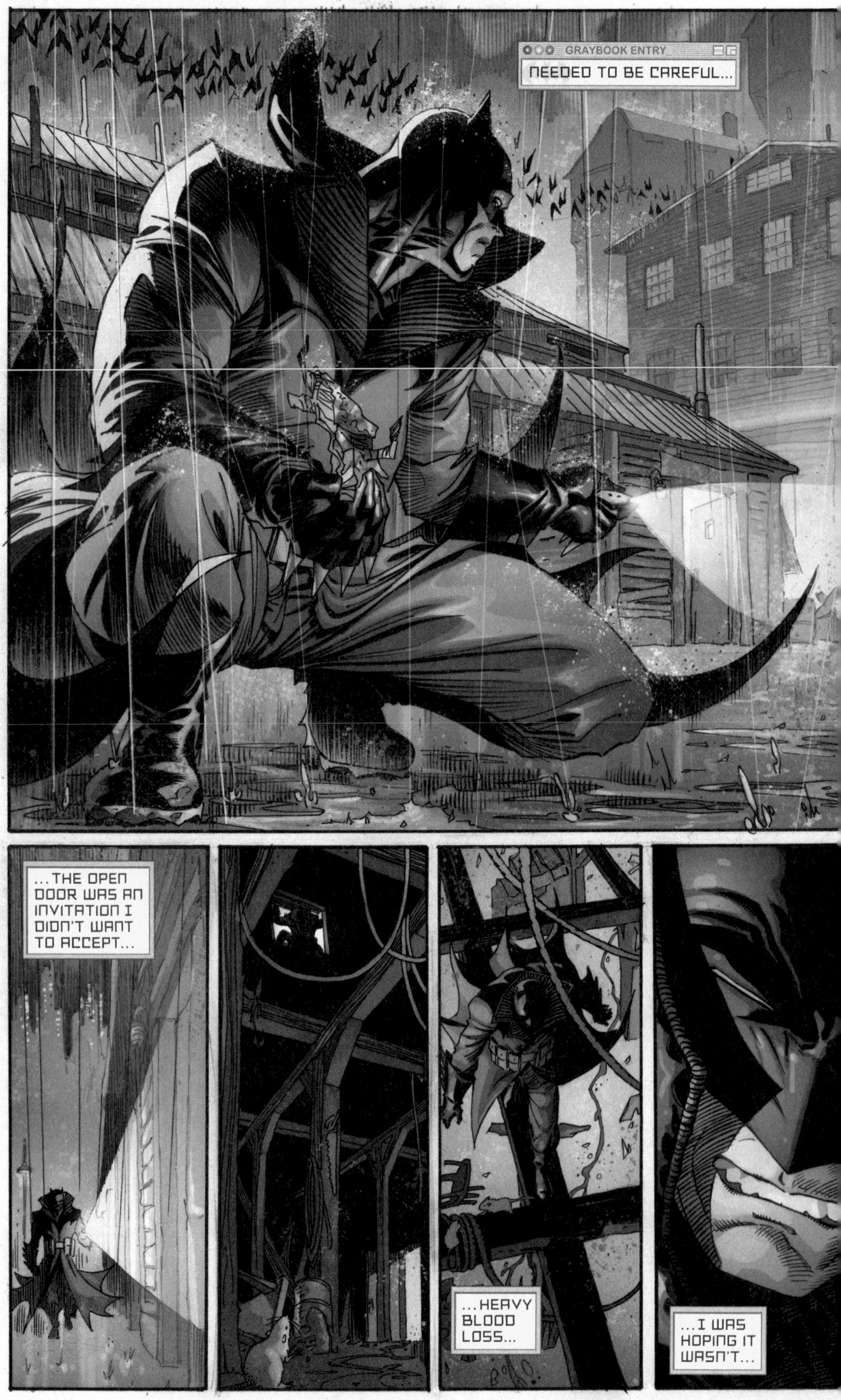
GRAYBOOK ENTRY
NEEDED TO BE CAREFUL...
...THE OPEN DOOR WAS AN INVITATION I DIDN'T WANT TO ACCEPT...
...HEAVY BLOOD LOSS...
...I WAS HOPING IT WASN'T...

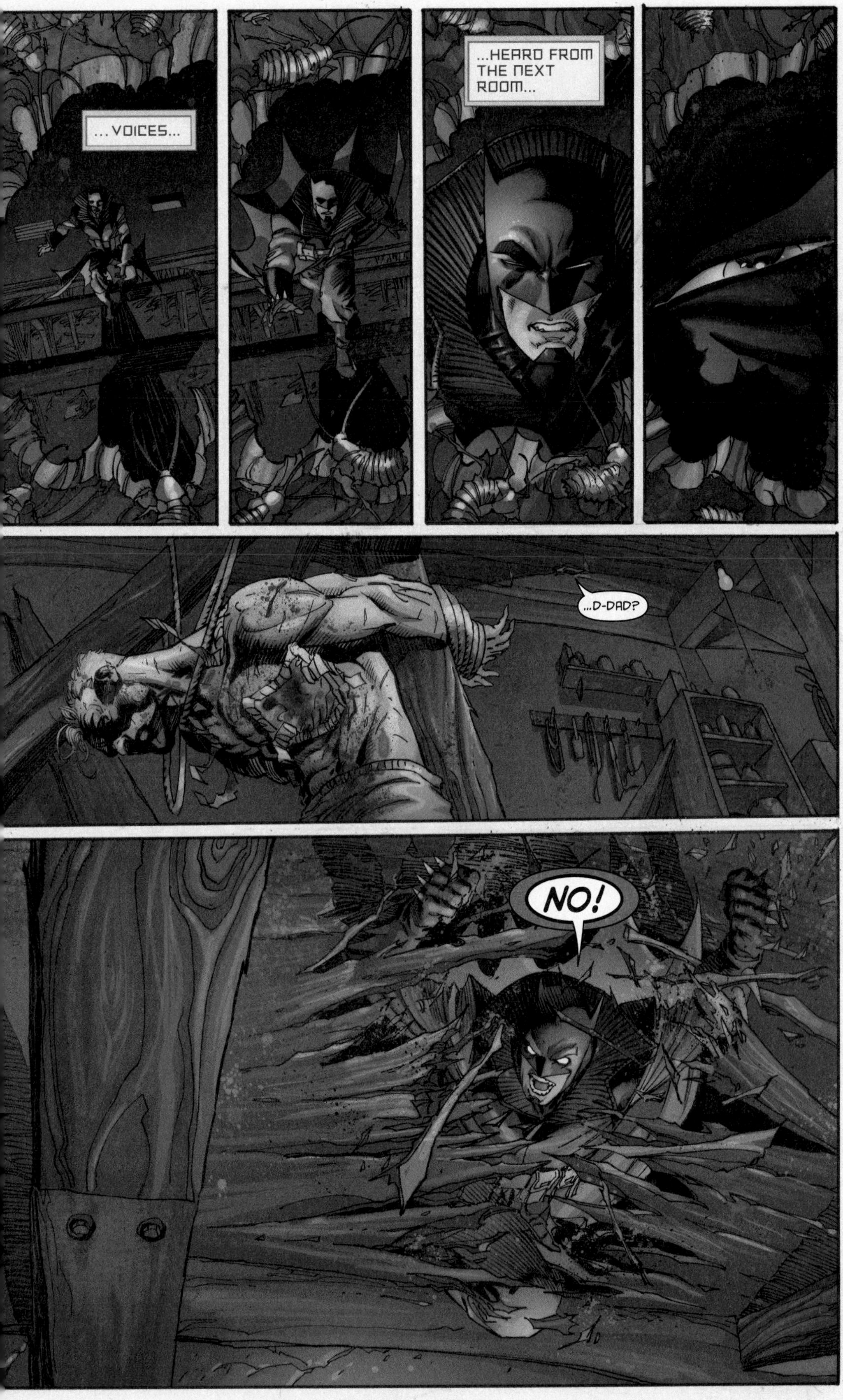
...VOICES...
...HEARD FROM THE NEXT ROOM...
...D-DAD?
NO!

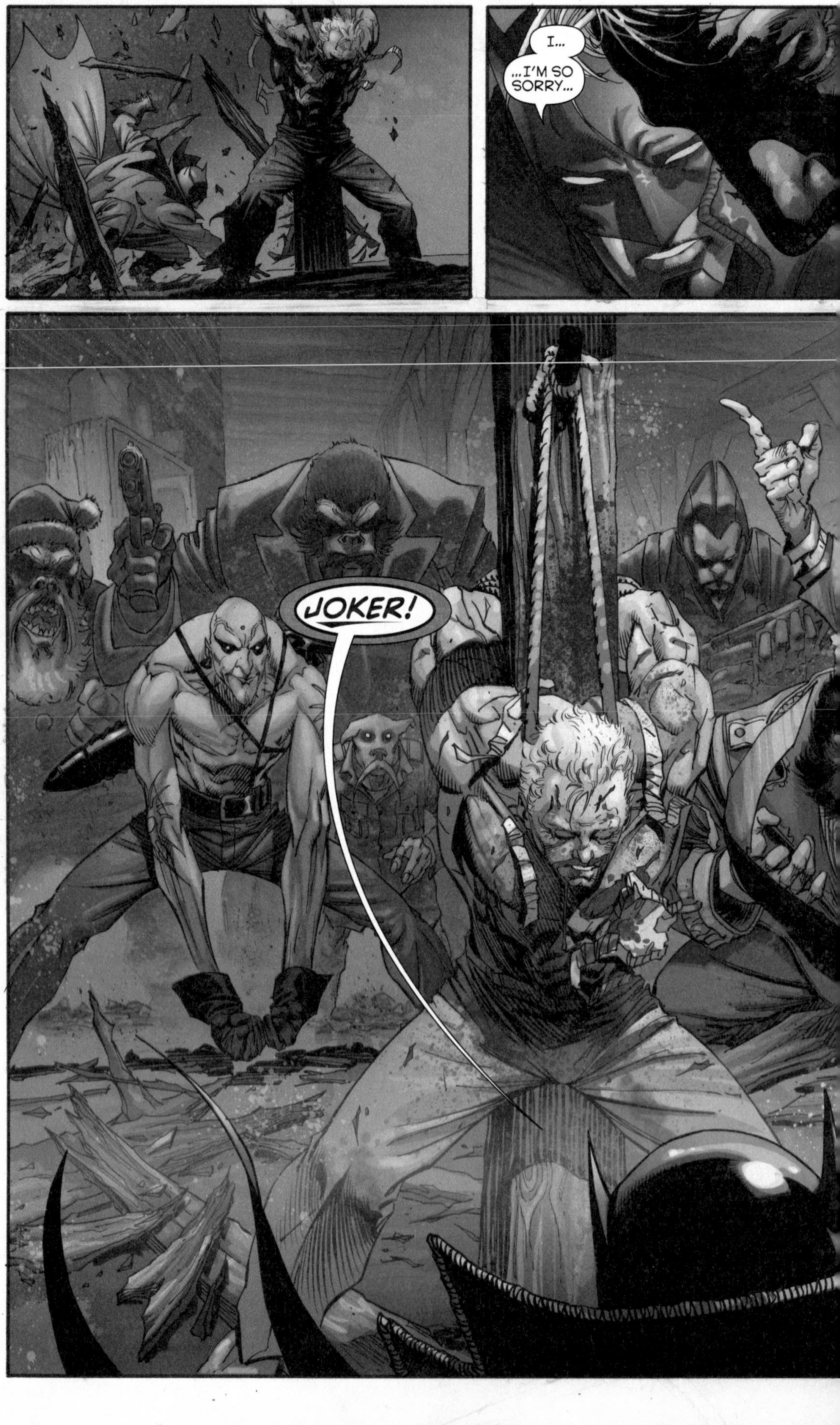
I...
...I'M SO SORRY...
JOKER!

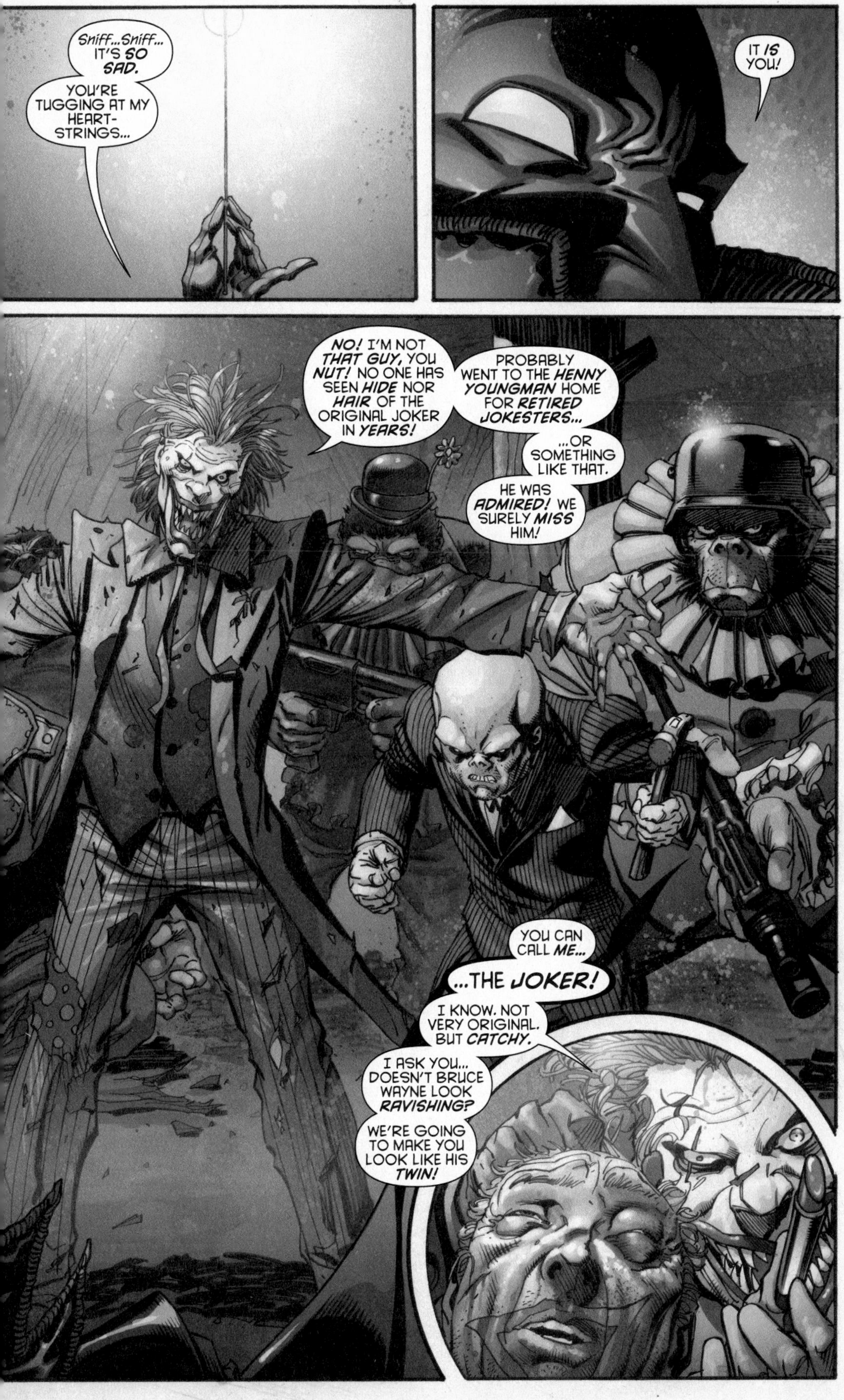
Sniff...Sniff... IT'S SO SAD.
YOU'RE TUGGING AT MY HEART-STRINGS...
IT IS YOU!
NO! I'M NOT THAT GUY, YOU NUT! NO ONE HAS SEEN HIDE NOR HAIR OF THE ORIGINAL JOKER IN YEARS!
PROBABLY WENT TO THE HENNY YOUNGMAN HOME FOR RETIRED JOKESTERS...
...OR SOMETHING LIKE THAT.
HE WAS ADMIRED! WE SURELY MISS HIM!
YOU CAN CALL ME...
...THE JOKER!
I KNOW. NOT VERY ORIGINAL. BUT CATCHY.
I ASK YOU... DOESN'T BRUCE WAYNE LOOK RAVISHING?
WE'RE GOING TO MAKE YOU LOOK LIKE HIS TWIN!

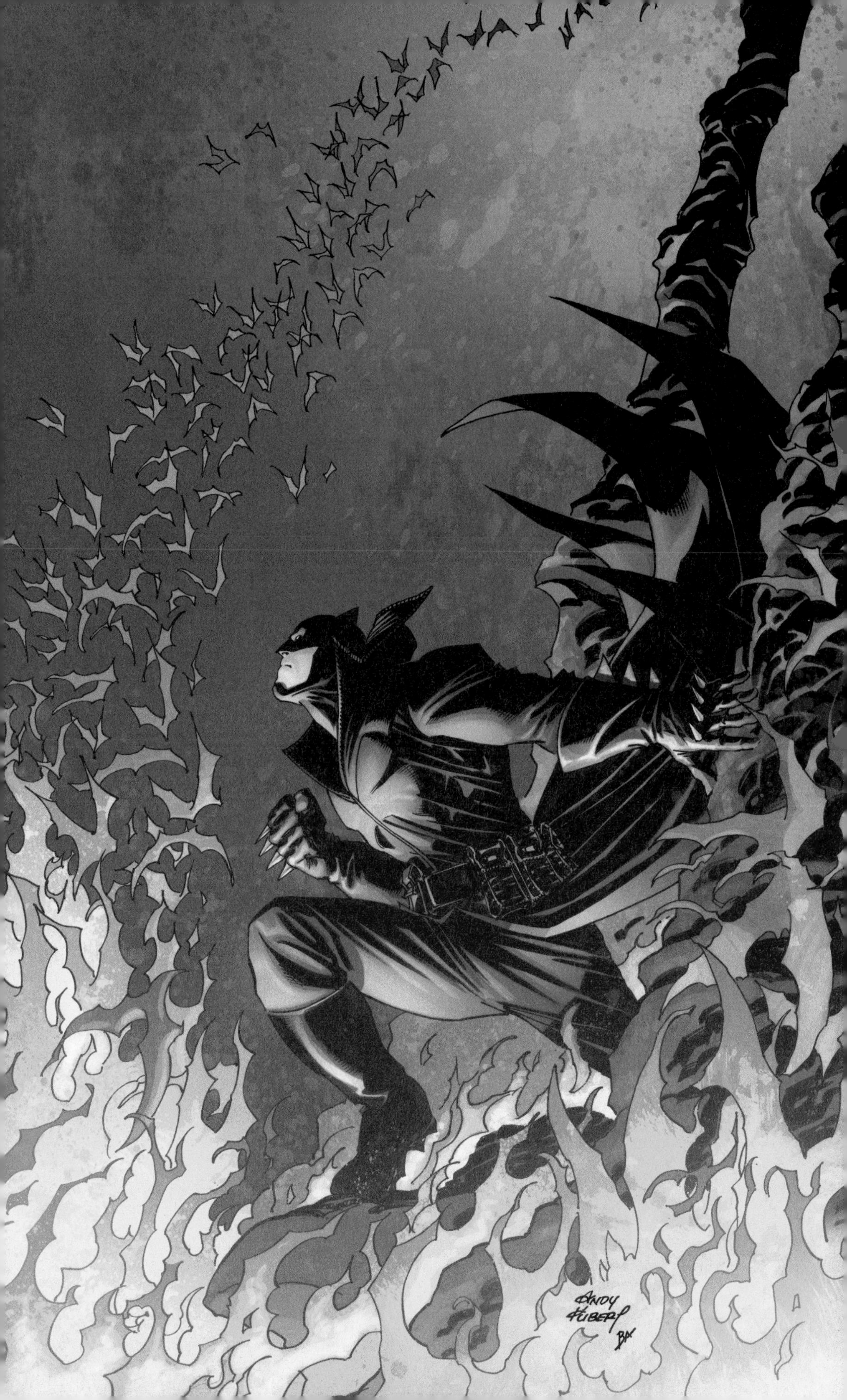
ANDY KUBERT
BA

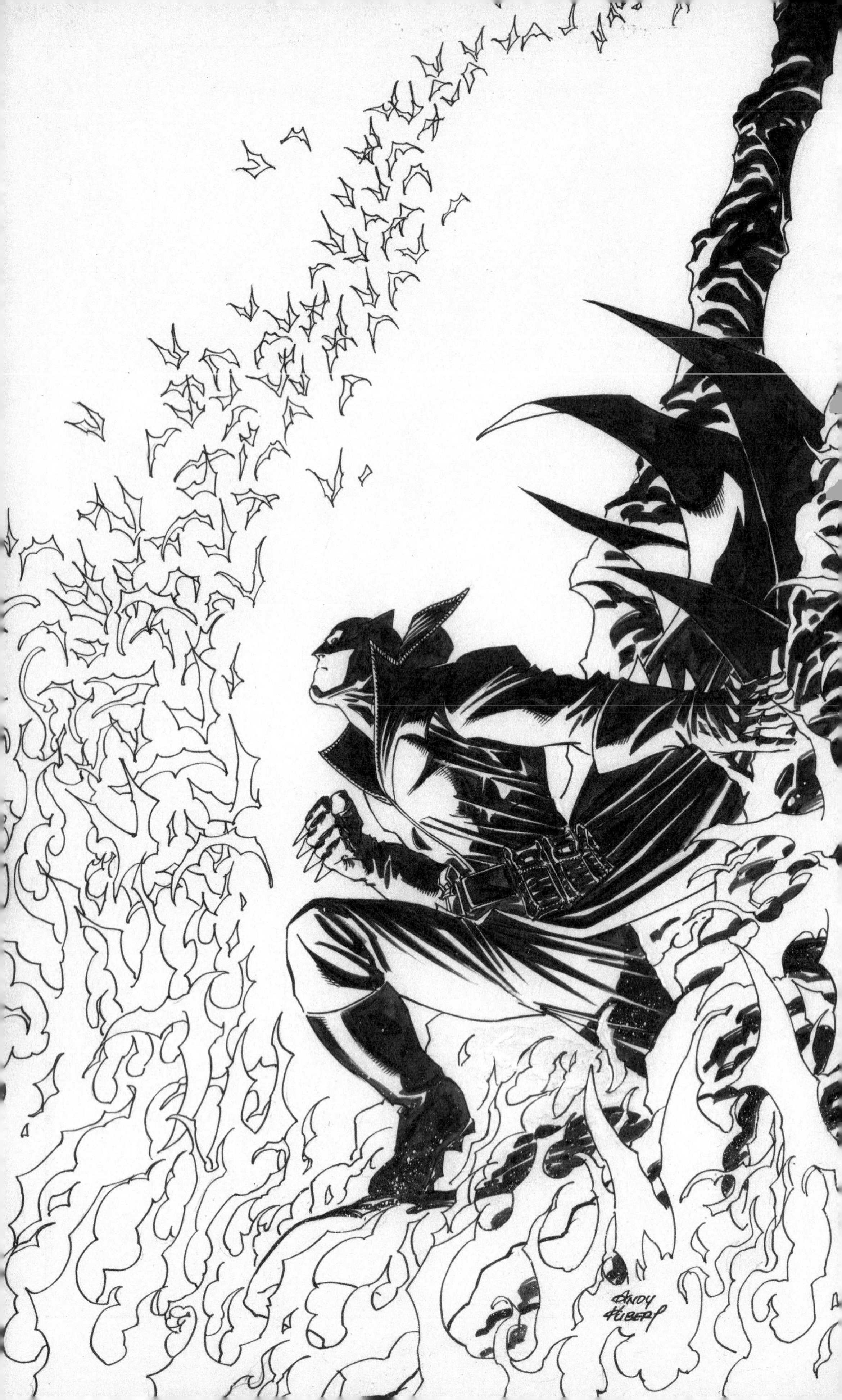
ANDY KUBERT

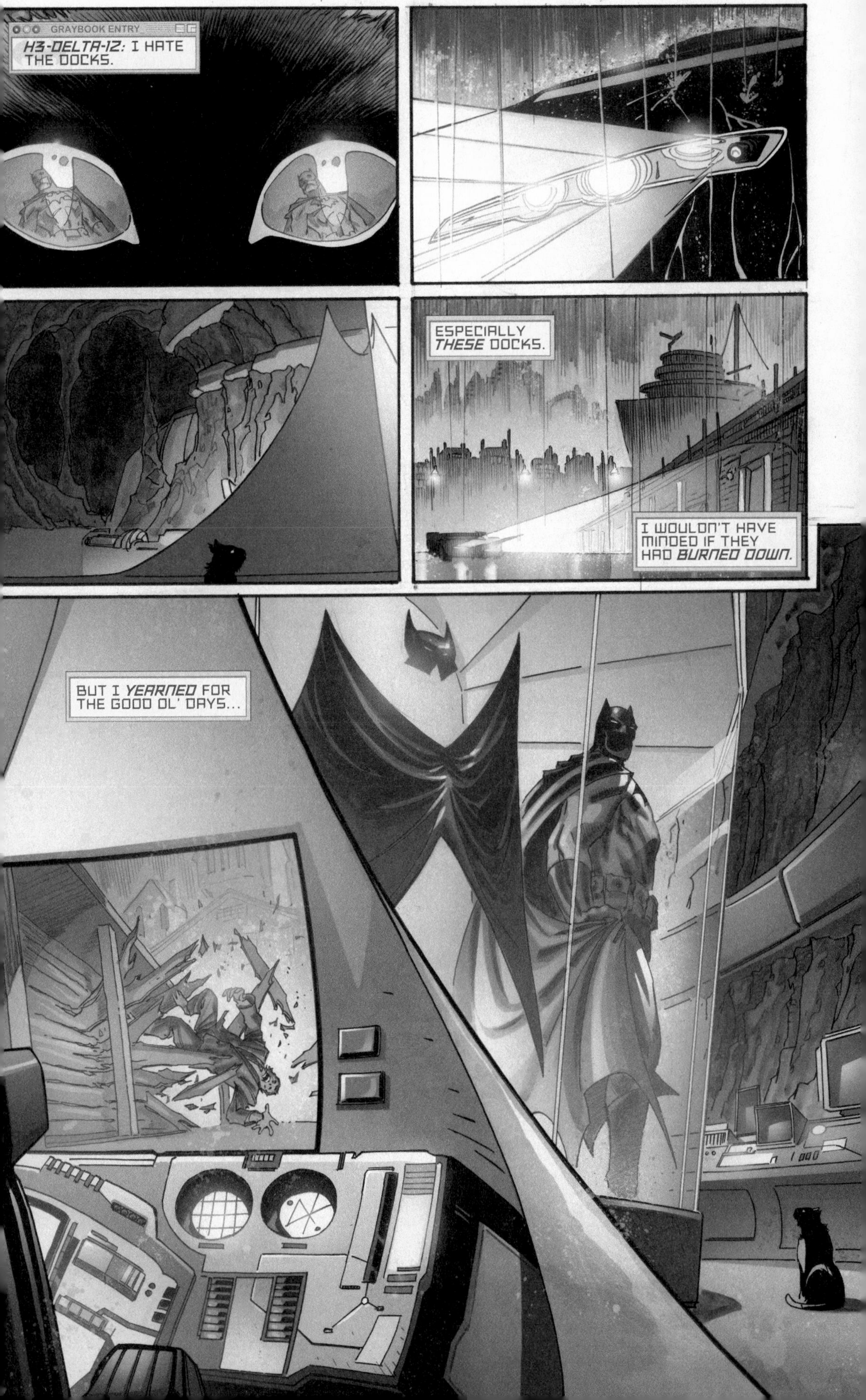
GRAYBOOK ENTRY
H3-DELTA-12: I HATE THE DOCKS.
ESPECIALLY THESE DOCKS.
I WOULDN'T HAVE MINDED IF THEY HAD BURNED DOWN.
BUT I YEARNED FOR THE GOOD OL' DAYS...

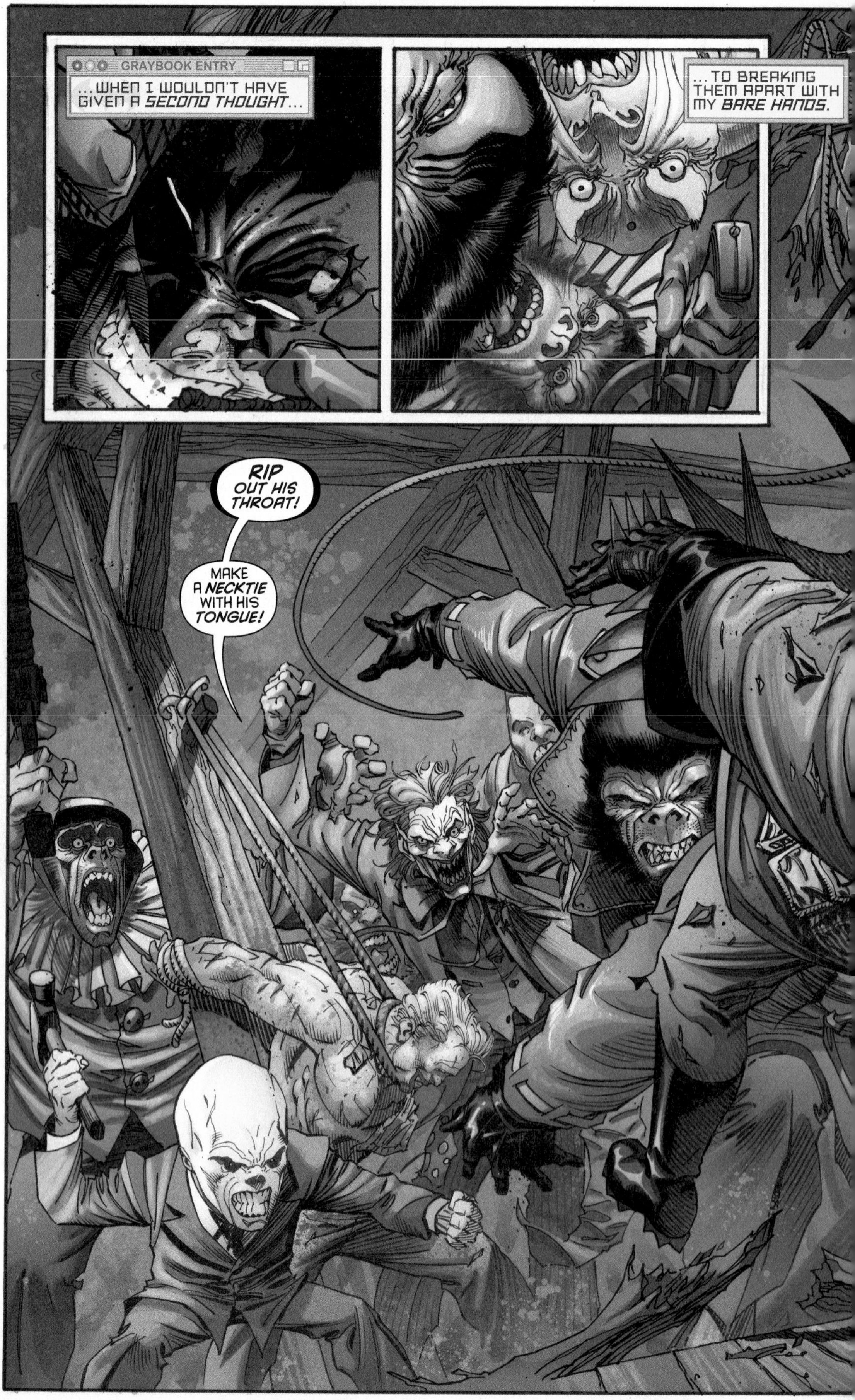
GRAYBOOK ENTRY
...WHEN I WOULDN'T HAVE GIVEN A SECOND THOUGHT...
...TO BREAKING THEM APART WITH MY BARE HANDS.
RIP OUT HIS THROAT!
MAKE A NECKTIE WITH HIS TONGUE!

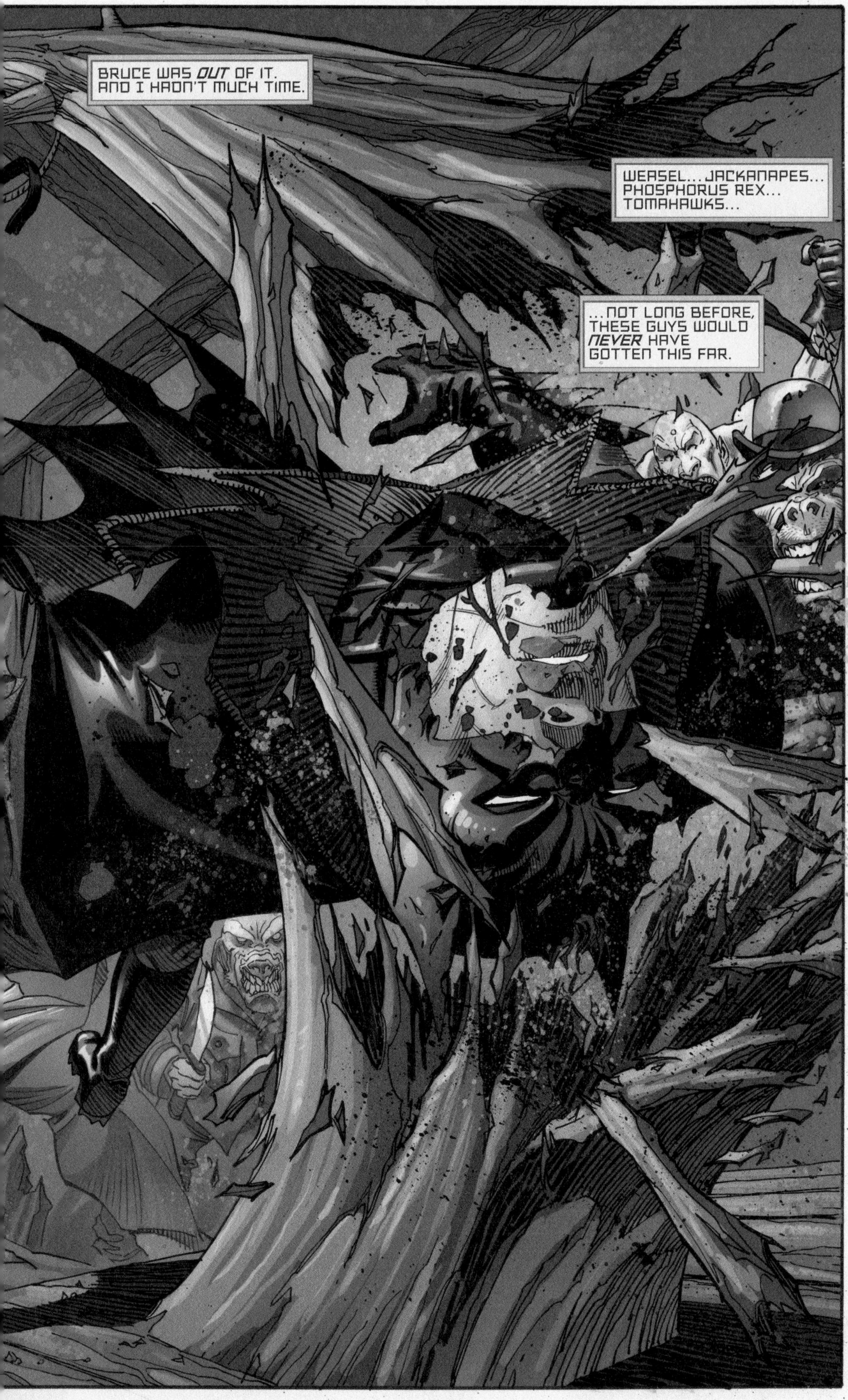
BRUCE WAS *OUT* OF IT. AND I HADN'T MUCH TIME.
WEASEL... JACKANAPES... PHOSPHORUS REX... TOMAHAWKS...
...NOT LONG BEFORE, THESE GUYS WOULD *NEVER* HAVE GOTTEN THIS FAR.

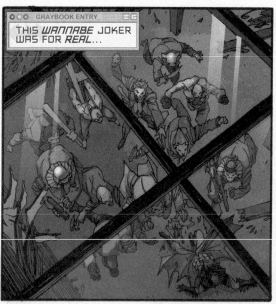

THIS *WANNABE* JOKER WAS FOR *REAL*...

...ALTHOUGH MUCH *UGLIER* THAN THE *ORIGINAL*, IF YOU CAN IMAGINE *THAT*.

SOMEDAY WHEN I HAVE SPARE TIME, I WANT TO HEAR *HIS* STORY.

AAAAHHHH!

DAMMIT!

THAT *HURT*!

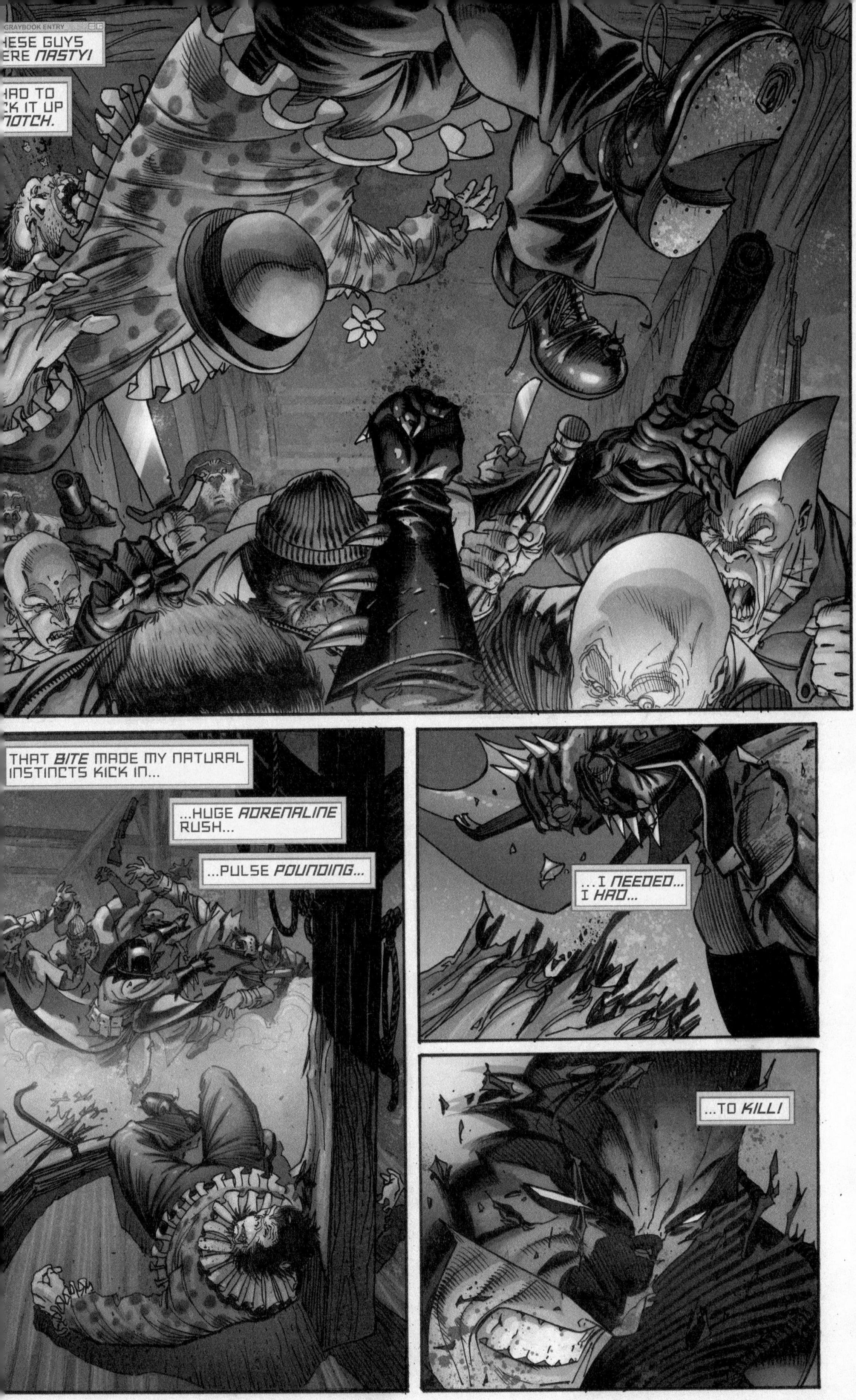
GRAYBOOK ENTRY
HESE GUYS ERE NASTY!
HAD TO CK IT UP NOTCH.
THAT BITE MADE MY NATURAL INSTINCTS KICK IN...
...HUGE ADRENALINE RUSH...
...PULSE POUNDING...
...I NEEDED... I HAD...
...TO KILL!

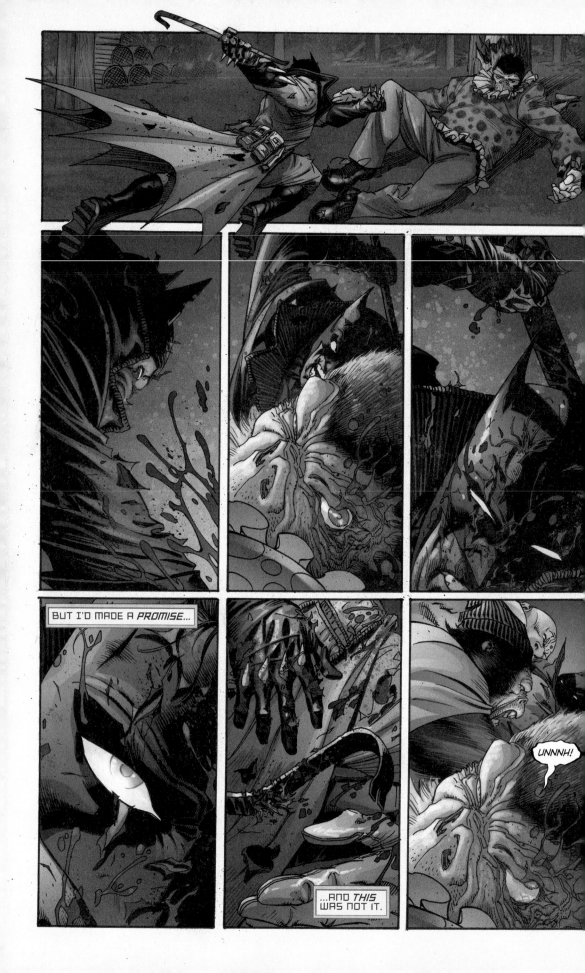

BUT I'D MADE A *PROMISE*...

...AND *THIS* WAS NOT IT.

UNNNH!

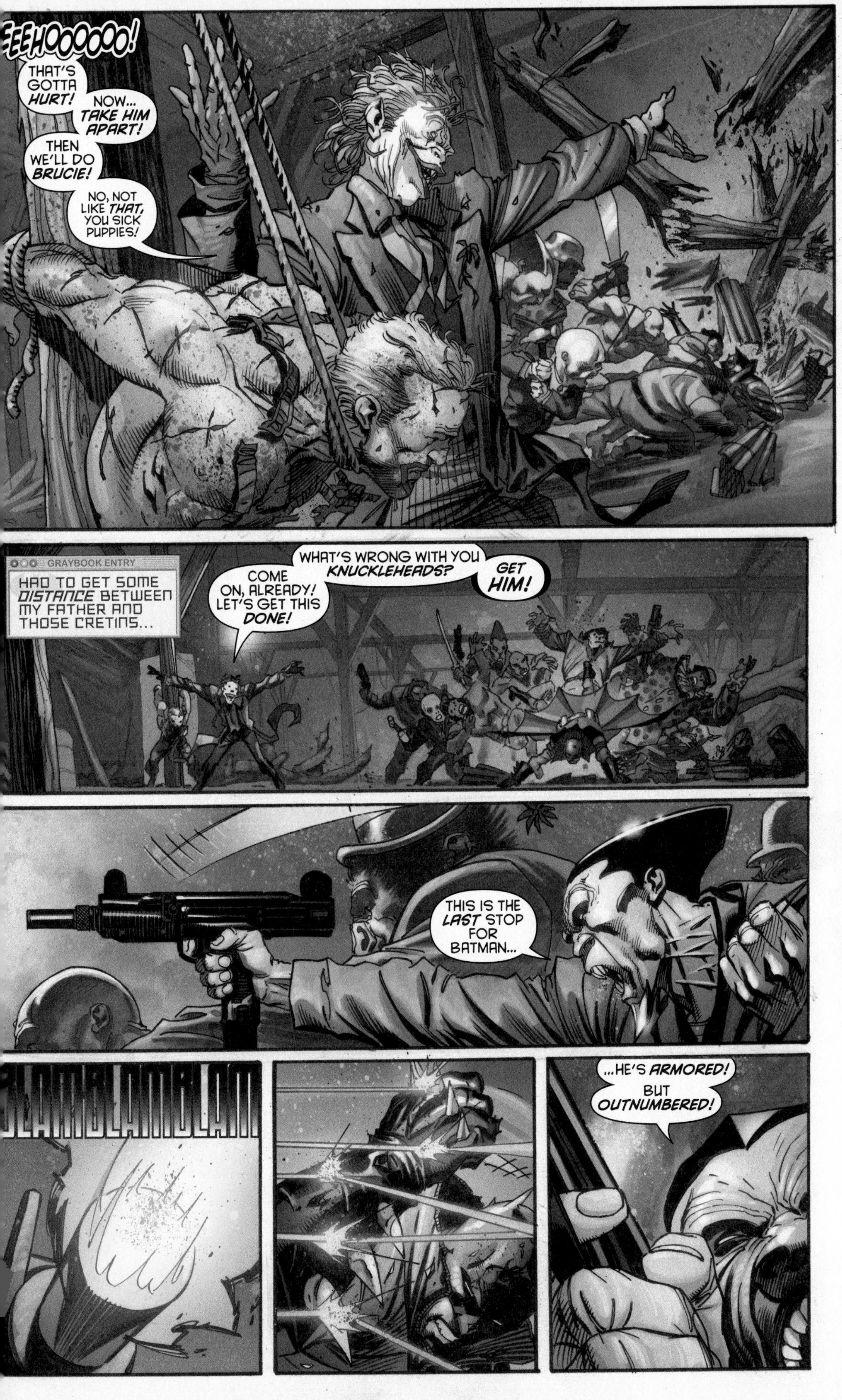
EEEHOOOOOO!
THAT'S GOTTA HURT!
NOW... TAKE HIM APART!
THEN WE'LL DO BRUCIE!
NO, NOT LIKE THAT, YOU SICK PUPPIES!
GRAYBOOK ENTRY
HAD TO GET SOME DISTANCE BETWEEN MY FATHER AND THOSE CRETINS...
COME ON, ALREADY! LET'S GET THIS DONE!
WHAT'S WRONG WITH YOU KNUCKLEHEADS?
GET HIM!
THIS IS THE LAST STOP FOR BATMAN...
BLAMBLAMBLAM
...HE'S ARMORED! BUT OUTNUMBERED!

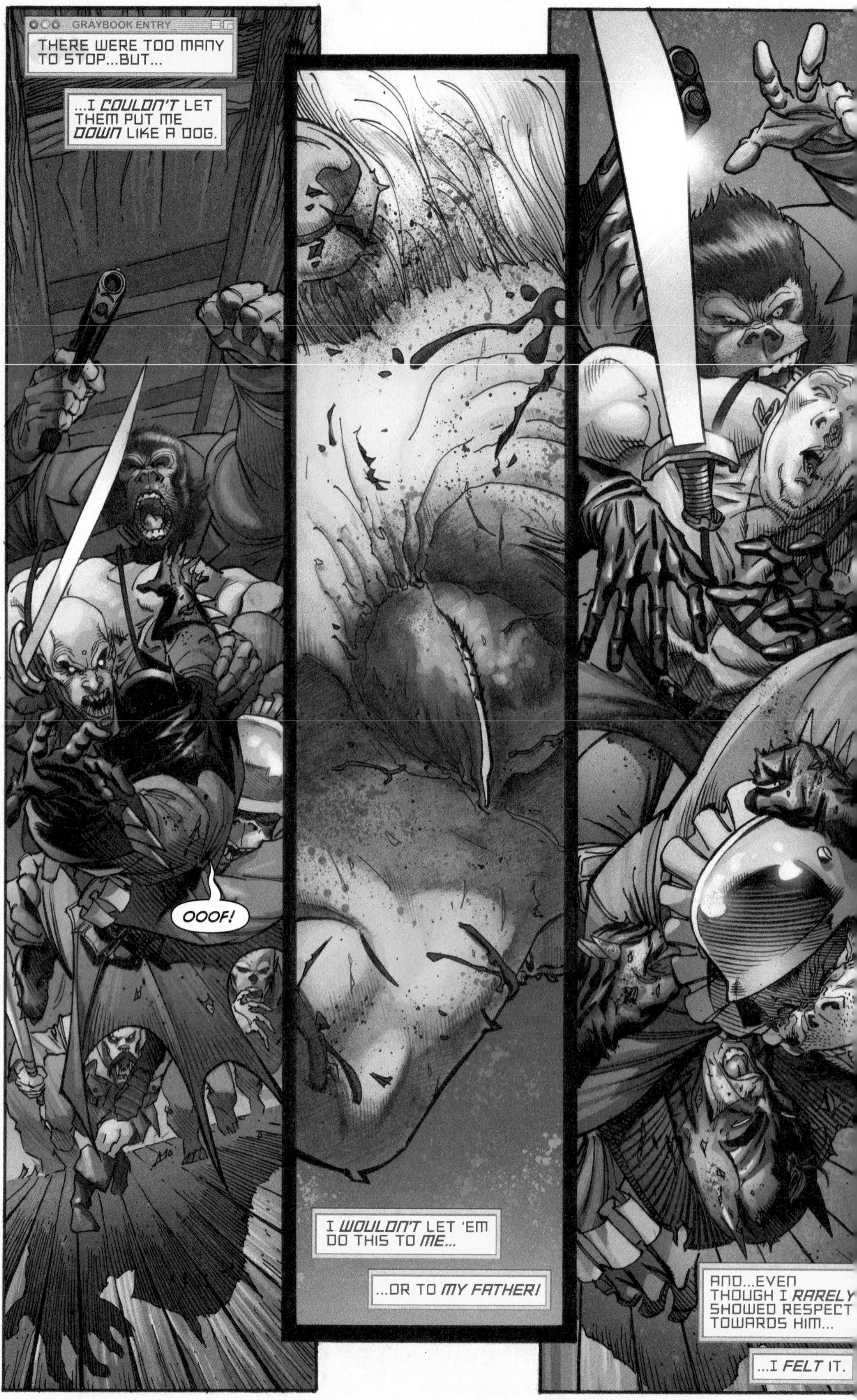
GRAYBOOK ENTRY
THERE WERE TOO MANY TO STOP...BUT...
...I COULDN'T LET THEM PUT ME DOWN LIKE A DOG.
OOOF!
I WOULDN'T LET 'EM DO THIS TO ME...
...OR TO MY FATHER!
AND...EVEN THOUGH I RARELY SHOWED RESPECT TOWARDS HIM...
...I FELT IT.

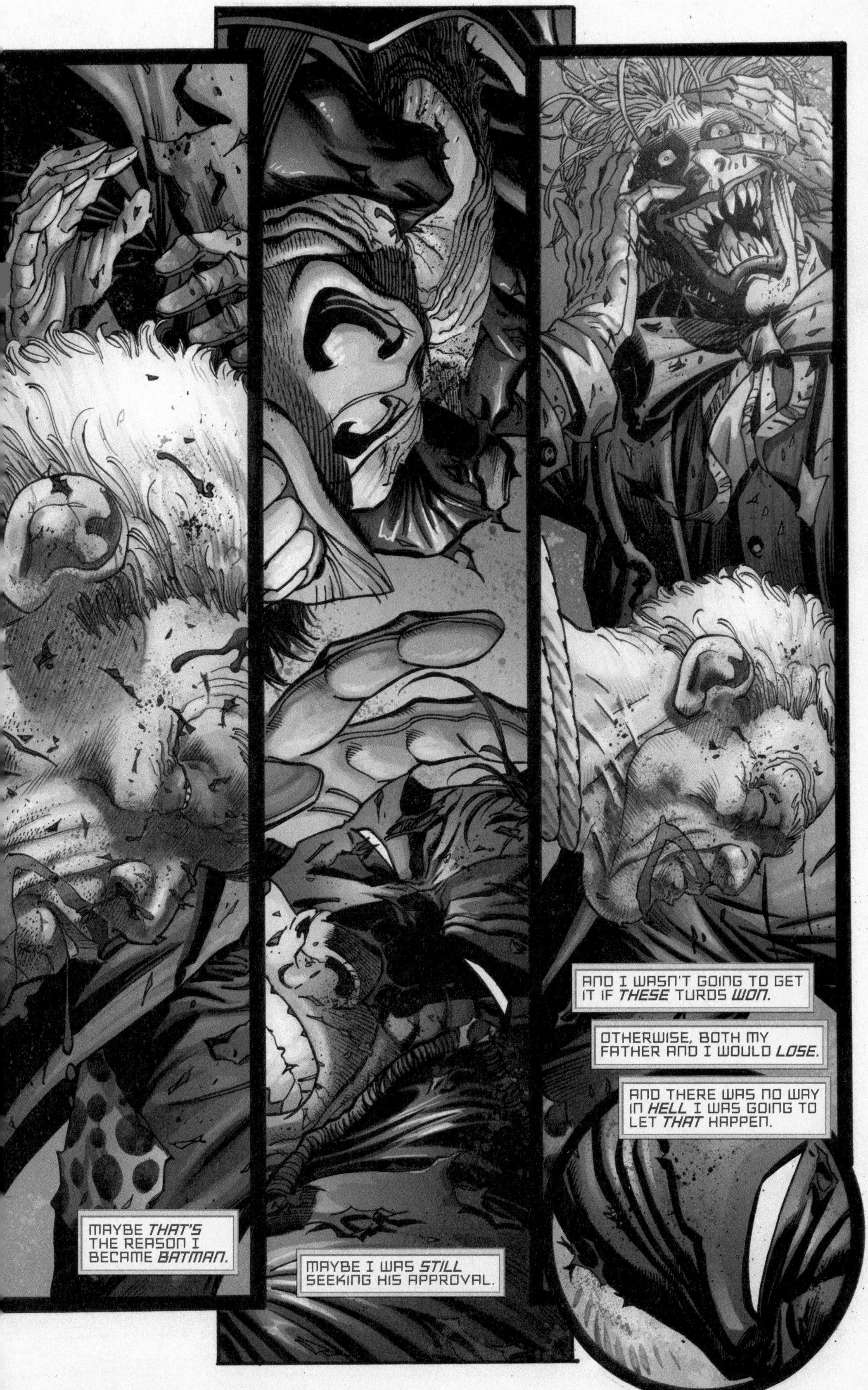
MAYBE THAT'S THE REASON I BECAME BATMAN.
MAYBE I WAS STILL SEEKING HIS APPROVAL.
AND I WASN'T GOING TO GET IT IF THESE TURDS WON.
OTHERWISE, BOTH MY FATHER AND I WOULD LOSE.
AND THERE WAS NO WAY IN HELL I WAS GOING TO LET THAT HAPPEN.

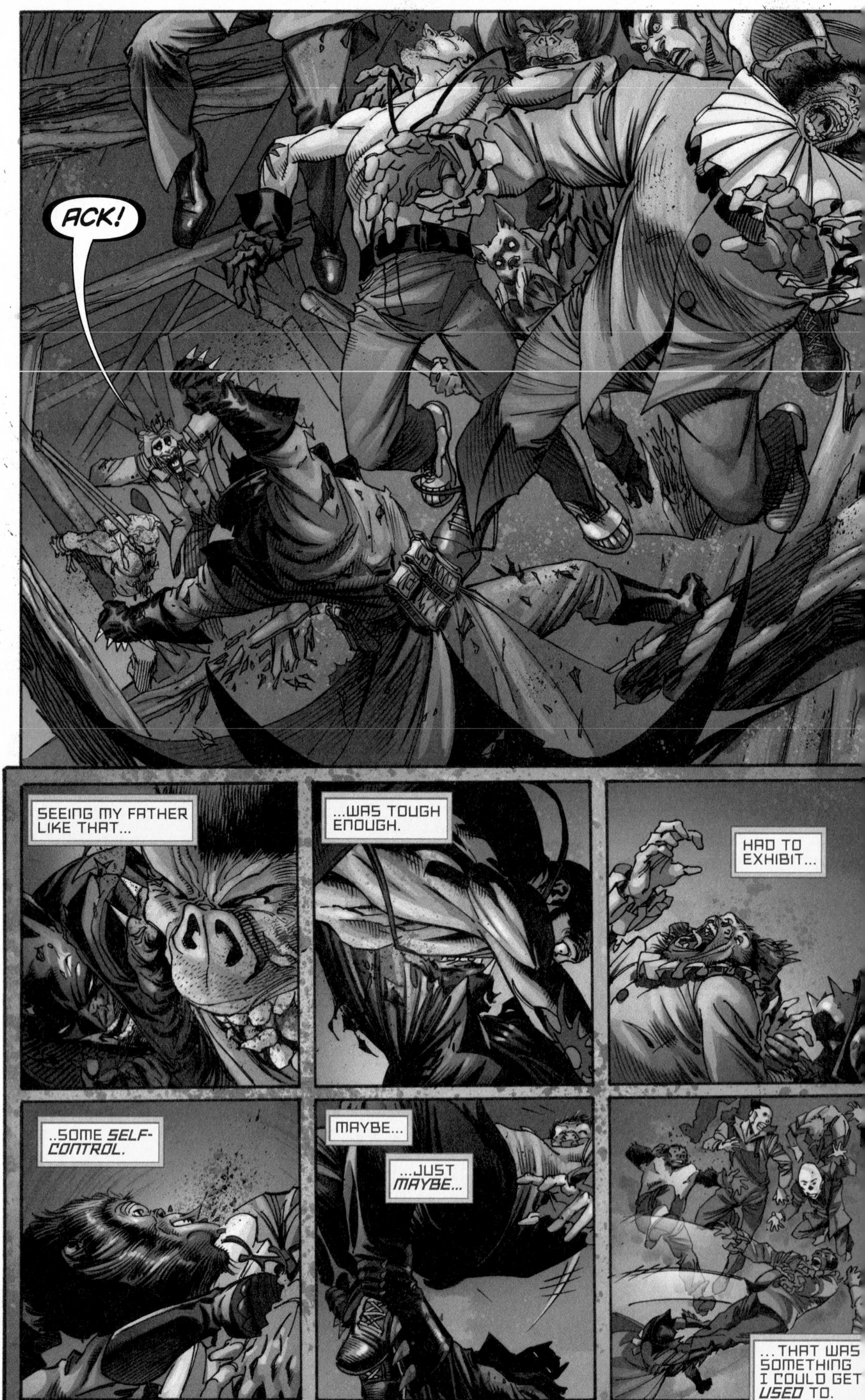
ACK!
SEEING MY FATHER LIKE THAT...
...WAS TOUGH ENOUGH.
HAD TO EXHIBIT...
..SOME SELF-CONTROL.
MAYBE...
...JUST MAYBE...
...THAT WAS SOMETHING I COULD GET USED TO.

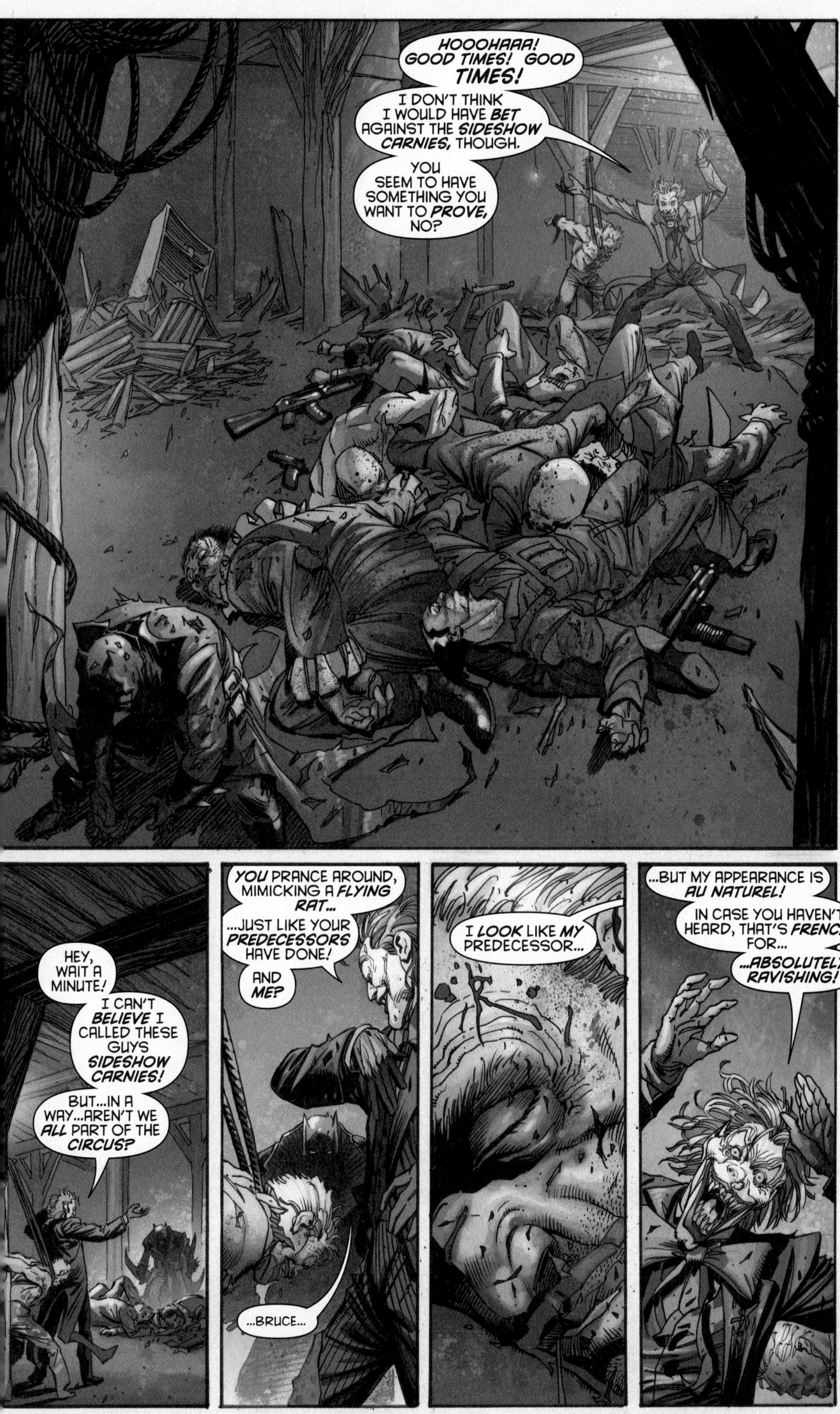

HOOOHAAA! GOOD TIMES! GOOD TIMES!
I DON'T THINK I WOULD HAVE BET AGAINST THE SIDESHOW CARNIES, THOUGH.
YOU SEEM TO HAVE SOMETHING YOU WANT TO PROVE, NO?
HEY, WAIT A MINUTE!
I CAN'T BELIEVE I CALLED THESE GUYS SIDESHOW CARNIES!
BUT...IN A WAY...AREN'T WE ALL PART OF THE CIRCUS?
YOU PRANCE AROUND, MIMICKING A FLYING RAT...
...JUST LIKE YOUR PREDECESSORS HAVE DONE!
AND ME?
...BRUCE...
I LOOK LIKE MY PREDECESSOR...
...BUT MY APPEARANCE IS AU NATUREL!
IN CASE YOU HAVEN'T HEARD, THAT'S FRENCH FOR...
...ABSOLUTELY RAVISHING!

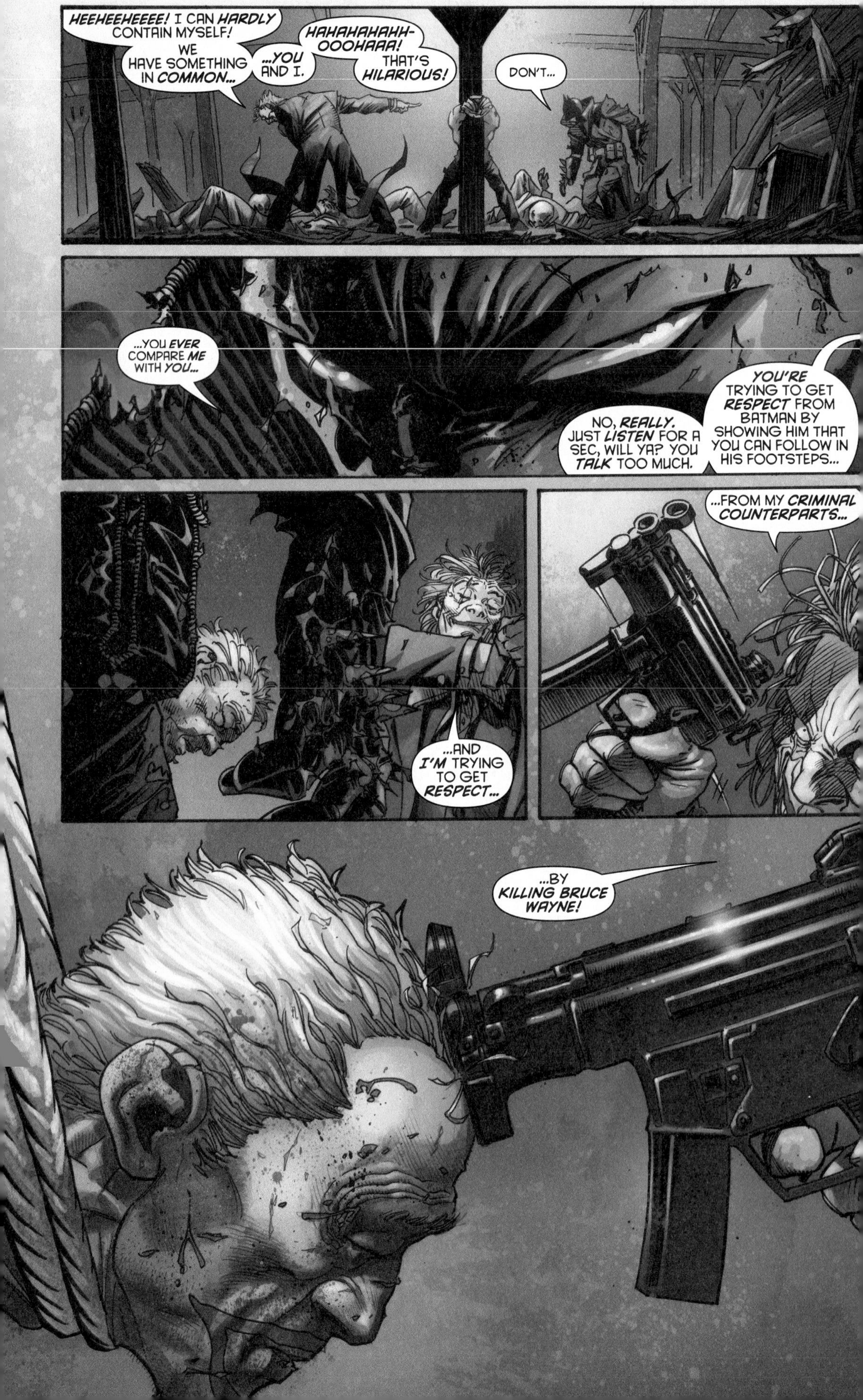
HEEHEEHEEEE! I CAN HARDLY CONTAIN MYSELF!
WE HAVE SOMETHING IN COMMON...
...YOU AND I.
HAHAHAHAHH-OOOHAAA! THAT'S HILARIOUS!
DON'T...
...YOU EVER COMPARE ME WITH YOU...
NO, REALLY. JUST LISTEN FOR A SEC, WILL YA? YOU TALK TOO MUCH.
YOU'RE TRYING TO GET RESPECT FROM BATMAN BY SHOWING HIM THAT YOU CAN FOLLOW IN HIS FOOTSTEPS...
...AND I'M TRYING TO GET RESPECT...
...FROM MY CRIMINAL COUNTERPARTS...
...BY KILLING BRUCE WAYNE!

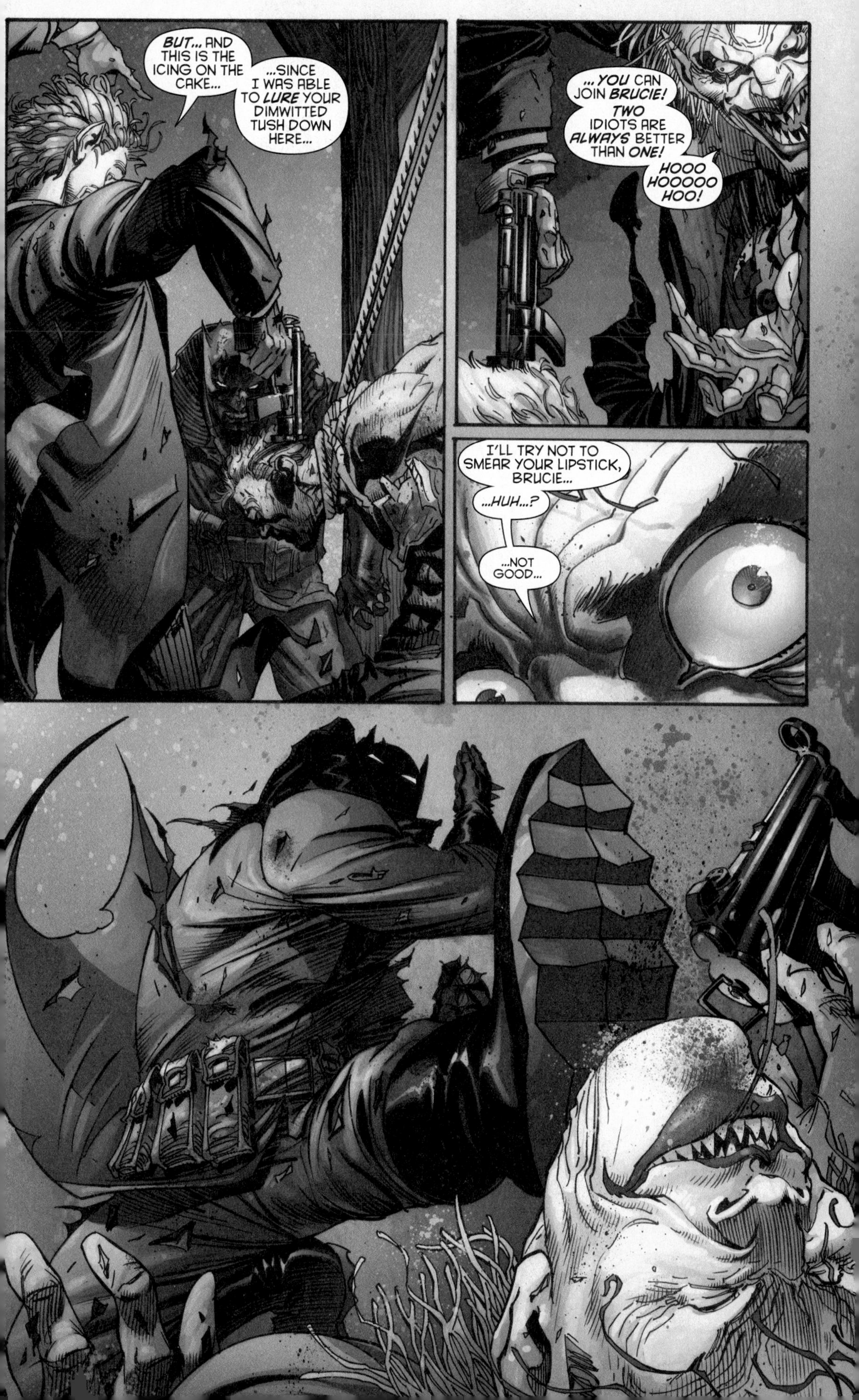
BUT... AND THIS IS THE ICING ON THE CAKE...
...SINCE I WAS ABLE TO LURE YOUR DIMWITTED TUSH DOWN HERE...
...YOU CAN JOIN BRUCIE! TWO IDIOTS ARE ALWAYS BETTER THAN ONE!
HOOO HOOOOO HOO!
I'LL TRY NOT TO SMEAR YOUR LIPSTICK, BRUCIE...
...HUH...?
...NOT GOOD...

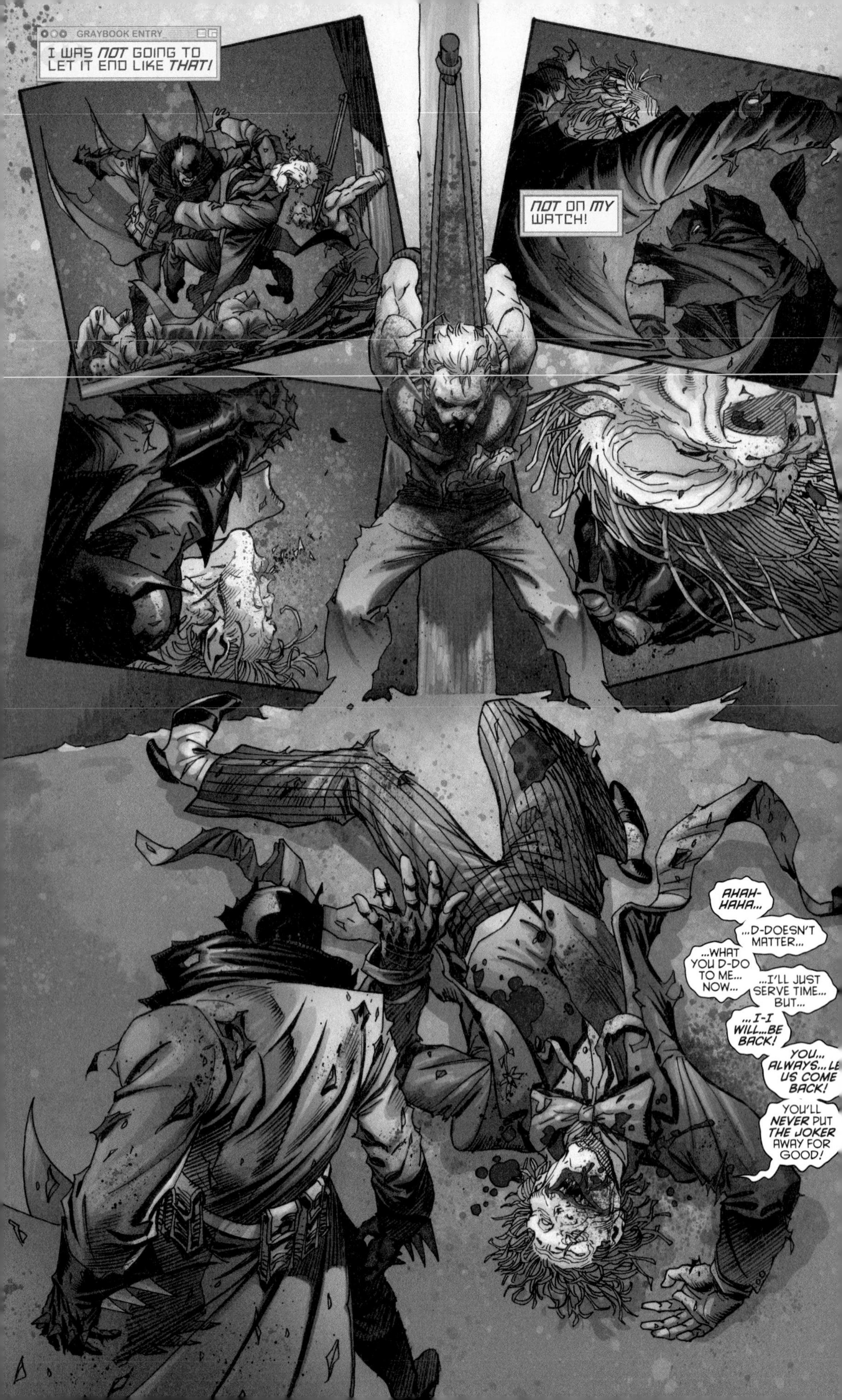
GRAYBOOK ENTRY
I WAS NOT GOING TO LET IT END LIKE THAT!
NOT ON MY WATCH!
AHAH-HAHA...
...D-DOESN'T MATTER...
...WHAT YOU D-DO TO ME... NOW...
...I'LL JUST SERVE TIME... BUT...
...I-I WILL...BE BACK!
YOU... ALWAYS...LE US COME BACK!
YOU'LL NEVER PUT THE JOKER AWAY FOR GOOD!

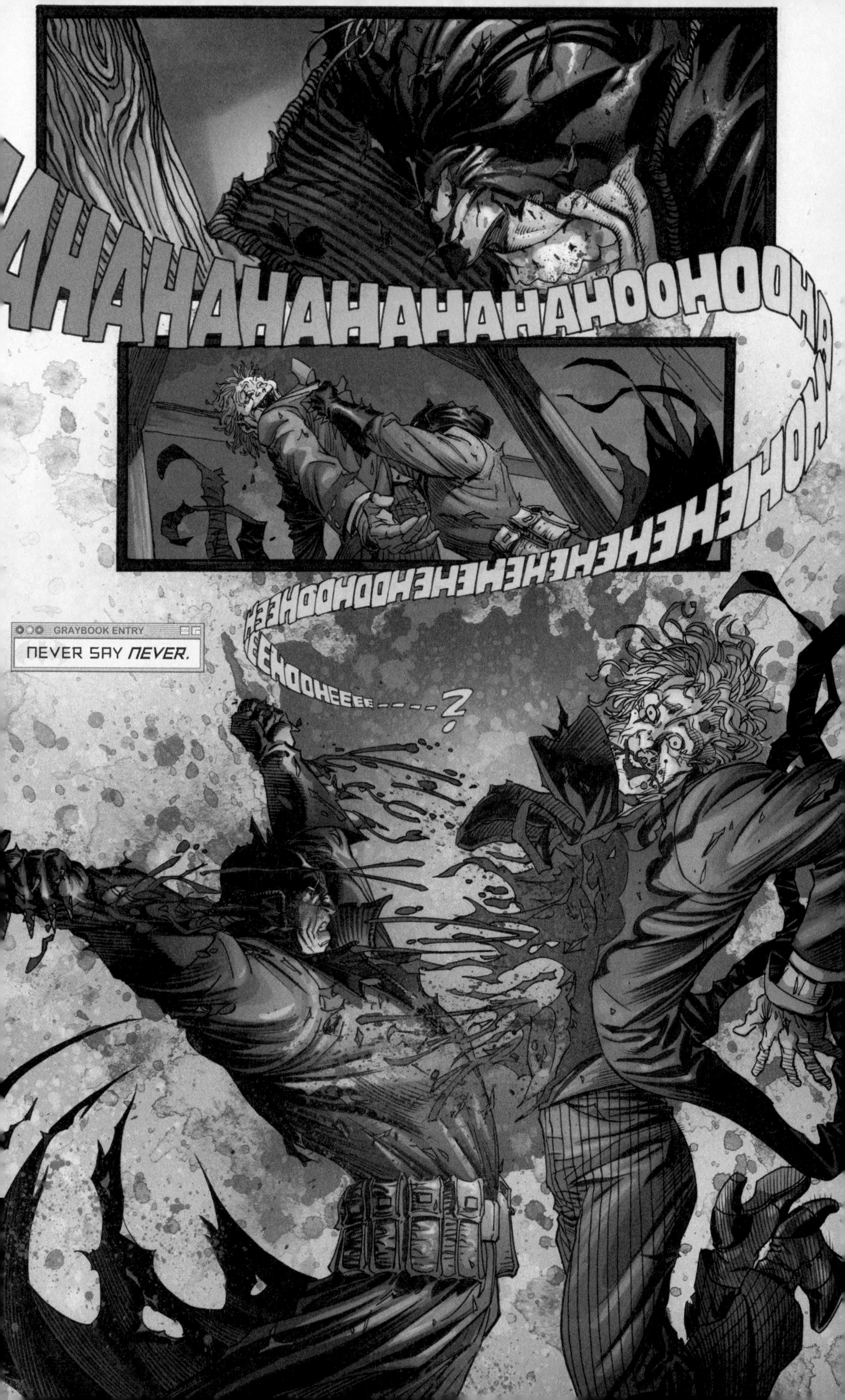

AHAHAHAHAHAHAHAHOOHOOHAHOHOHEHEHEHEHEHOOHOOHEEHEEHOOHEEEE----?
GRAYBOOK ENTRY
NEVER SAY *NEVER.*

I STILL FEEL THAT A *PART* OF ME LET MY FATHER DOWN.

BUT THERE WAS *ANOTHER* PART OF ME THAT FELT *REJUVENATED.* AS IF MY BATTERIES HAD BEEN RECHARGED.

BRUCE...

...I'M SO... VERY SORRY ABOUT... WHAT HAS HAPPENED TO YOU...

...UHNN....

...I'LL NEVER...

...LET THAT HAPPEN...

...TO YOU..

...AGAIN...

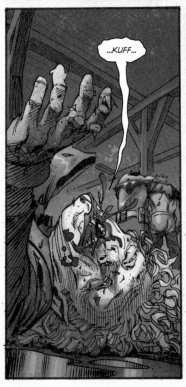

...KUFF...

HeeHe →KOFF←

...NOT...

...DEAD...

..YET--?

POK

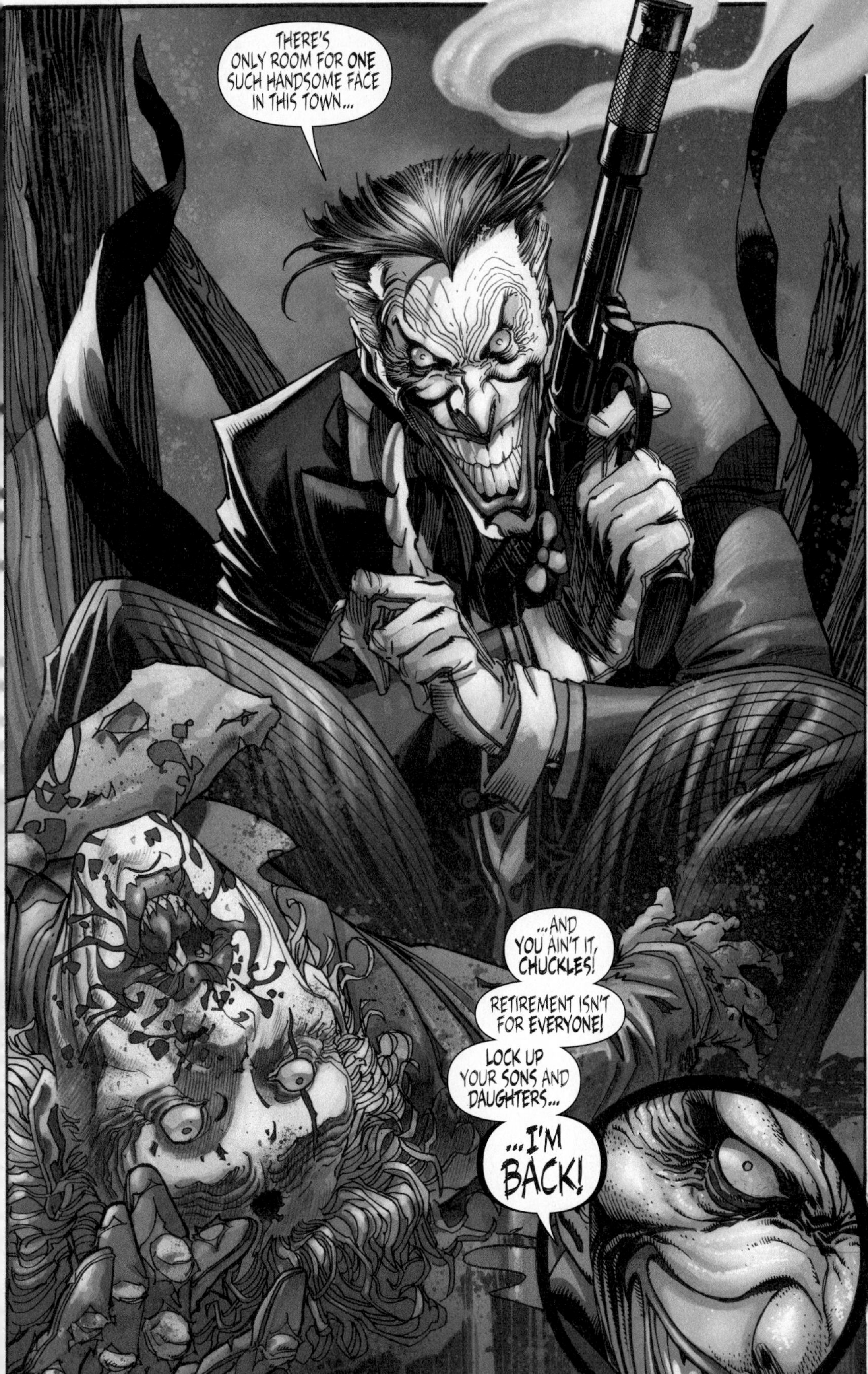
THERE'S ONLY ROOM FOR ONE SUCH HANDSOME FACE IN THIS TOWN...
...AND YOU AIN'T IT, CHUCKLES!
RETIREMENT ISN'T FOR EVERYONE!
LOCK UP YOUR SONS AND DAUGHTERS...
...I'M BACK!

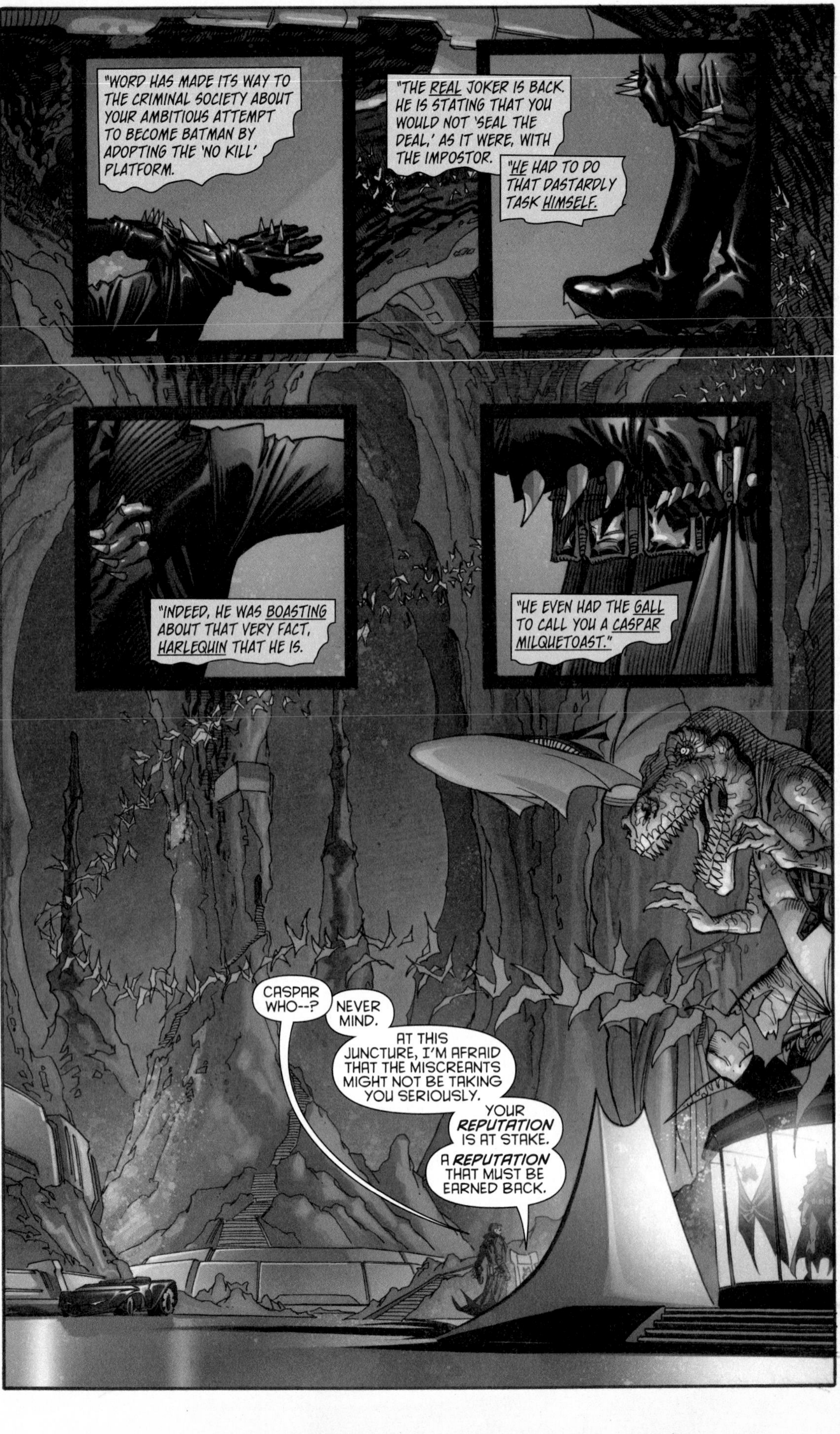

"WORD HAS MADE ITS WAY TO THE CRIMINAL SOCIETY ABOUT YOUR AMBITIOUS ATTEMPT TO BECOME BATMAN BY ADOPTING THE 'NO KILL' PLATFORM.
"THE REAL JOKER IS BACK. HE IS STATING THAT YOU WOULD NOT 'SEAL THE DEAL,' AS IT WERE, WITH THE IMPOSTOR.
"HE HAD TO DO THAT DASTARDLY TASK HIMSELF.
"INDEED, HE WAS BOASTING ABOUT THAT VERY FACT, HARLEQUIN THAT HE IS.
"HE EVEN HAD THE GALL TO CALL YOU A CASPAR MILQUETOAST."
CASPAR WHO--?
NEVER MIND.
AT THIS JUNCTURE, I'M AFRAID THAT THE MISCREANTS MIGHT NOT BE TAKING YOU SERIOUSLY.
YOUR REPUTATION IS AT STAKE.
A REPUTATION THAT MUST BE EARNED BACK.

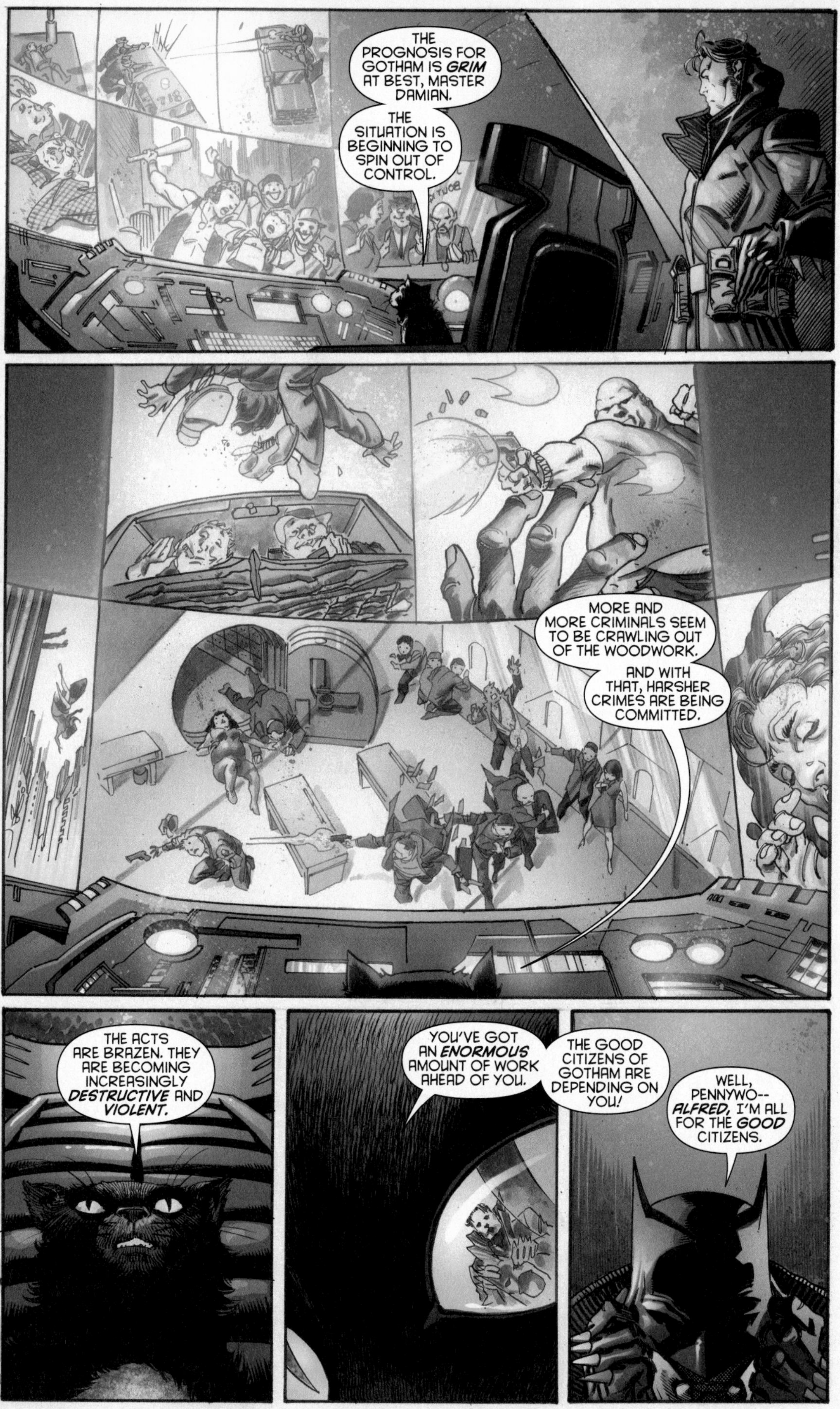
THE PROGNOSIS FOR GOTHAM IS GRIM AT BEST, MASTER DAMIAN.
THE SITUATION IS BEGINNING TO SPIN OUT OF CONTROL.
MORE AND MORE CRIMINALS SEEM TO BE CRAWLING OUT OF THE WOODWORK.
AND WITH THAT, HARSHER CRIMES ARE BEING COMMITTED.
THE ACTS ARE BRAZEN. THEY ARE BECOMING INCREASINGLY DESTRUCTIVE AND VIOLENT.
YOU'VE GOT AN ENORMOUS AMOUNT OF WORK AHEAD OF YOU.
THE GOOD CITIZENS OF GOTHAM ARE DEPENDING ON YOU!
WELL, PENNYWO-- ALFRED, I'M ALL FOR THE GOOD CITIZENS.

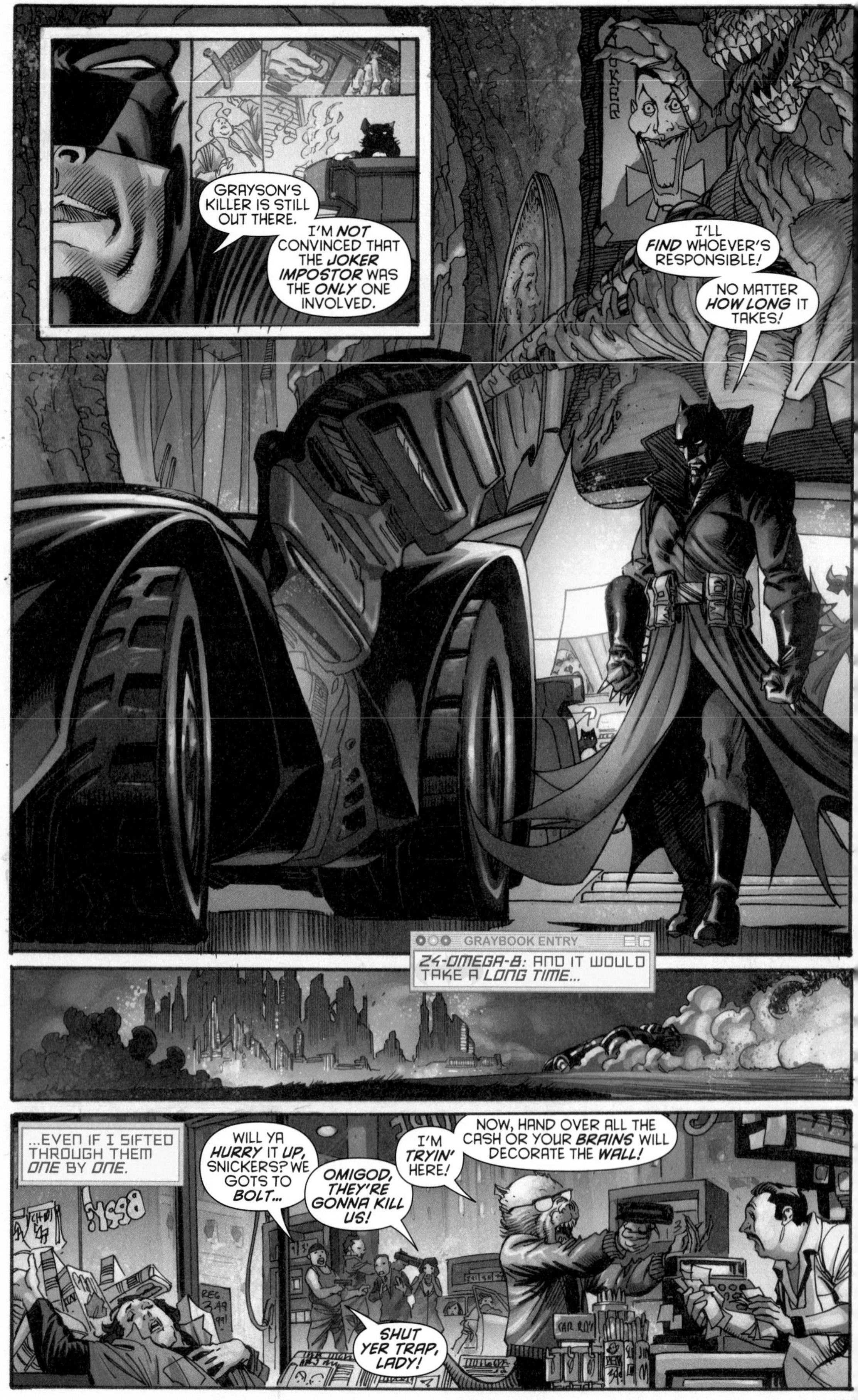

GRAYSON'S KILLER IS STILL OUT THERE.
I'M NOT CONVINCED THAT THE JOKER IMPOSTOR WAS THE ONLY ONE INVOLVED.
I'LL FIND WHOEVER'S RESPONSIBLE!
NO MATTER HOW LONG IT TAKES!
GRAYBOOK ENTRY_
24-OMEGA-8: AND IT WOULD TAKE A LONG TIME...
...EVEN IF I SIFTED THROUGH THEM ONE BY ONE.
WILL YA HURRY IT UP, SNICKERS? WE GOTS TO BOLT...
OMIGOD, THEY'RE GONNA KILL US!
I'M TRYIN' HERE!
NOW, HAND OVER ALL THE CASH OR YOUR BRAINS WILL DECORATE THE WALL!
SHUT YER TRAP, LADY!

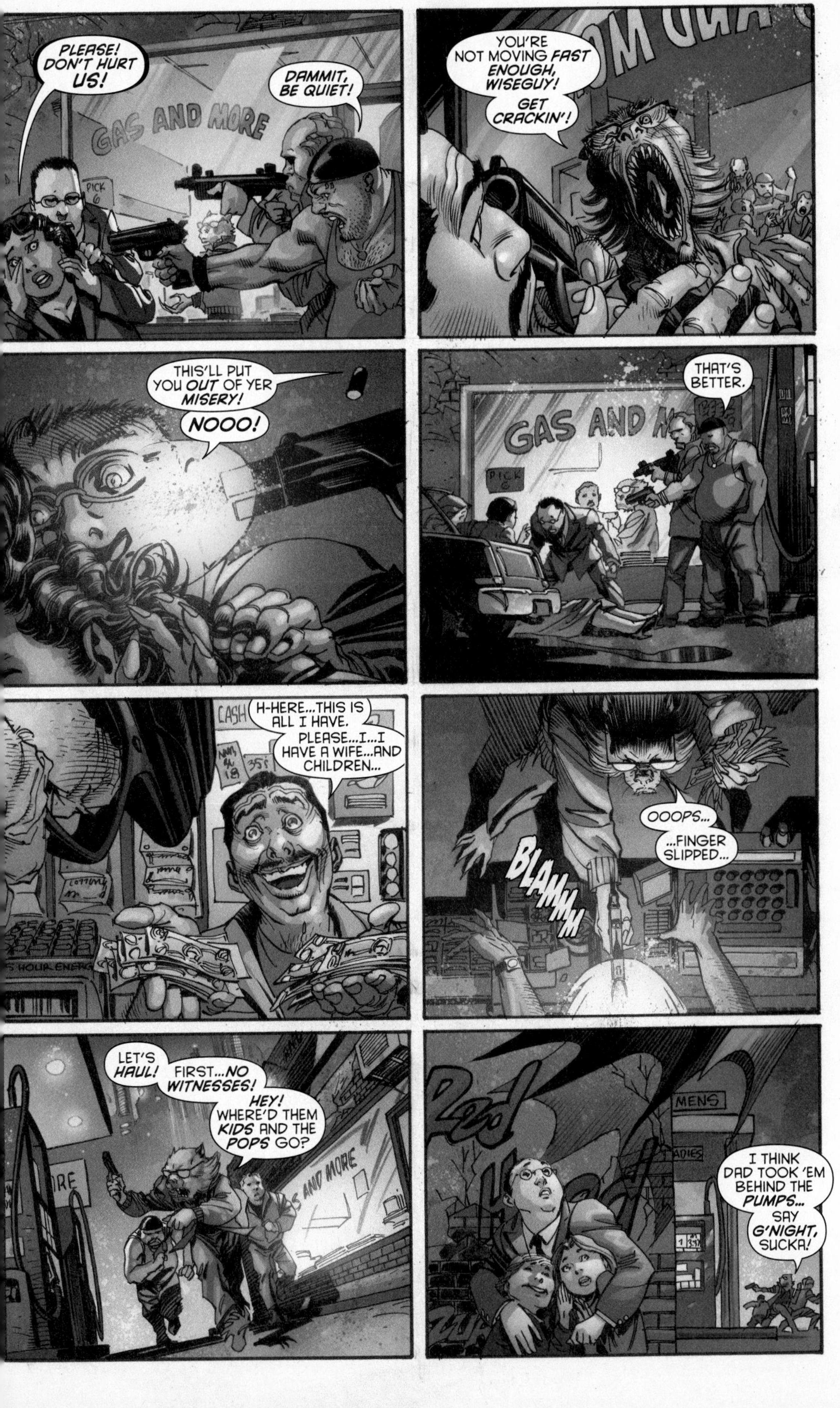
PLEASE! DON'T HURT US!
DAMMIT, BE QUIET!
GAS AND MORE
PICK 6
YOU'RE NOT MOVING FAST ENOUGH, WISEGUY!
GET CRACKIN'!
THIS'LL PUT YOU OUT OF YER MISERY!
NOOO!
THAT'S BETTER.
GAS AND M
PICK 6
CASH
H-HERE...THIS IS ALL I HAVE.
PLEASE...I...I HAVE A WIFE...AND CHILDREN...
OOOPS...
...FINGER SLIPPED...
BLAMMM
LET'S HAUL!
FIRST...NO WITNESSES!
HEY! WHERE'D THEM KIDS AND THE POPS GO?
S AND MORE
MENS
I THINK DAD TOOK 'EM BEHIND THE PUMPS...
SAY G'NIGHT, SUCKA!

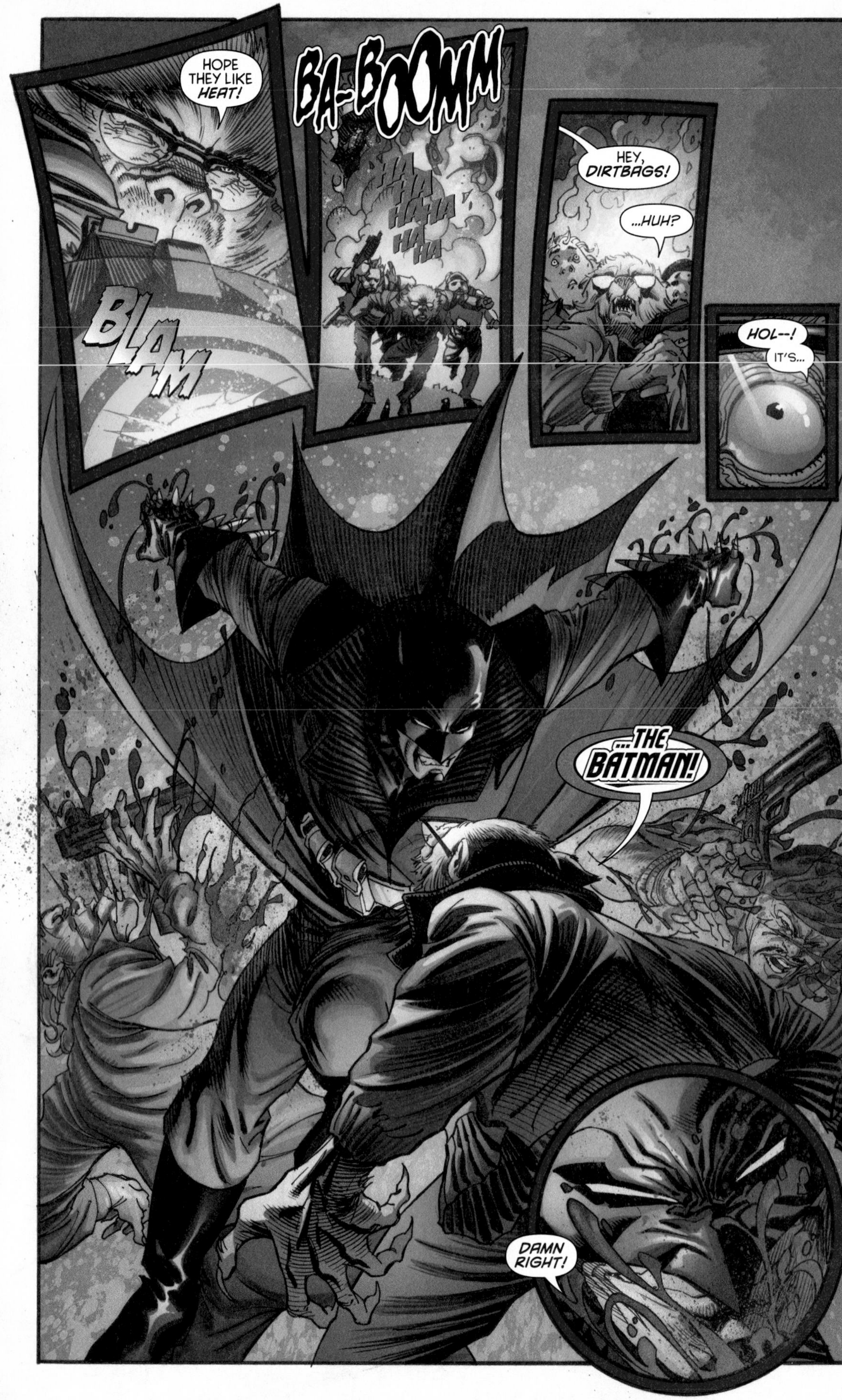
HOPE THEY LIKE HEAT!
BLAM
BA-BOOMM
HA HA HAHA HAHA HA HA
HEY, DIRTBAGS!
...HUH?
HOL--!
IT'S...
...THE BATMAN!
DAMN RIGHT!

DAMIAN: SON OF BATMAN 1
Variant cover by **Tony S. Daniel**, **Sandu Florea** & **Tomeu Morey**

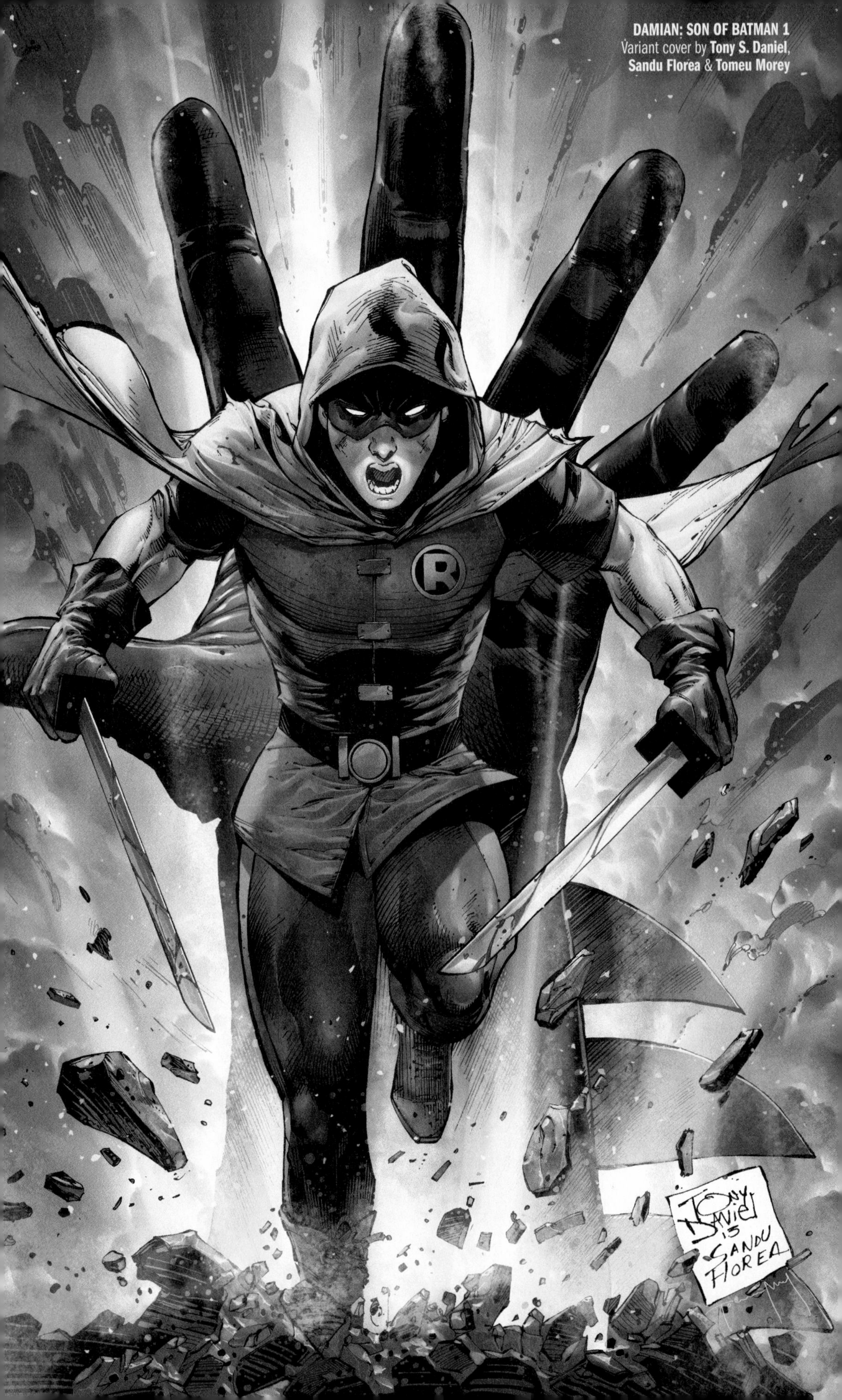
TONY DANIEL '15
SANDU FLOREA

DAMIAN: SON OF BATMAN 2
Variant cover by **Chris Burnham** & **Nathan Fairbairn**

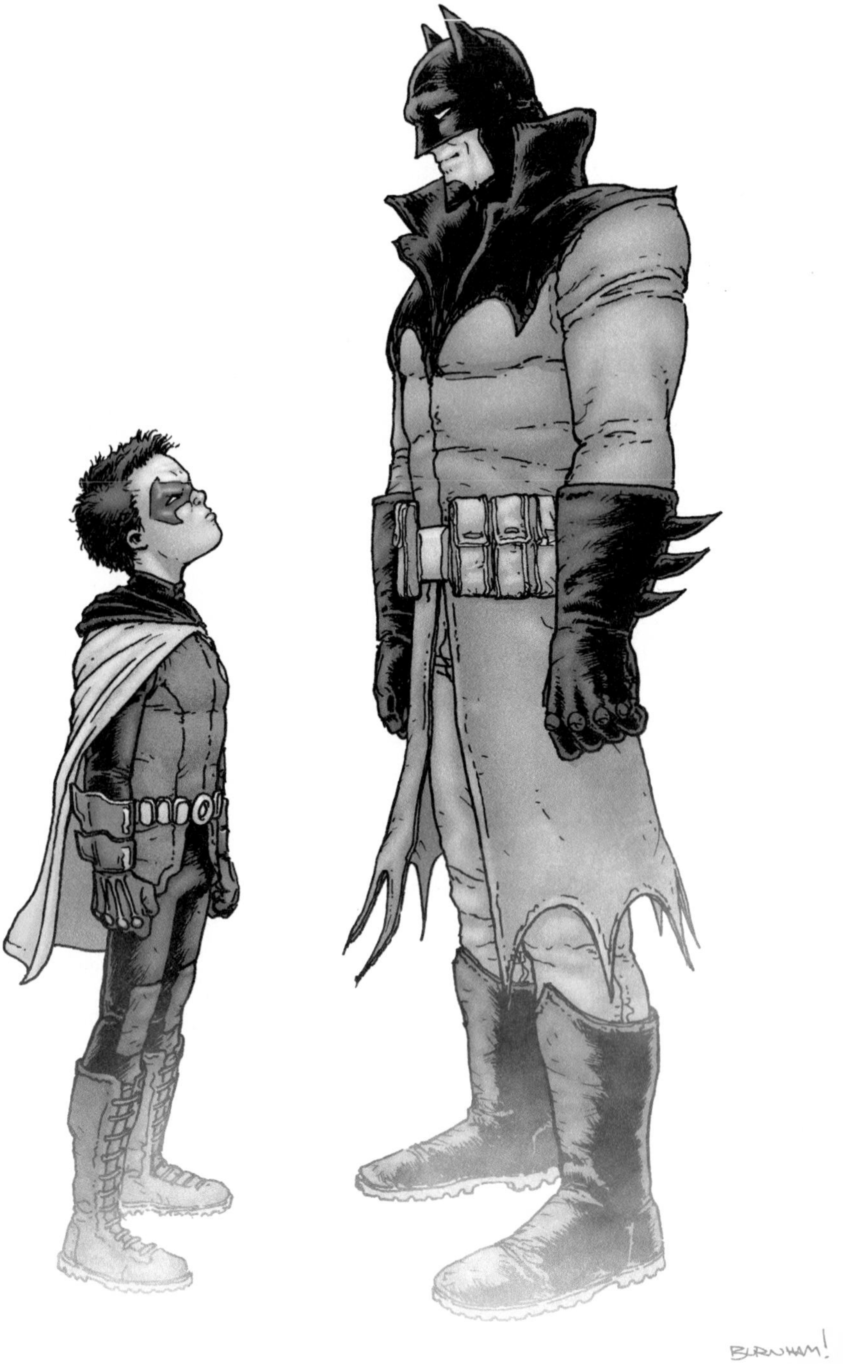
BURNHAM!

DAMIAN: SON OF BATMAN 3
Variant cover by **Dustin Nguyen**

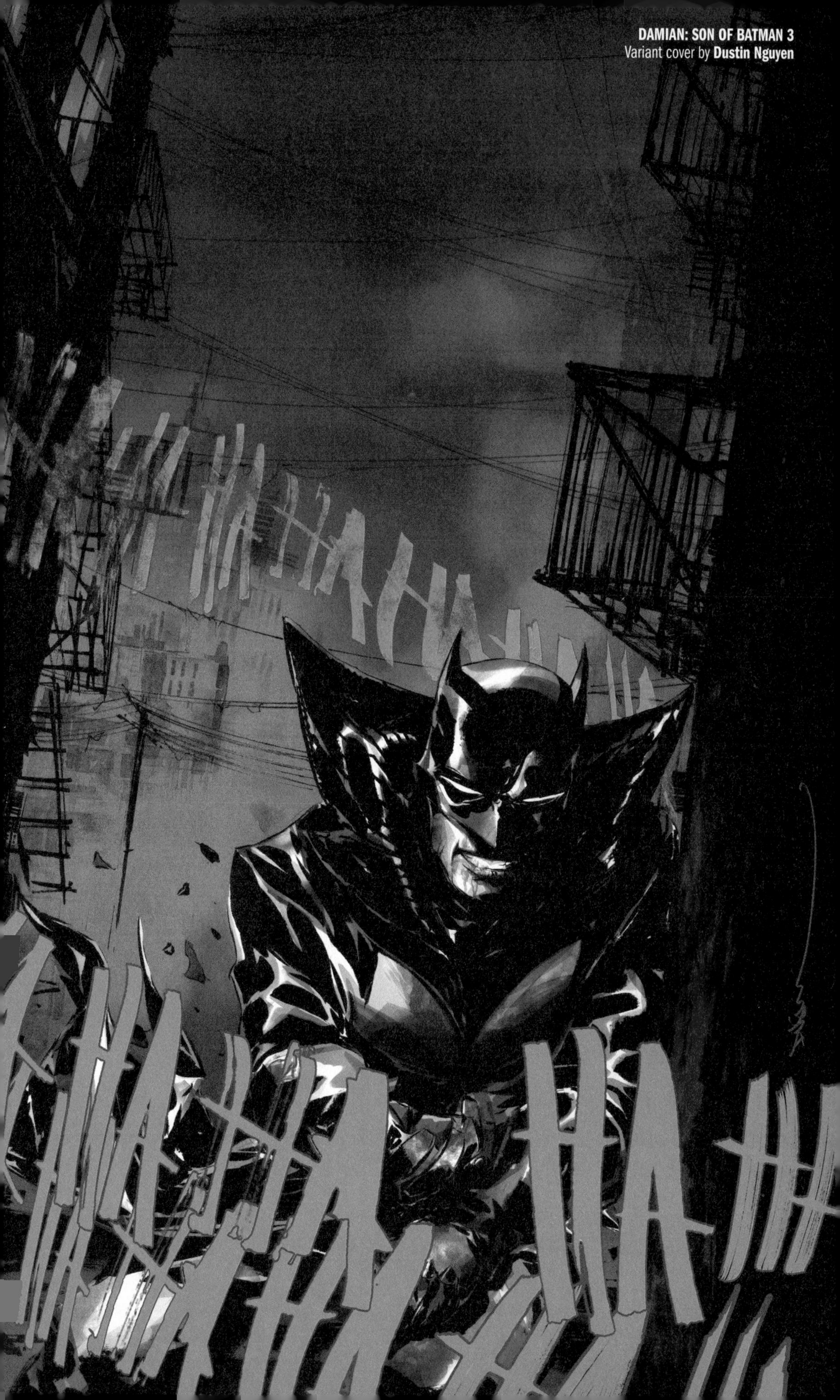

DAMIAN: SON OF BATMAN 4
Variant cover by **Pat Gleason**, **Mick Gray** & **John Kalisz**

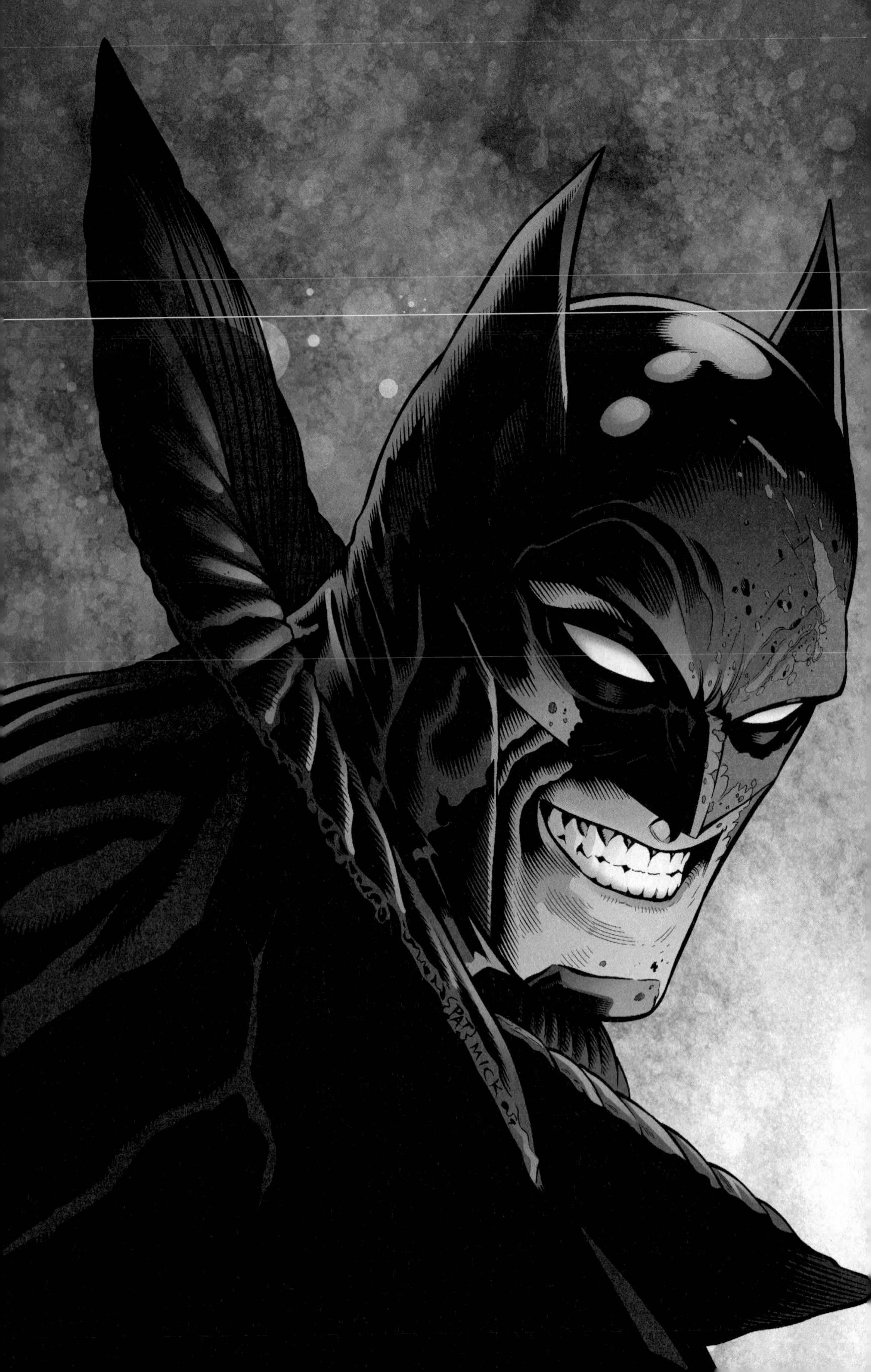

BETHLEHEM

GRANT ANDY
MORRISON KUBERT
WRITER   PENCILLER

JESSE JARED K.
DELPERDANG FLETCHER
INKER   LETTERER

GUY
MAJOR
COLORIST

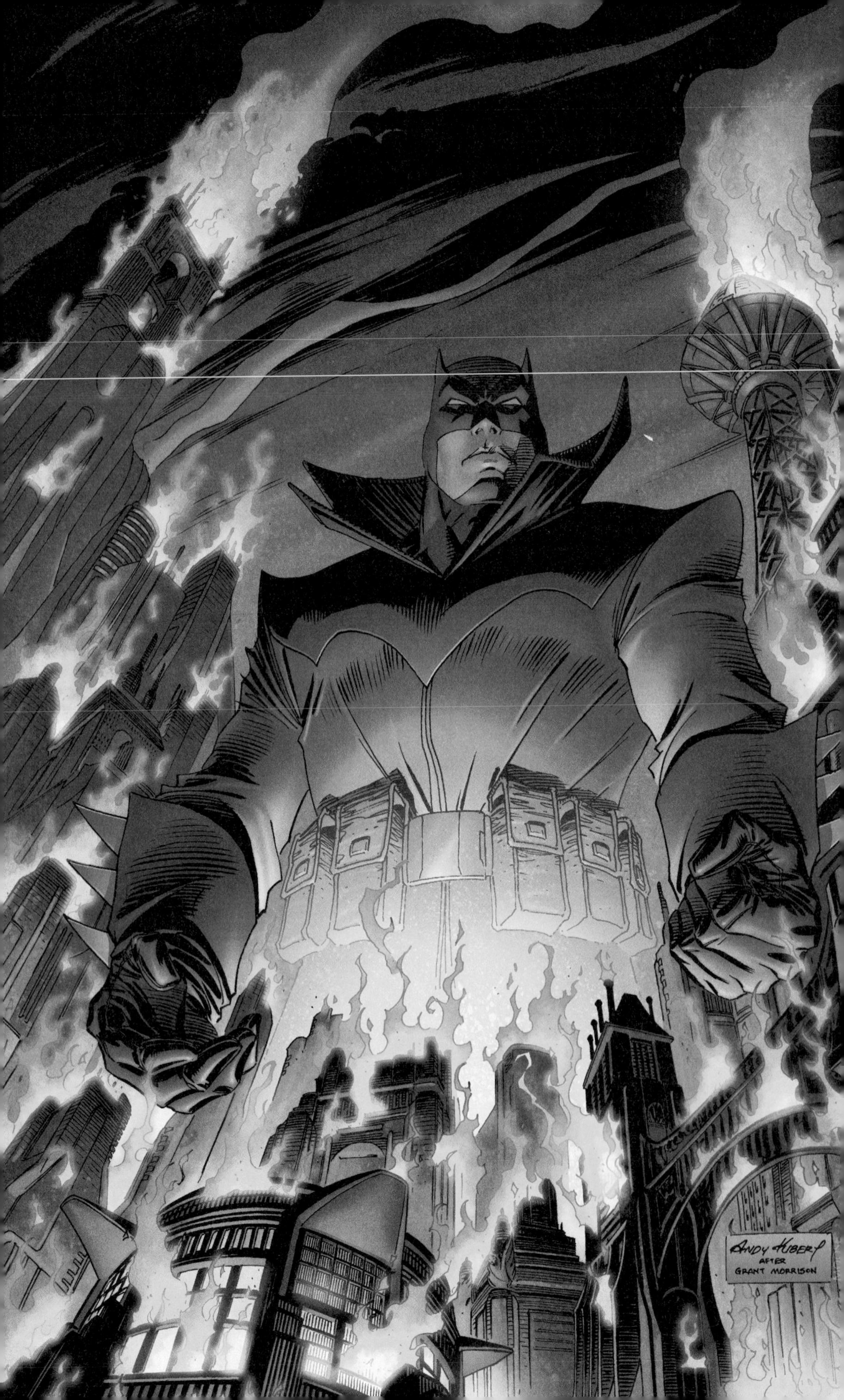
ANDY KUBERT
AFTER
GRANT MORRISON

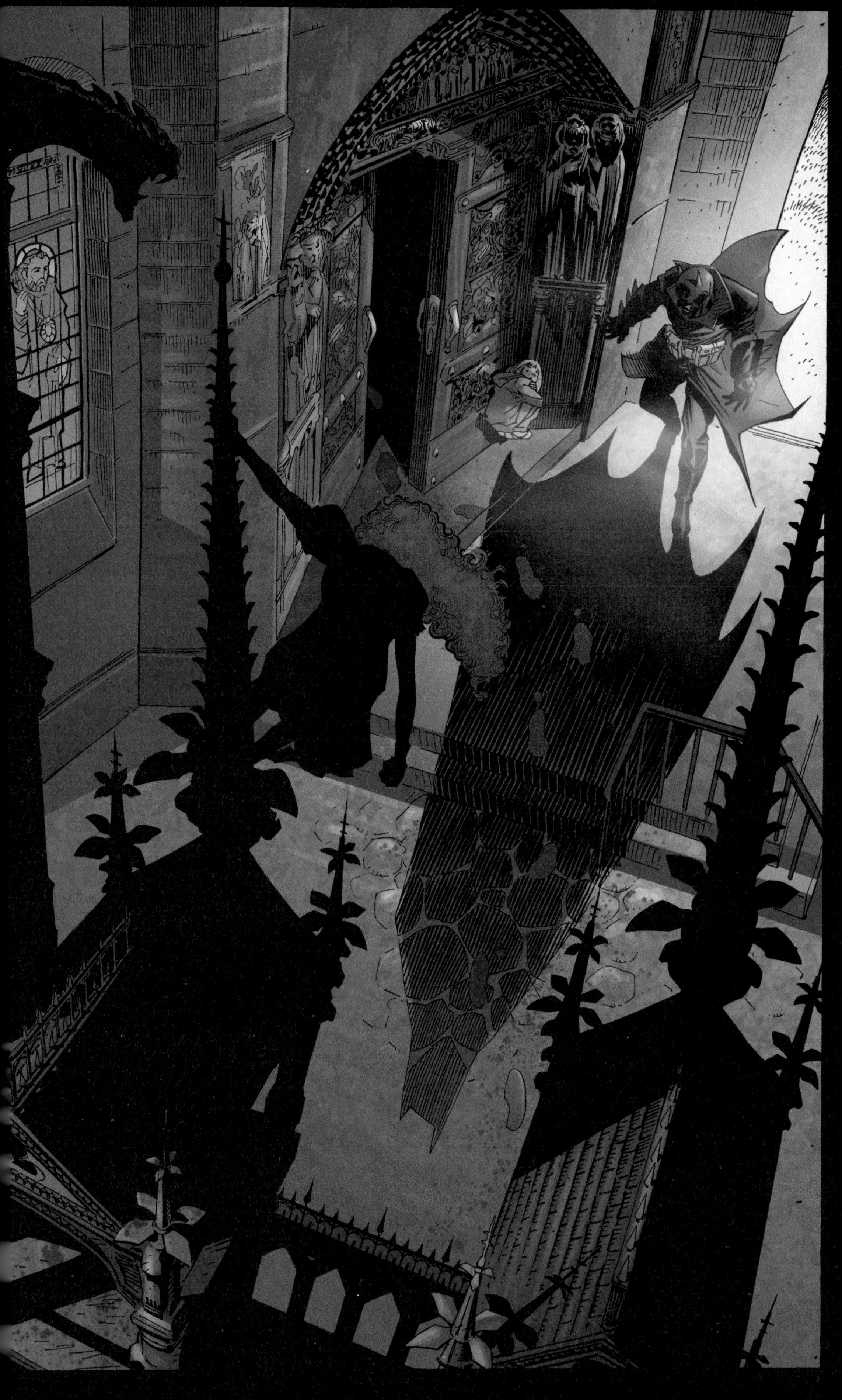

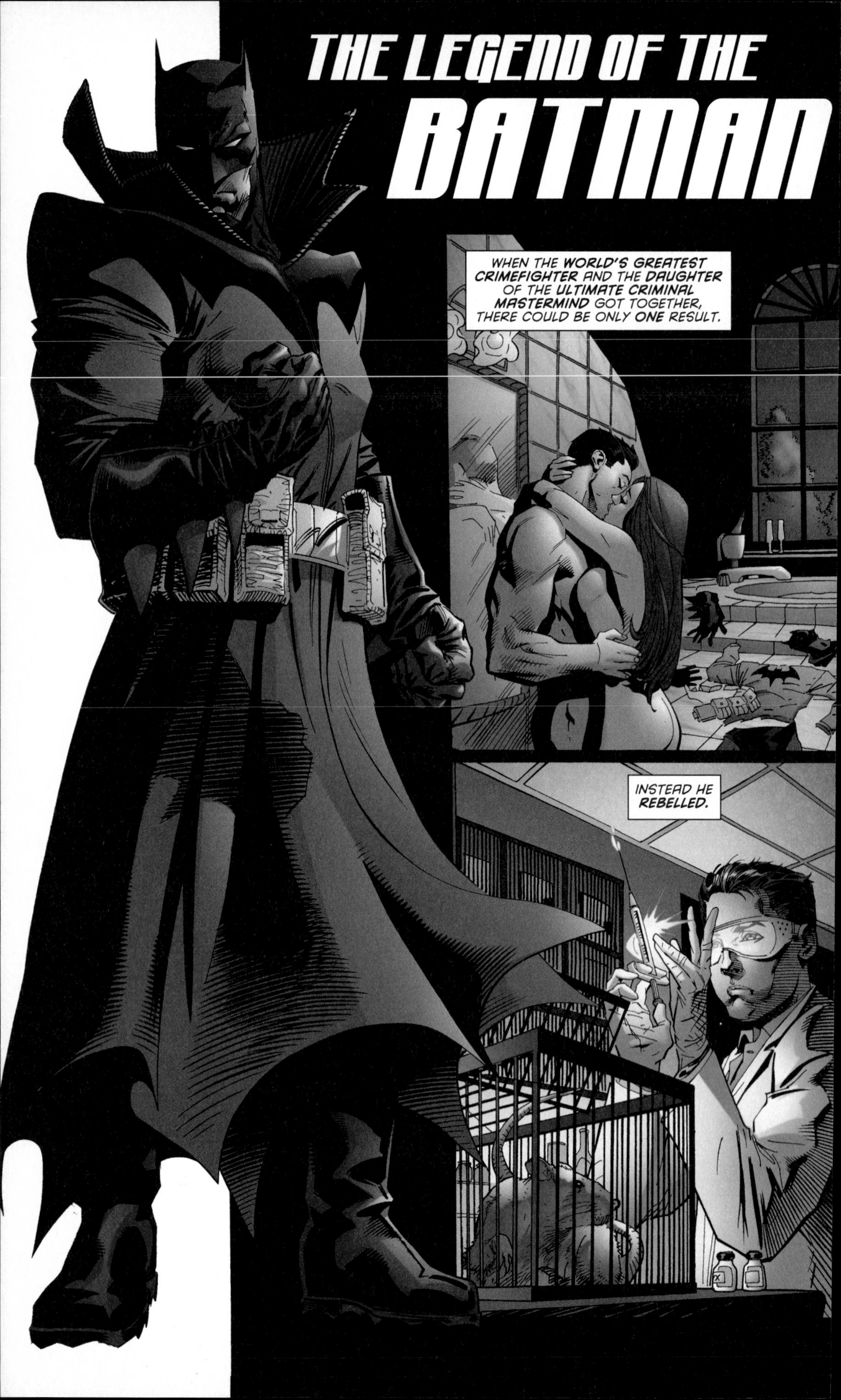
THE LEGEND OF THE BATMAN
WHEN THE WORLD'S GREATEST CRIMEFIGHTER AND THE DAUGHTER OF THE ULTIMATE CRIMINAL MASTERMIND GOT TOGETHER, THERE COULD BE ONLY ONE RESULT.
INSTEAD HE REBELLED.

WHO HE IS AND HOW HE CAME TO BE...

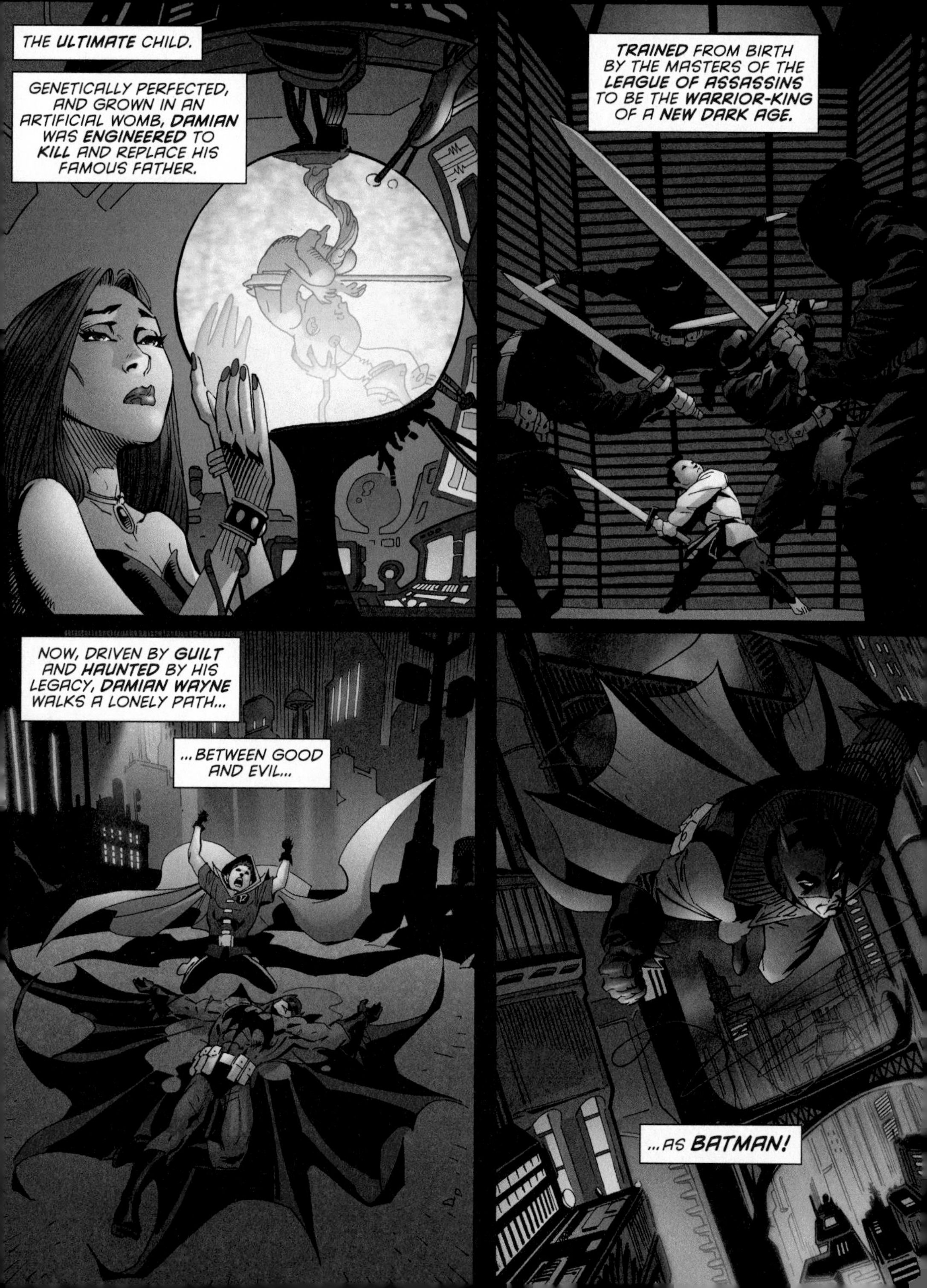

THE ULTIMATE CHILD.
GENETICALLY PERFECTED, AND GROWN IN AN ARTIFICIAL WOMB, DAMIAN WAS ENGINEERED TO KILL AND REPLACE HIS FAMOUS FATHER.
TRAINED FROM BIRTH BY THE MASTERS OF THE LEAGUE OF ASSASSINS TO BE THE WARRIOR-KING OF A NEW DARK AGE.
NOW, DRIVEN BY GUILT AND HAUNTED BY HIS LEGACY, DAMIAN WAYNE WALKS A LONELY PATH...
...BETWEEN GOOD AND EVIL...
...AS BATMAN!

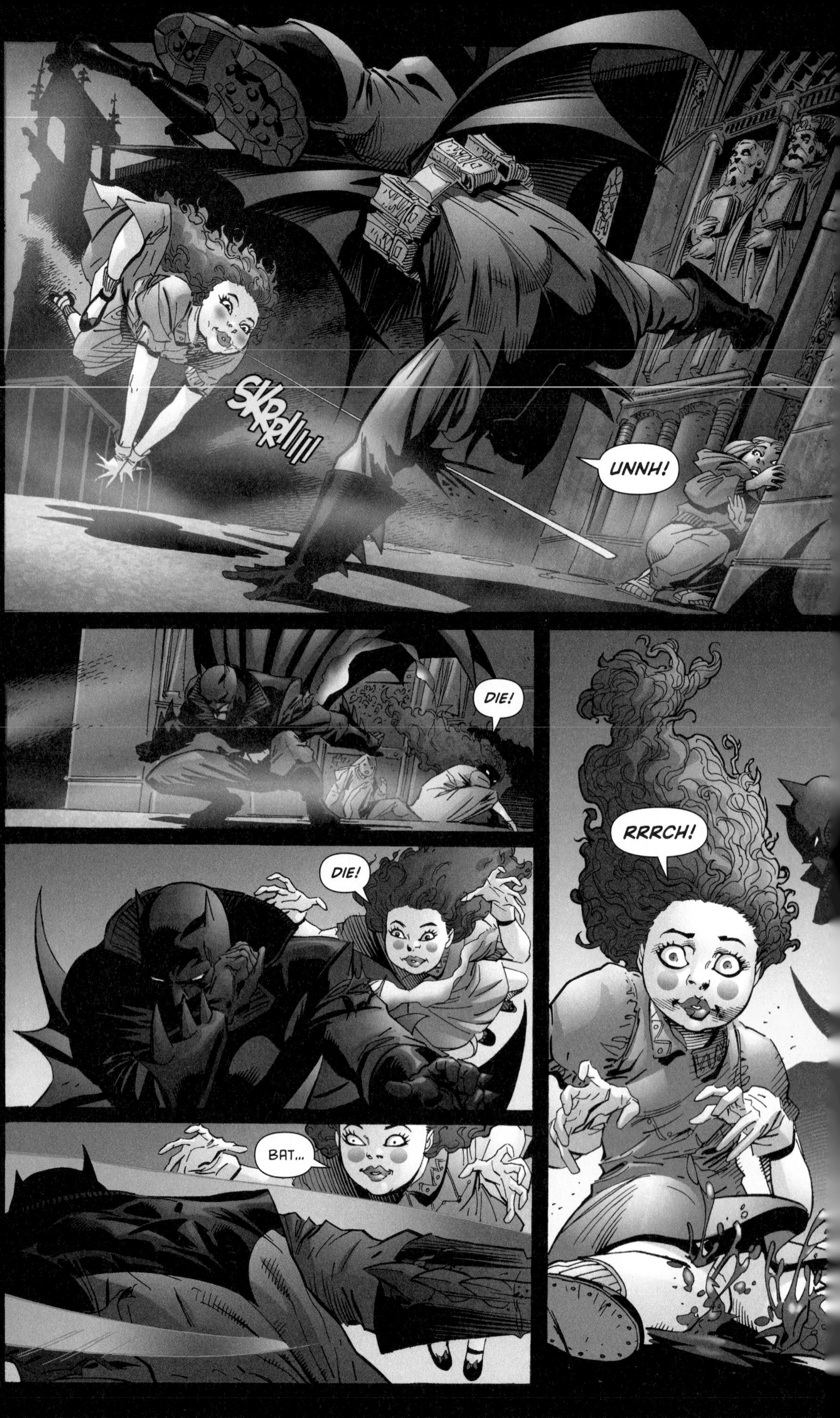
SKRRIIII
UNNH!
DIE!
DIE!
BAT...
RRRCH!

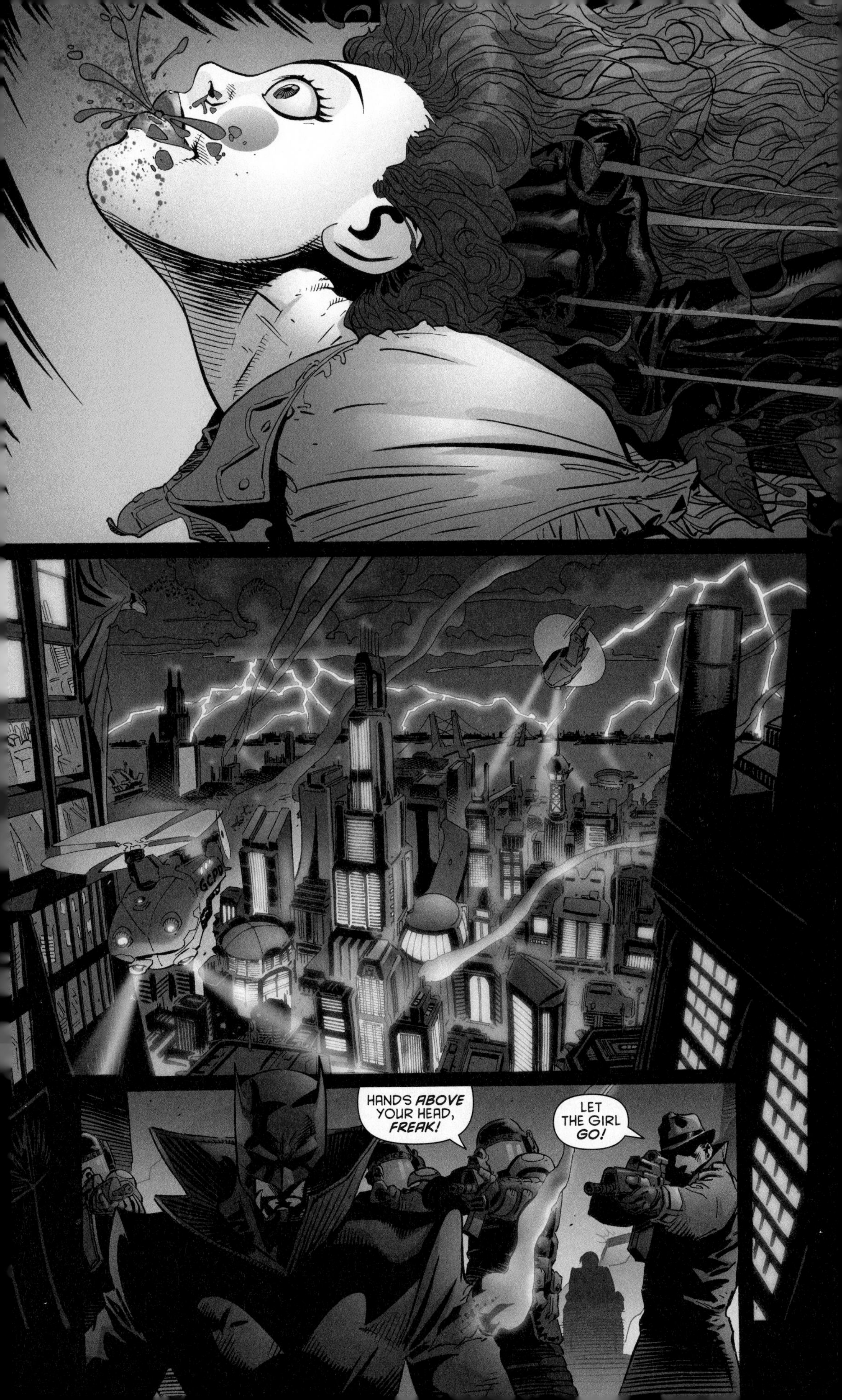
HANDS ABOVE YOUR HEAD, FREAK!
LET THE GIRL GO!

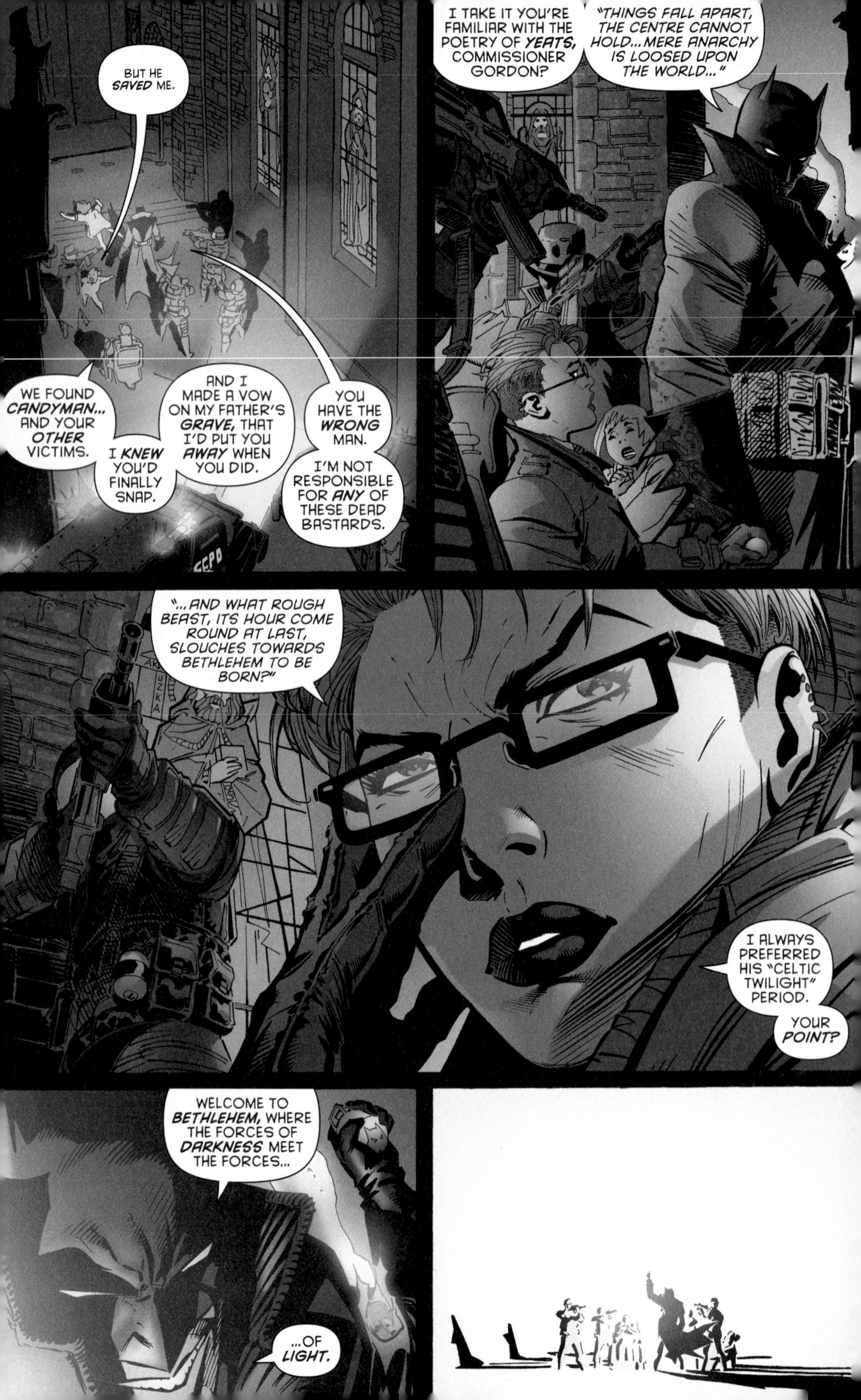
BUT HE SAVED ME.
WE FOUND CANDYMAN... AND YOUR OTHER VICTIMS.
I KNEW YOU'D FINALLY SNAP.
AND I MADE A VOW ON MY FATHER'S GRAVE, THAT I'D PUT YOU AWAY WHEN YOU DID.
YOU HAVE THE WRONG MAN.
I'M NOT RESPONSIBLE FOR ANY OF THESE DEAD BASTARDS.
I TAKE IT YOU'RE FAMILIAR WITH THE POETRY OF YEATS, COMMISSIONER GORDON?
"THINGS FALL APART, THE CENTRE CANNOT HOLD... MERE ANARCHY IS LOOSED UPON THE WORLD..."
"...AND WHAT ROUGH BEAST, ITS HOUR COME ROUND AT LAST, SLOUCHES TOWARDS BETHLEHEM TO BE BORN?"
I ALWAYS PREFERRED HIS "CELTIC TWILIGHT" PERIOD.
YOUR POINT?
WELCOME TO BETHLEHEM, WHERE THE FORCES OF DARKNESS MEET THE FORCES...
...OF LIGHT.

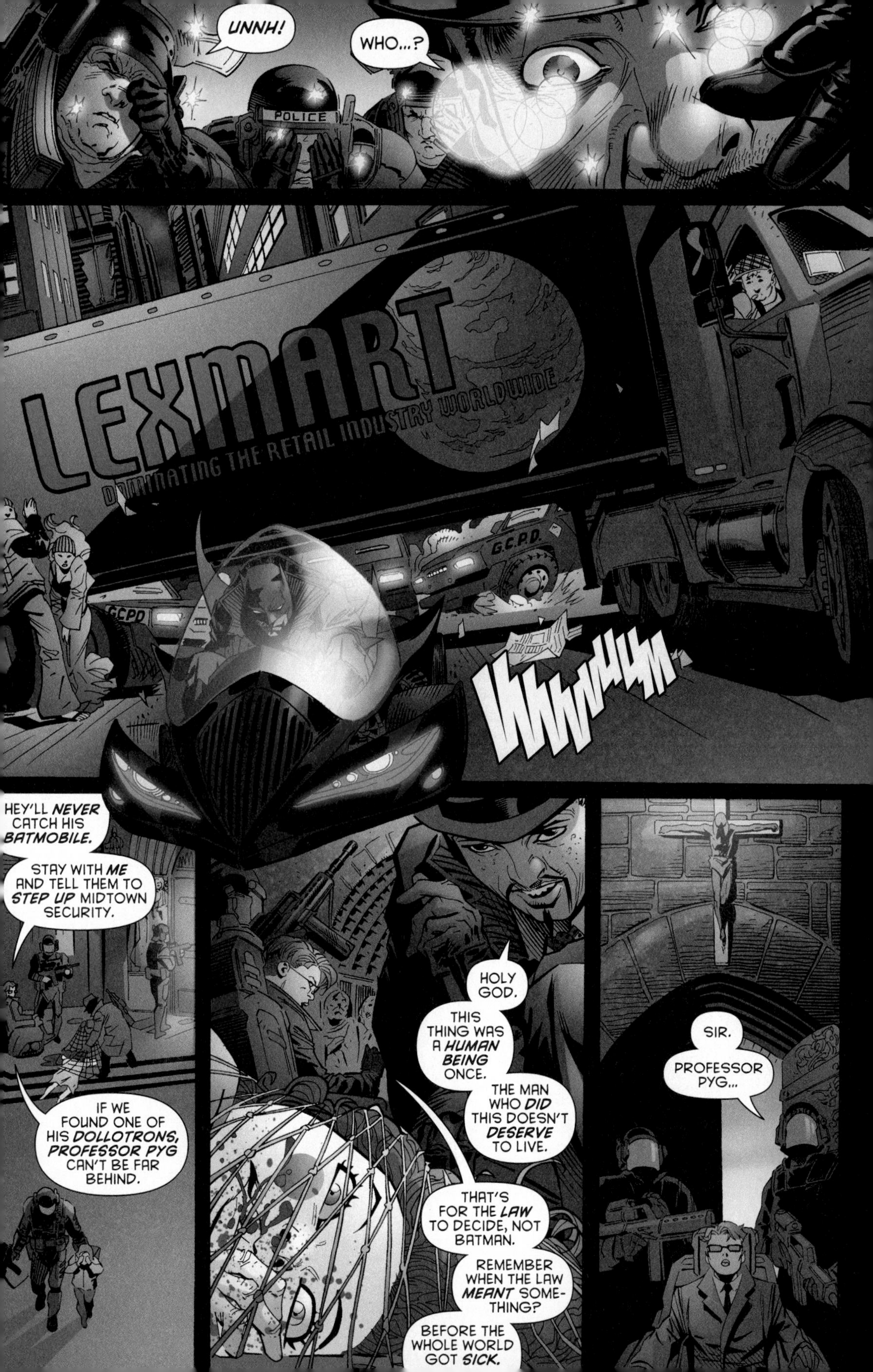

UNNH!
WHO...?
POLICE
LEXMART
DOMINATING THE RETAIL INDUSTRY WORLDWIDE
G.C.P.D.
GCPD
VVVVVVUUM
HEY'LL NEVER CATCH HIS BATMOBILE.
STAY WITH ME AND TELL THEM TO STEP UP MIDTOWN SECURITY.
IF WE FOUND ONE OF HIS DOLLOTRONS, PROFESSOR PYG CAN'T BE FAR BEHIND.
HOLY GOD.
THIS THING WAS A HUMAN BEING ONCE.
THE MAN WHO DID THIS DOESN'T DESERVE TO LIVE.
THAT'S FOR THE LAW TO DECIDE, NOT BATMAN.
REMEMBER WHEN THE LAW MEANT SOME-THING?
BEFORE THE WHOLE WORLD GOT SICK.
SIR.
PROFESSOR PYG...

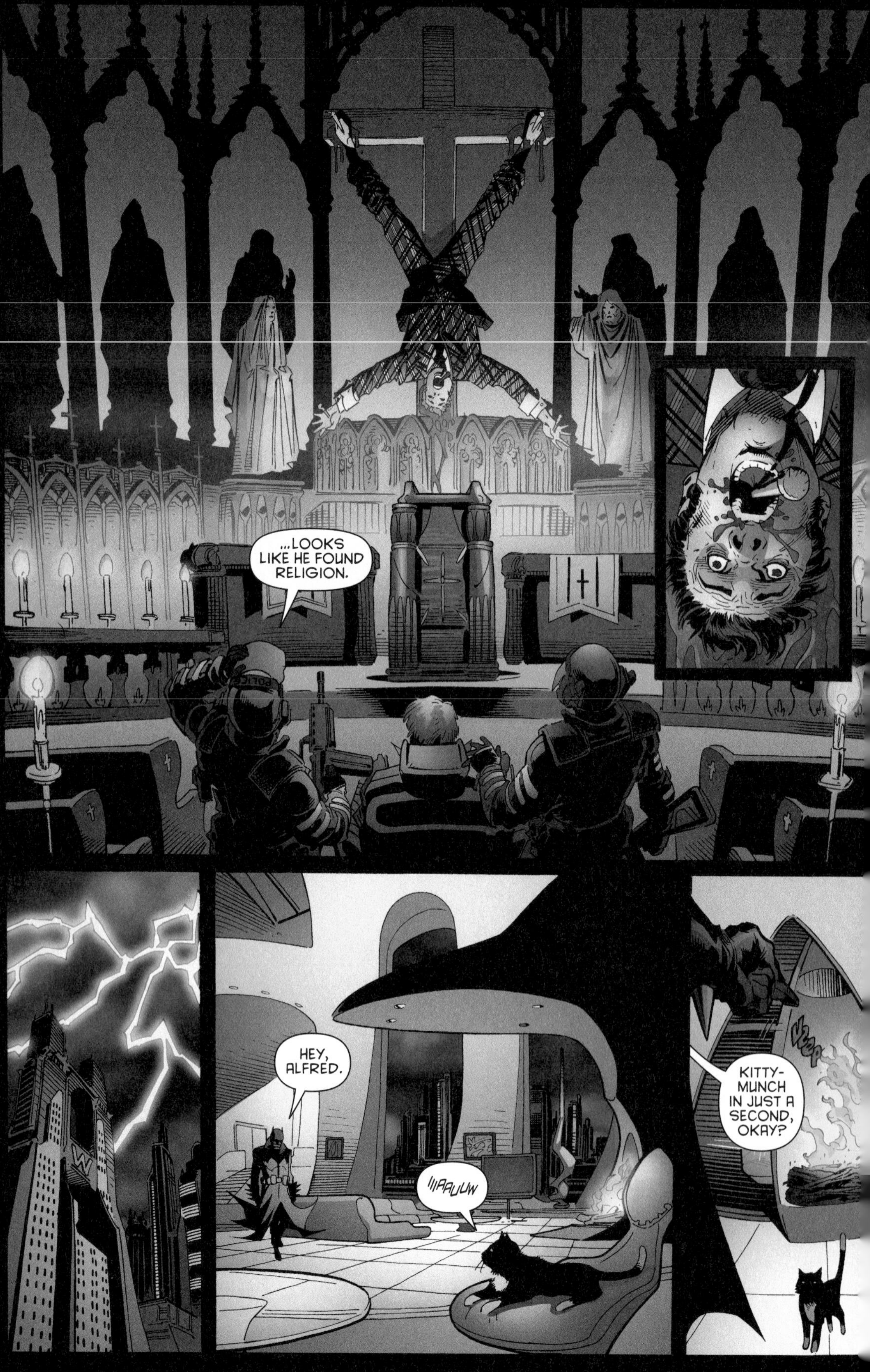
...LOOKS LIKE HE FOUND RELIGION.
HEY, ALFRED.
IIIAAUUW
KITTY-MUNCH IN JUST A SECOND, OKAY?

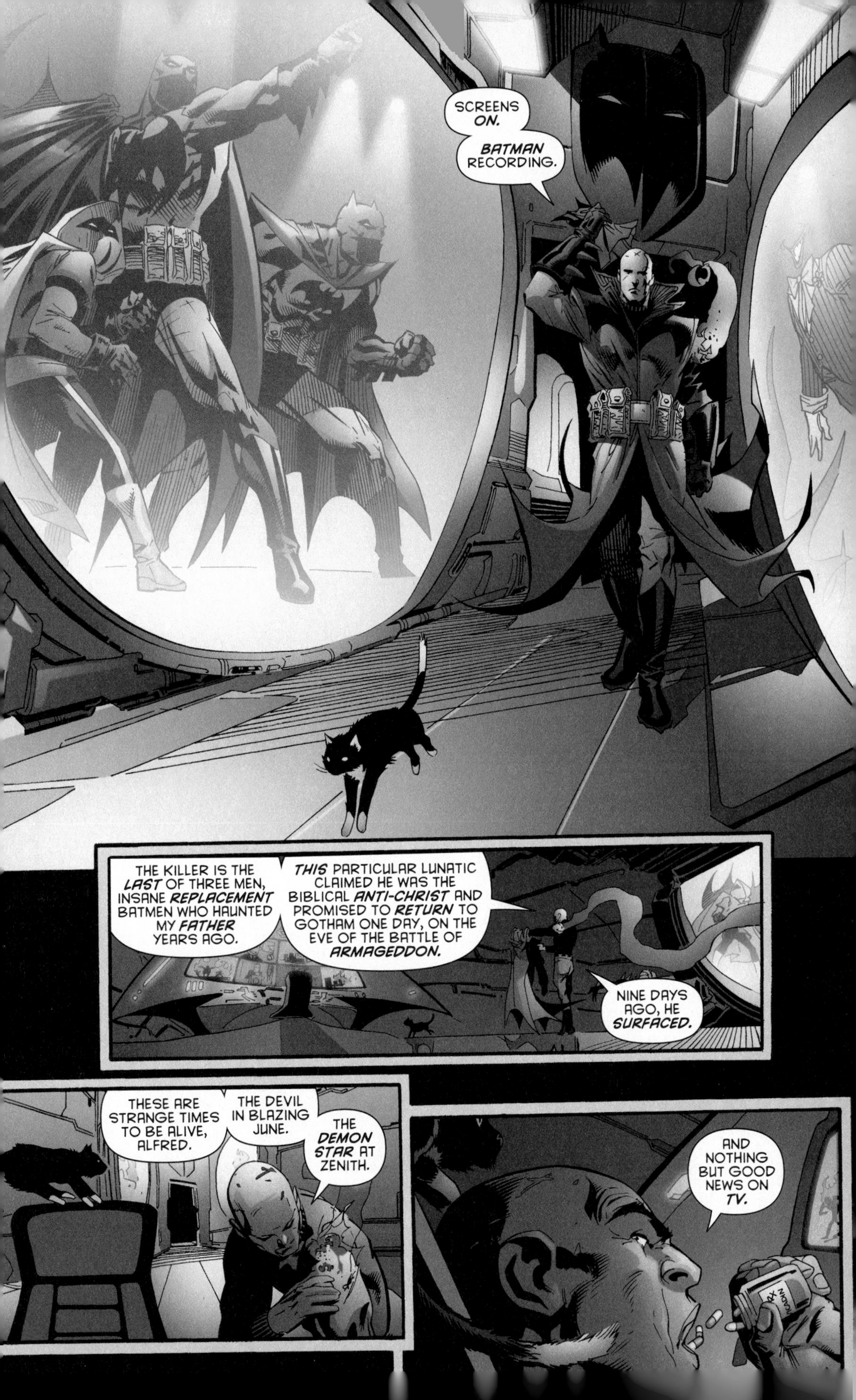
SCREENS ON.
BATMAN RECORDING.
THE KILLER IS THE LAST OF THREE MEN, INSANE REPLACEMENT BATMEN WHO HAUNTED MY FATHER YEARS AGO.
THIS PARTICULAR LUNATIC CLAIMED HE WAS THE BIBLICAL ANTI-CHRIST AND PROMISED TO RETURN TO GOTHAM ONE DAY, ON THE EVE OF THE BATTLE OF ARMAGEDDON.
NINE DAYS AGO, HE SURFACED.
THESE ARE STRANGE TIMES TO BE ALIVE, ALFRED.
THE DEVIL IN BLAZING JUNE.
THE DEMON STAR AT ZENITH.
AND NOTHING BUT GOOD NEWS ON TV.

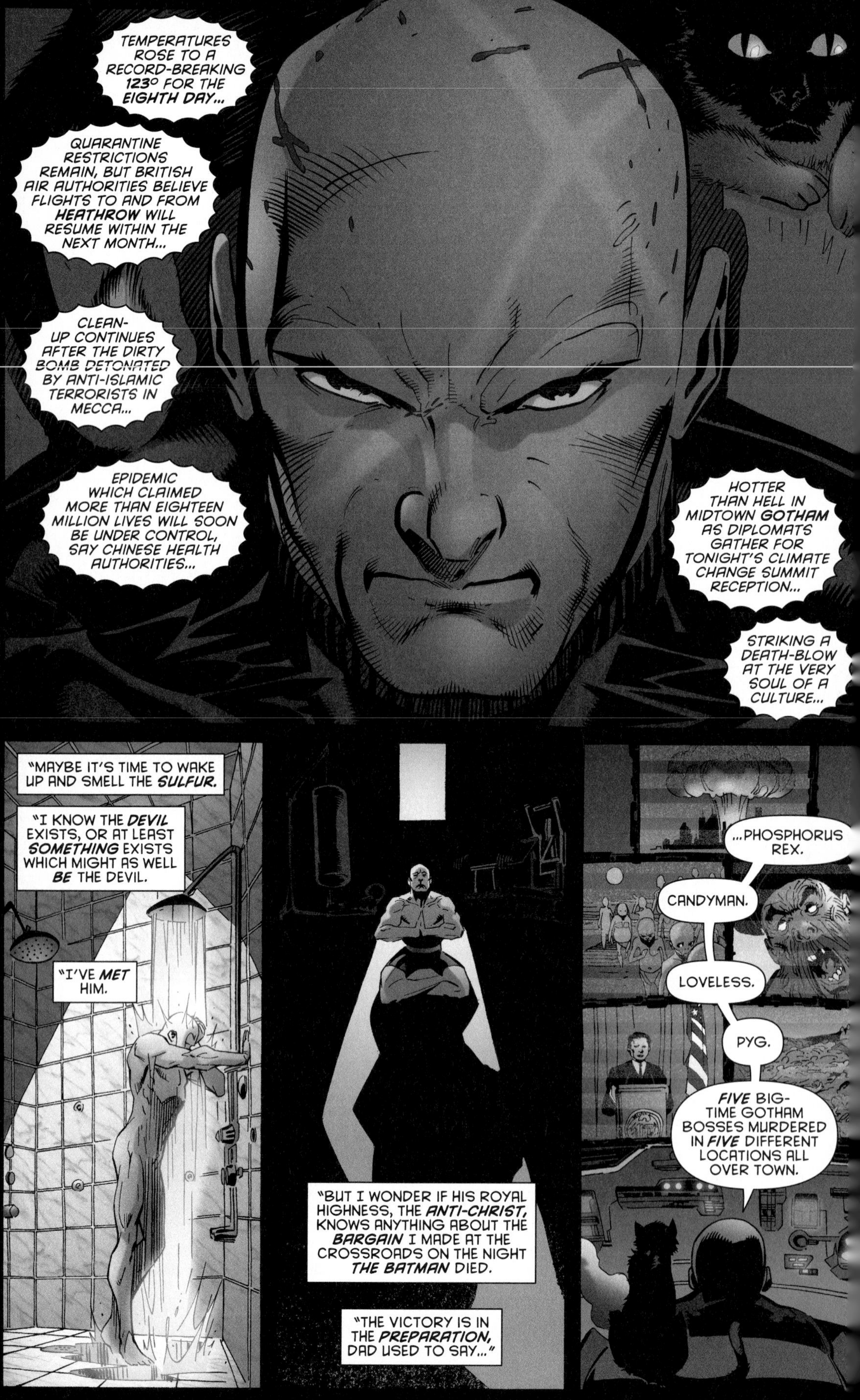
TEMPERATURES ROSE TO A RECORD-BREAKING 123° FOR THE EIGHTH DAY...
QUARANTINE RESTRICTIONS REMAIN, BUT BRITISH AIR AUTHORITIES BELIEVE FLIGHTS TO AND FROM HEATHROW WILL RESUME WITHIN THE NEXT MONTH...
CLEAN-UP CONTINUES AFTER THE DIRTY BOMB DETONATED BY ANTI-ISLAMIC TERRORISTS IN MECCA...
EPIDEMIC WHICH CLAIMED MORE THAN EIGHTEEN MILLION LIVES WILL SOON BE UNDER CONTROL, SAY CHINESE HEALTH AUTHORITIES...
HOTTER THAN HELL IN MIDTOWN GOTHAM AS DIPLOMATS GATHER FOR TONIGHT'S CLIMATE CHANGE SUMMIT RECEPTION...
STRIKING A DEATH-BLOW AT THE VERY SOUL OF A CULTURE...
"MAYBE IT'S TIME TO WAKE UP AND SMELL THE SULFUR.
"I KNOW THE DEVIL EXISTS, OR AT LEAST SOMETHING EXISTS WHICH MIGHT AS WELL BE THE DEVIL.
"I'VE MET HIM.
"BUT I WONDER IF HIS ROYAL HIGHNESS, THE ANTI-CHRIST, KNOWS ANYTHING ABOUT THE BARGAIN I MADE AT THE CROSSROADS ON THE NIGHT THE BATMAN DIED.
"THE VICTORY IS IN THE PREPARATION, DAD USED TO SAY..."
...PHOSPHORUS REX.
CANDYMAN.
LOVELESS.
PYG.
FIVE BIG-TIME GOTHAM BOSSES MURDERED IN FIVE DIFFERENT LOCATIONS ALL OVER TOWN.

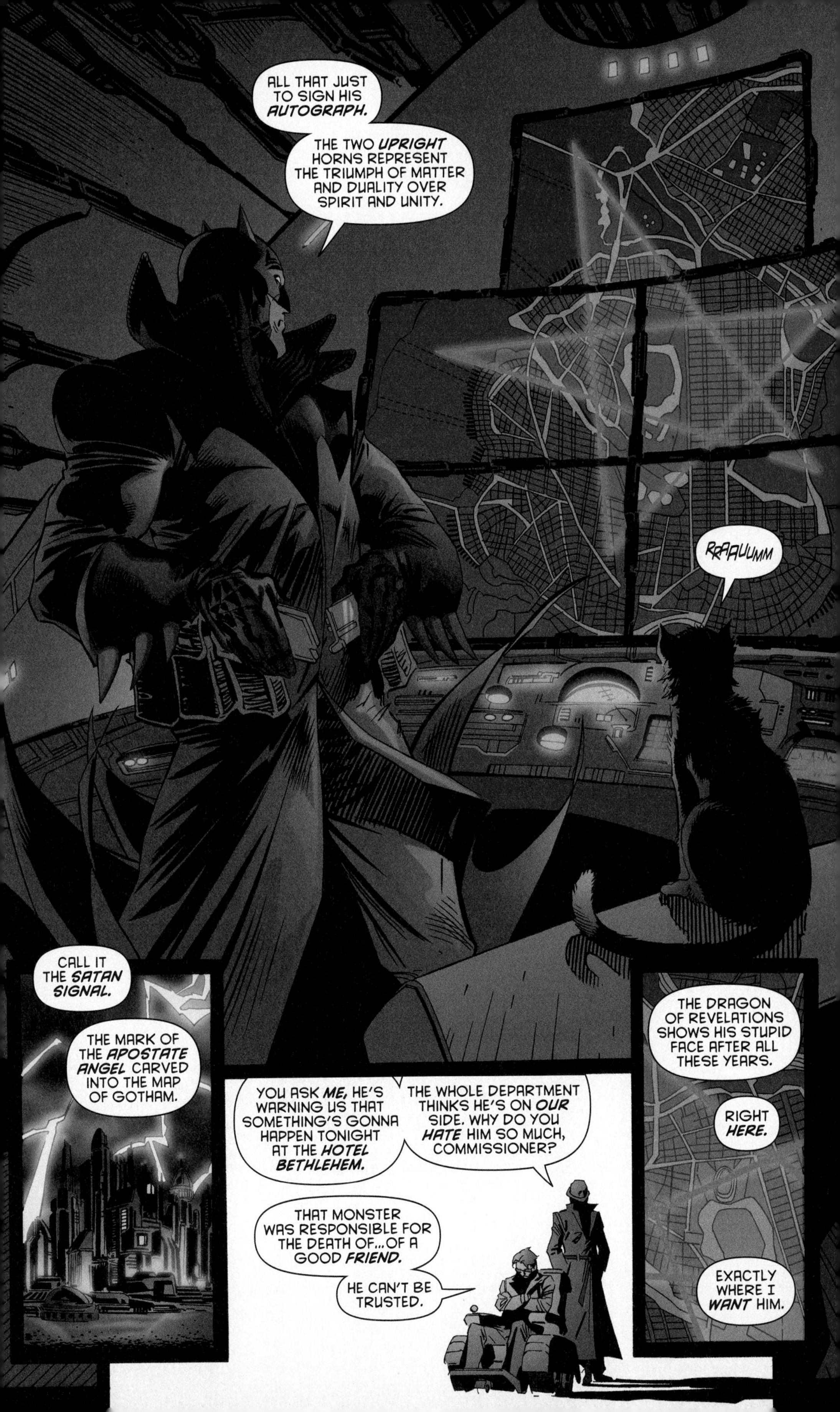
ALL THAT JUST TO SIGN HIS AUTOGRAPH.
THE TWO UPRIGHT HORNS REPRESENT THE TRIUMPH OF MATTER AND DUALITY OVER SPIRIT AND UNITY.
RRRAUUMM
CALL IT THE SATAN SIGNAL.
THE MARK OF THE APOSTATE ANGEL CARVED INTO THE MAP OF GOTHAM.
YOU ASK ME, HE'S WARNING US THAT SOMETHING'S GONNA HAPPEN TONIGHT AT THE HOTEL BETHLEHEM.
THE WHOLE DEPARTMENT THINKS HE'S ON OUR SIDE. WHY DO YOU HATE HIM SO MUCH, COMMISSIONER?
THAT MONSTER WAS RESPONSIBLE FOR THE DEATH OF...OF A GOOD FRIEND.
HE CAN'T BE TRUSTED.
THE DRAGON OF REVELATIONS SHOWS HIS STUPID FACE AFTER ALL THESE YEARS.
RIGHT HERE.
EXACTLY WHERE I WANT HIM.

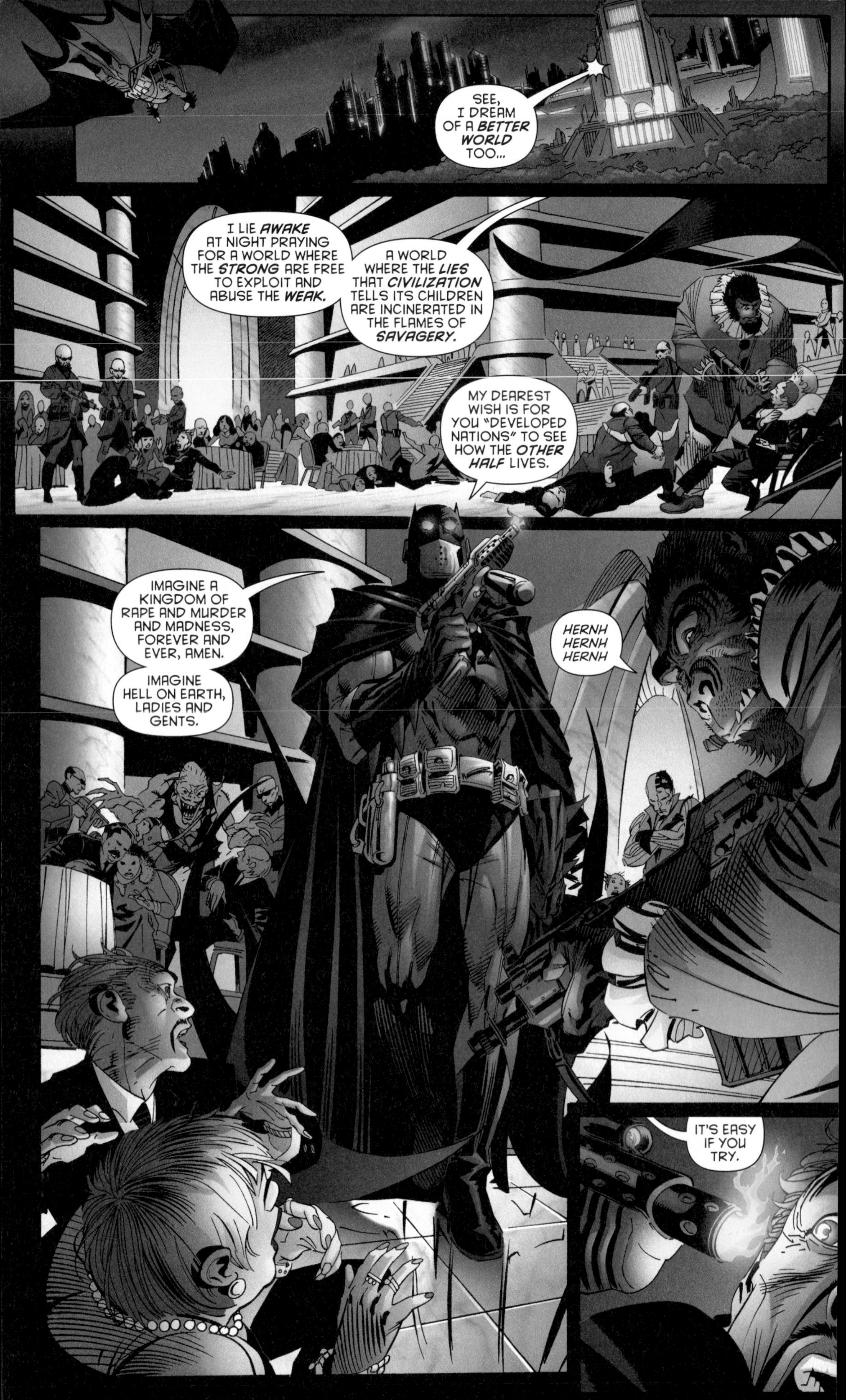
SEE, I DREAM OF A BETTER WORLD TOO...
I LIE AWAKE AT NIGHT PRAYING FOR A WORLD WHERE THE STRONG ARE FREE TO EXPLOIT AND ABUSE THE WEAK.
A WORLD WHERE THE LIES THAT CIVILIZATION TELLS ITS CHILDREN ARE INCINERATED IN THE FLAMES OF SAVAGERY.
MY DEAREST WISH IS FOR YOU "DEVELOPED NATIONS" TO SEE HOW THE OTHER HALF LIVES.
IMAGINE A KINGDOM OF RAPE AND MURDER AND MADNESS, FOREVER AND EVER, AMEN.
IMAGINE HELL ON EARTH, LADIES AND GENTS.
HERNH HERNH HERNH
IT'S EASY IF YOU TRY.

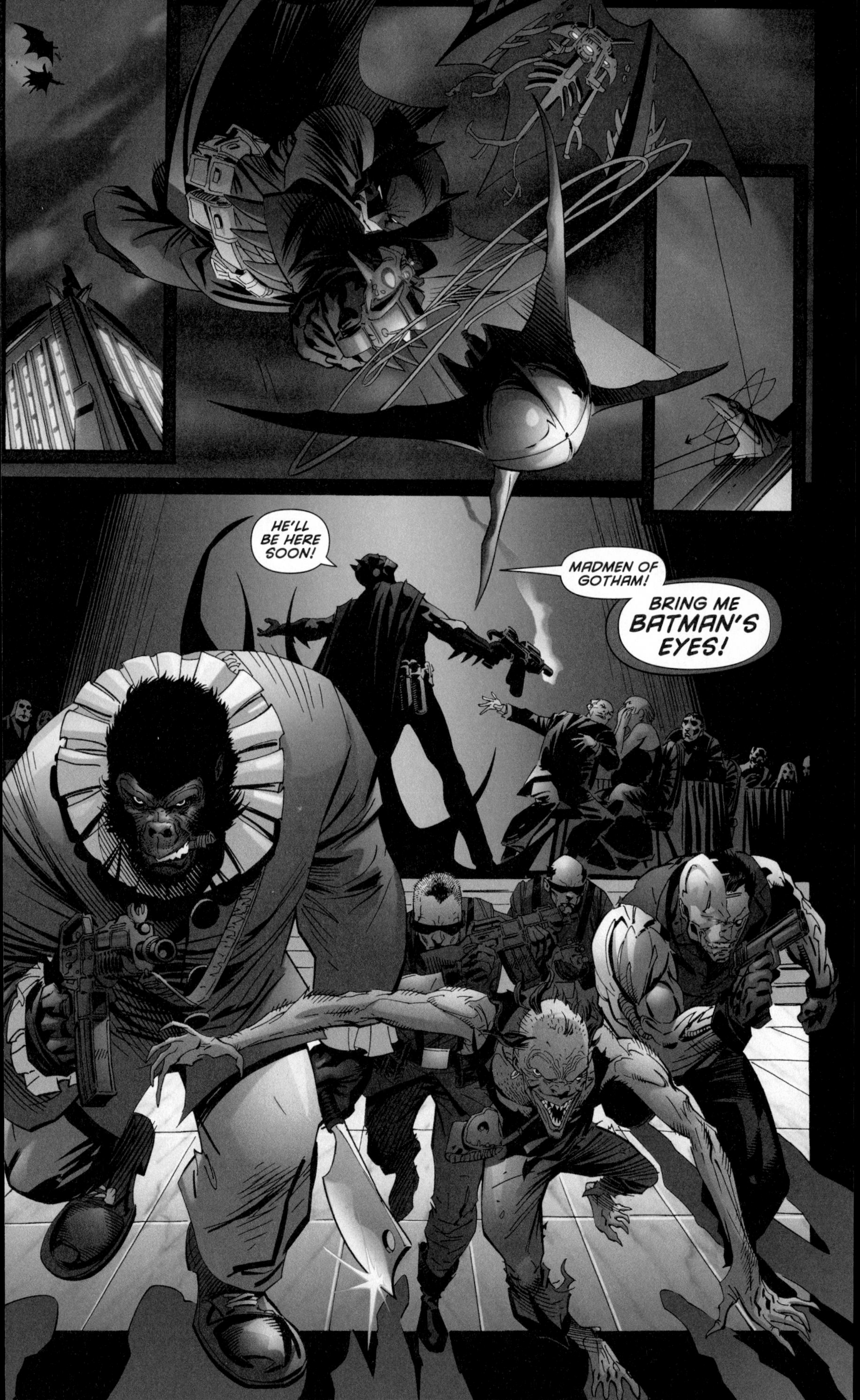
HE'LL BE HERE SOON!
MADMEN OF GOTHAM!
BRING ME BATMAN'S EYES!

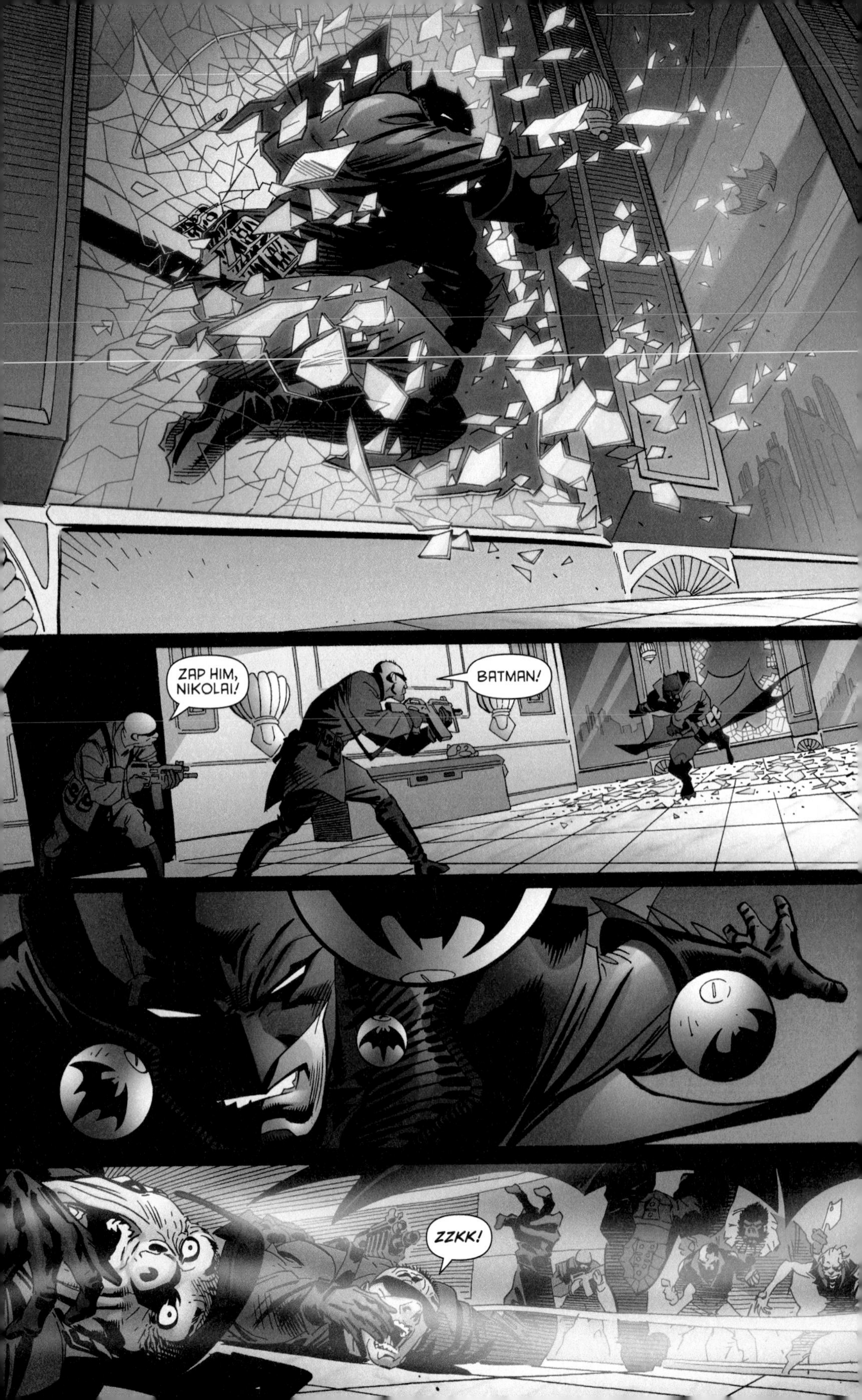
ZAP HIM, NIKOLAI!
BATMAN!
ZZKK!

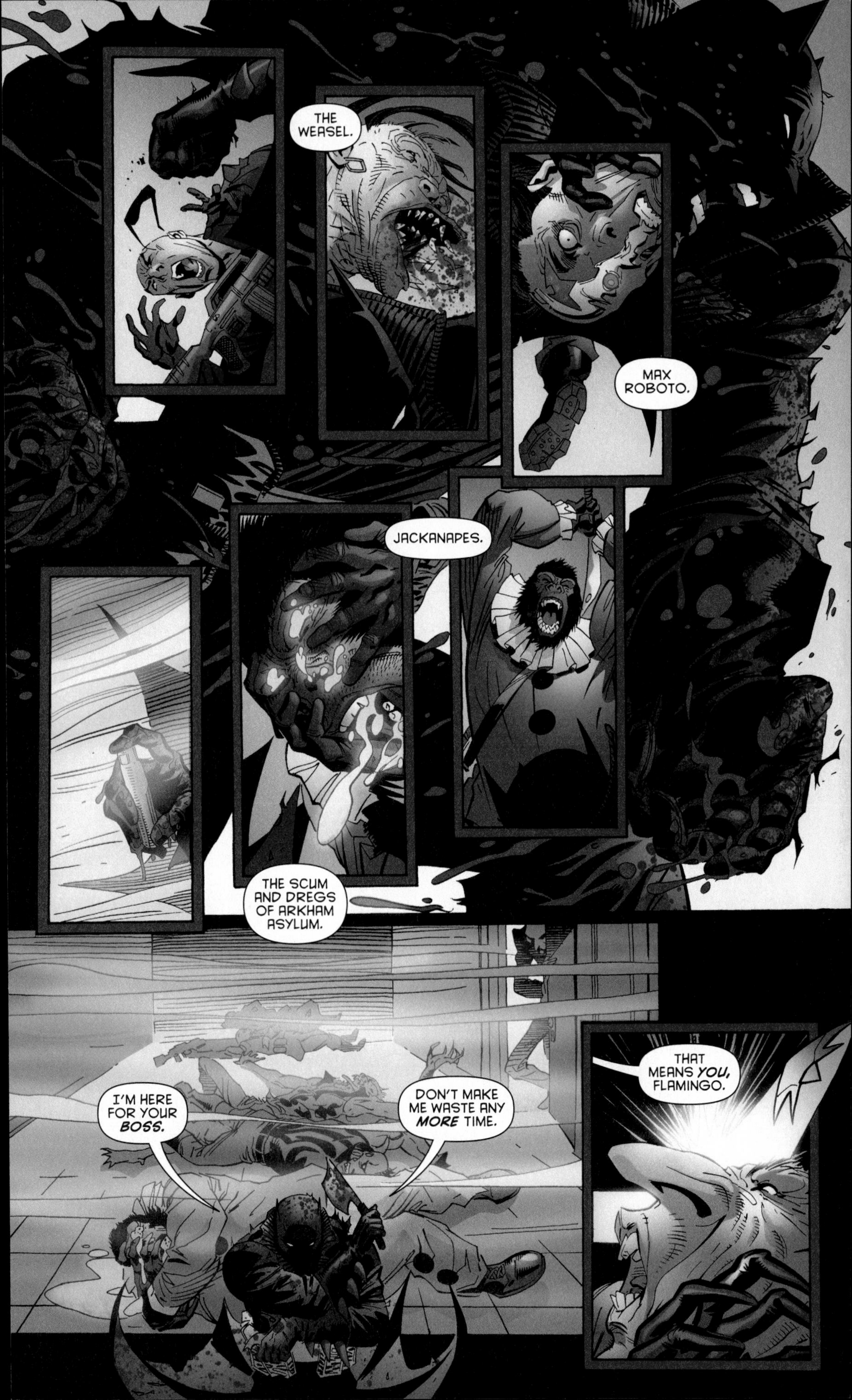
THE WEASEL.
MAX ROBOTO.
JACKANAPES.
THE SCUM AND DREGS OF ARKHAM ASYLUM.
I'M HERE FOR YOUR BOSS.
DON'T MAKE ME WASTE ANY MORE TIME.
THAT MEANS YOU, FLAMINGO.

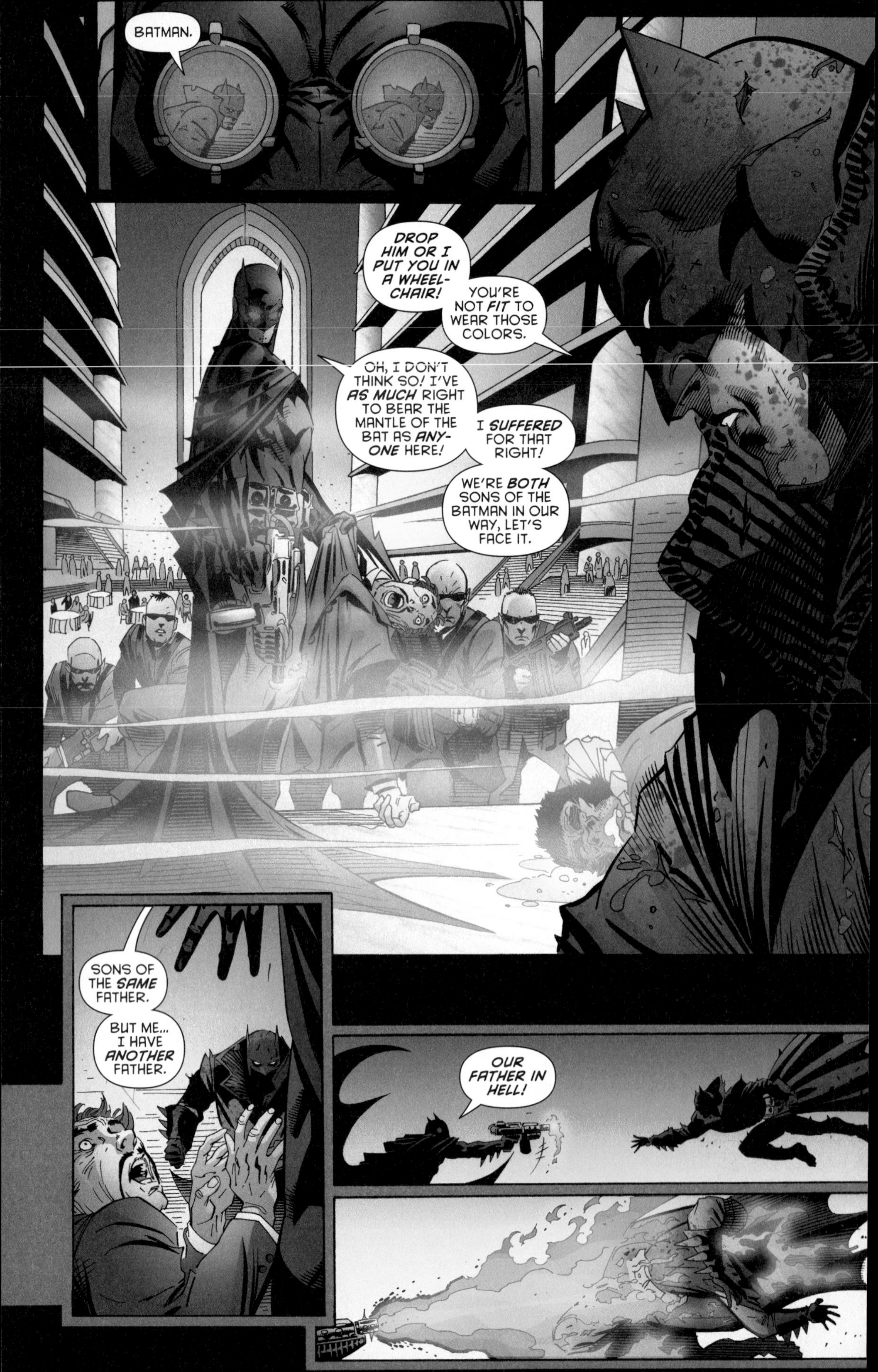
BATMAN.
DROP HIM OR I PUT YOU IN A WHEEL-CHAIR!
YOU'RE NOT FIT TO WEAR THOSE COLORS.
OH, I DON'T THINK SO! I'VE AS MUCH RIGHT TO BEAR THE MANTLE OF THE BAT AS ANY-ONE HERE!
I SUFFERED FOR THAT RIGHT!
WE'RE BOTH SONS OF THE BATMAN IN OUR WAY, LET'S FACE IT.
SONS OF THE SAME FATHER.
BUT ME... I HAVE ANOTHER FATHER.
OUR FATHER IN HELL!

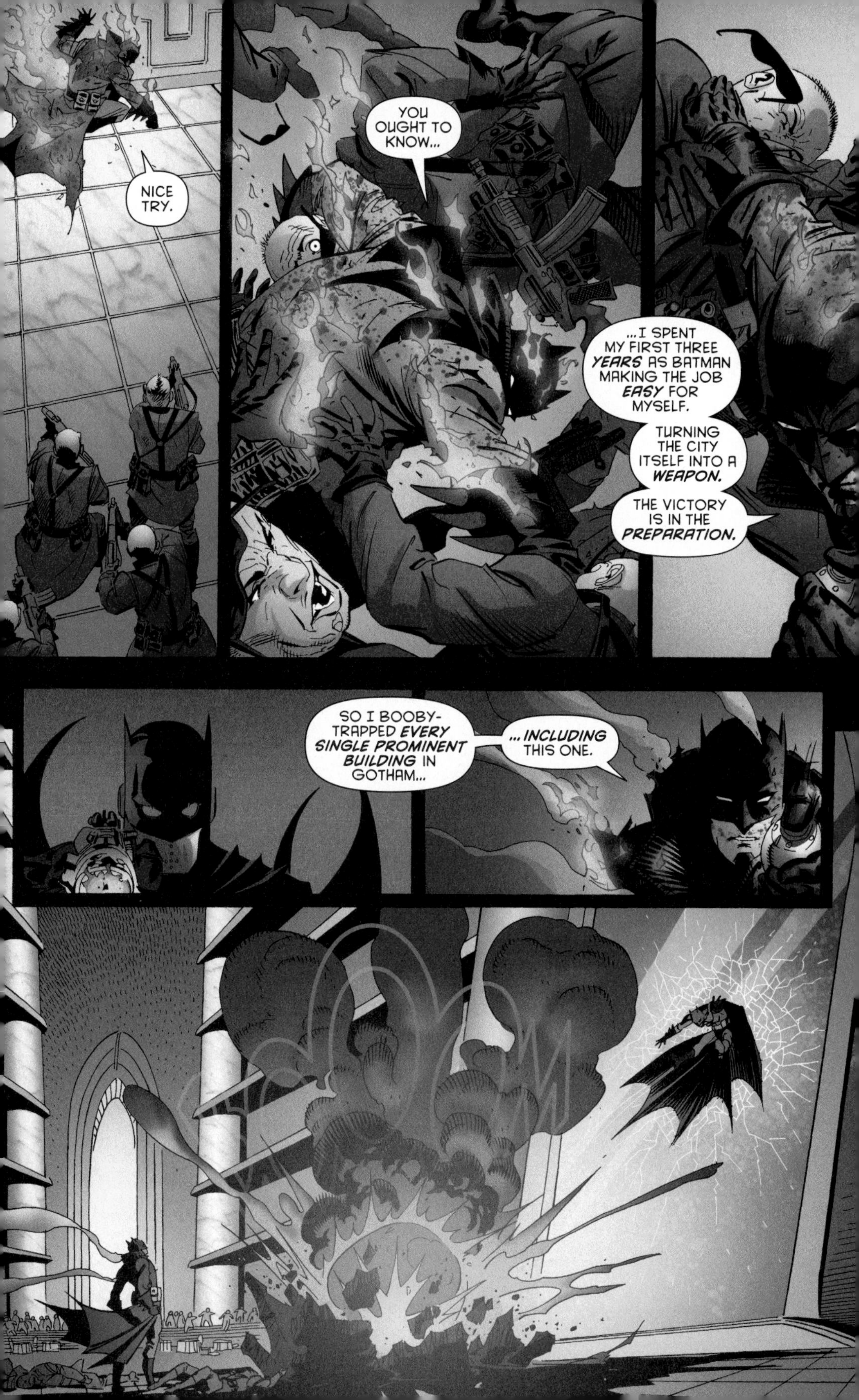

NICE TRY.
YOU OUGHT TO KNOW...
...I SPENT MY FIRST THREE YEARS AS BATMAN MAKING THE JOB EASY FOR MYSELF.
TURNING THE CITY ITSELF INTO A WEAPON.
THE VICTORY IS IN THE PREPARATION.
SO I BOOBY-TRAPPED EVERY SINGLE PROMINENT BUILDING IN GOTHAM...
...INCLUDING THIS ONE.

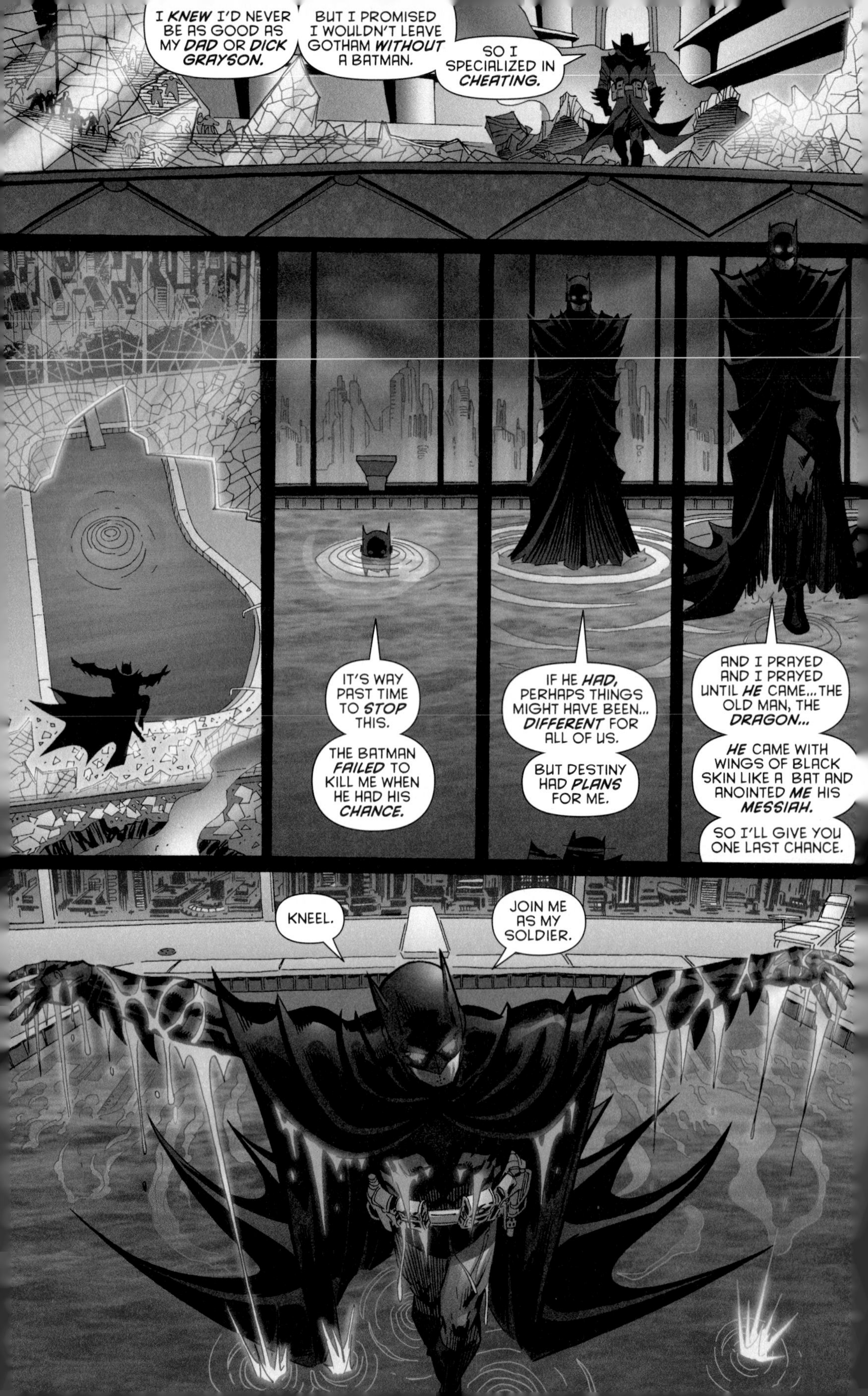
I KNEW I'D NEVER BE AS GOOD AS MY DAD OR DICK GRAYSON.
BUT I PROMISED I WOULDN'T LEAVE GOTHAM WITHOUT A BATMAN.
SO I SPECIALIZED IN CHEATING.
IT'S WAY PAST TIME TO STOP THIS.
THE BATMAN FAILED TO KILL ME WHEN HE HAD HIS CHANCE.
IF HE HAD, PERHAPS THINGS MIGHT HAVE BEEN... DIFFERENT FOR ALL OF US.
BUT DESTINY HAD PLANS FOR ME.
AND I PRAYED AND I PRAYED UNTIL HE CAME... THE OLD MAN, THE DRAGON...
HE CAME WITH WINGS OF BLACK SKIN LIKE A BAT AND ANOINTED ME HIS MESSIAH.
SO I'LL GIVE YOU ONE LAST CHANCE.
KNEEL.
JOIN ME AS MY SOLDIER.

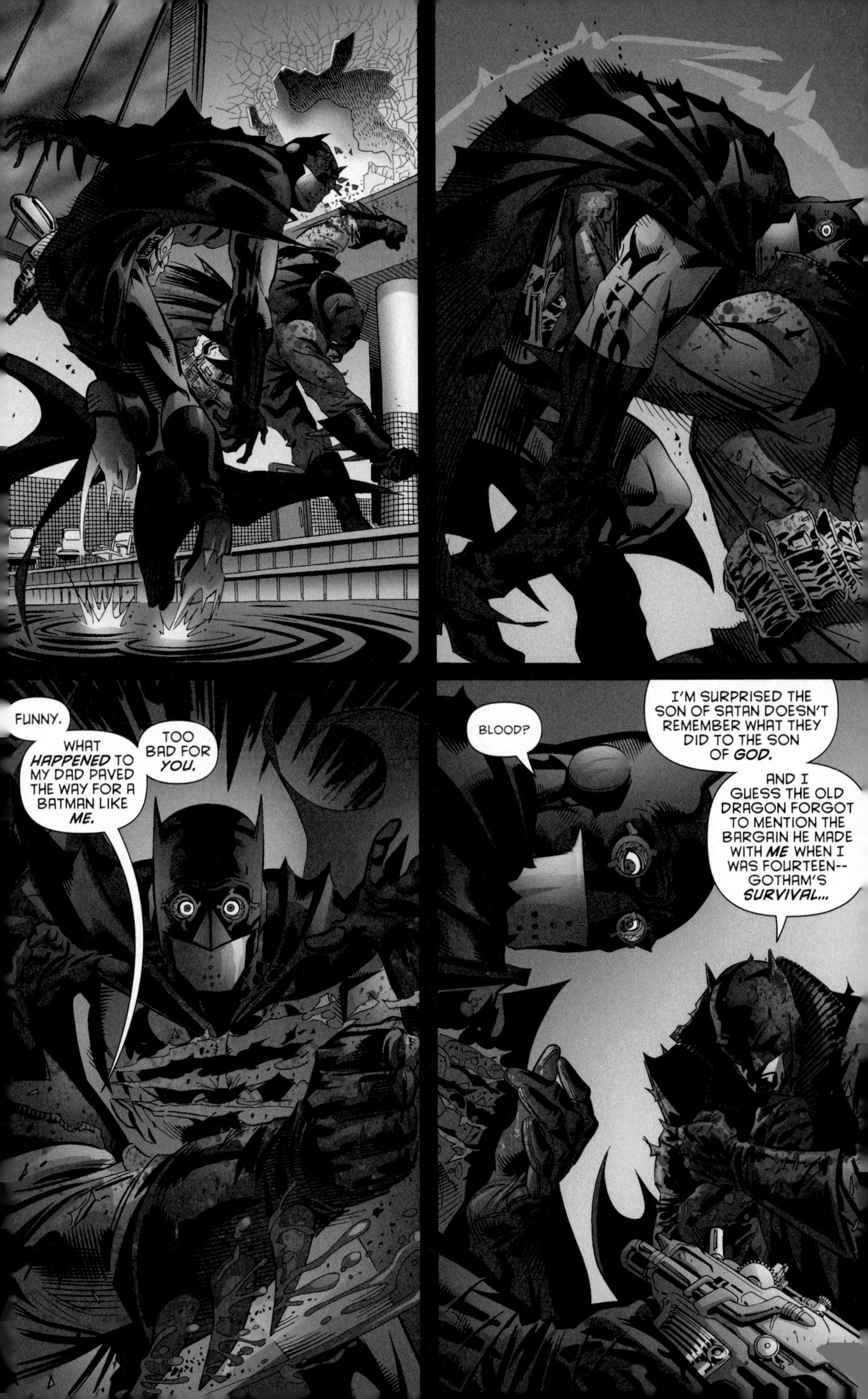

FUNNY.
WHAT HAPPENED TO MY DAD PAVED THE WAY FOR A BATMAN LIKE ME.
TOO BAD FOR YOU.
BLOOD?
I'M SURPRISED THE SON OF SATAN DOESN'T REMEMBER WHAT THEY DID TO THE SON OF GOD.
AND I GUESS THE OLD DRAGON FORGOT TO MENTION THE BARGAIN HE MADE WITH ME WHEN I WAS FOURTEEN-- GOTHAM'S SURVIVAL...

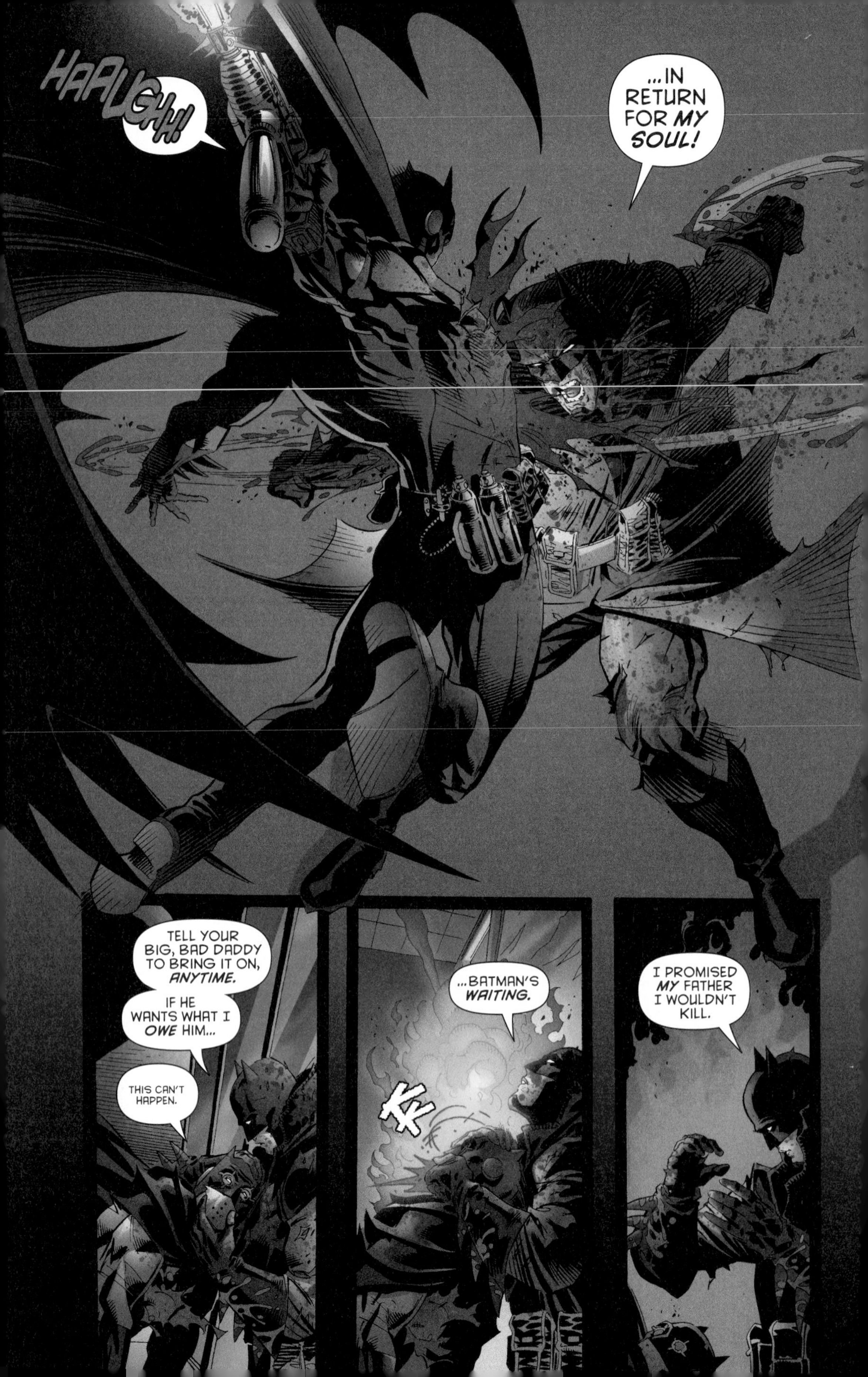
HAAUGHH!
...IN RETURN FOR MY SOUL!
TELL YOUR BIG, BAD DADDY TO BRING IT ON, ANYTIME.
IF HE WANTS WHAT I OWE HIM...
THIS CAN'T HAPPEN.
...BATMAN'S WAITING.
KK
I PROMISED MY FATHER I WOULDN'T KILL.

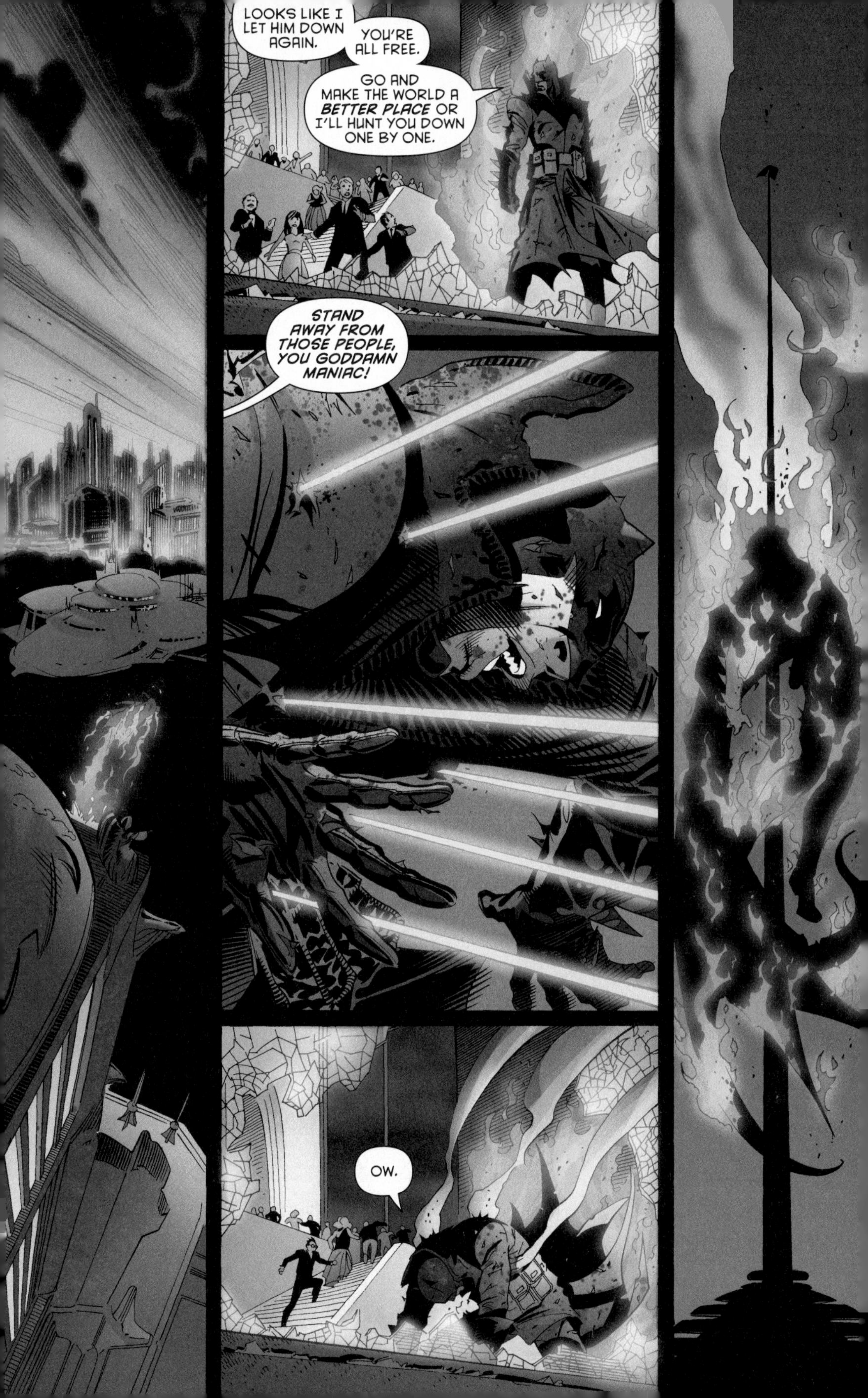
LOOKS LIKE I LET HIM DOWN AGAIN.
YOU'RE ALL FREE.
GO AND MAKE THE WORLD A BETTER PLACE OR I'LL HUNT YOU DOWN ONE BY ONE.
STAND AWAY FROM THOSE PEOPLE, YOU GODDAMN MANIAC!
OW.

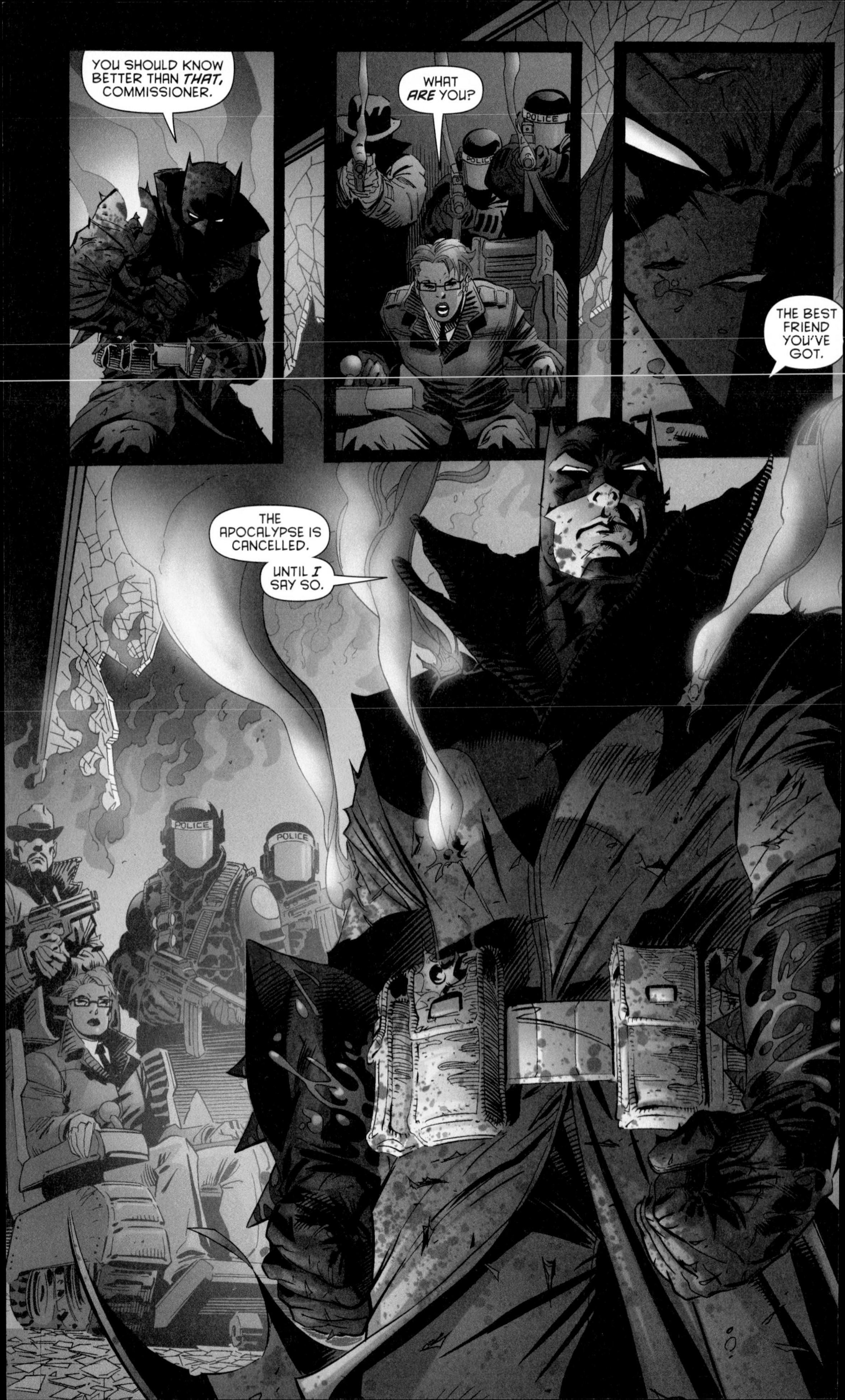
YOU SHOULD KNOW BETTER THAN *THAT,* COMMISSIONER.
WHAT *ARE* YOU?
THE BEST FRIEND YOU'VE GOT.
THE APOCALYPSE IS CANCELLED.
UNTIL *I* SAY SO.

TIME AND THE BATMAN

GRANT MORRISON
WRITER

ANDY KUBERT
ARTIST

JARED K. FLETCHER
LETTERER

BRAD ANDERSON
COLORIST

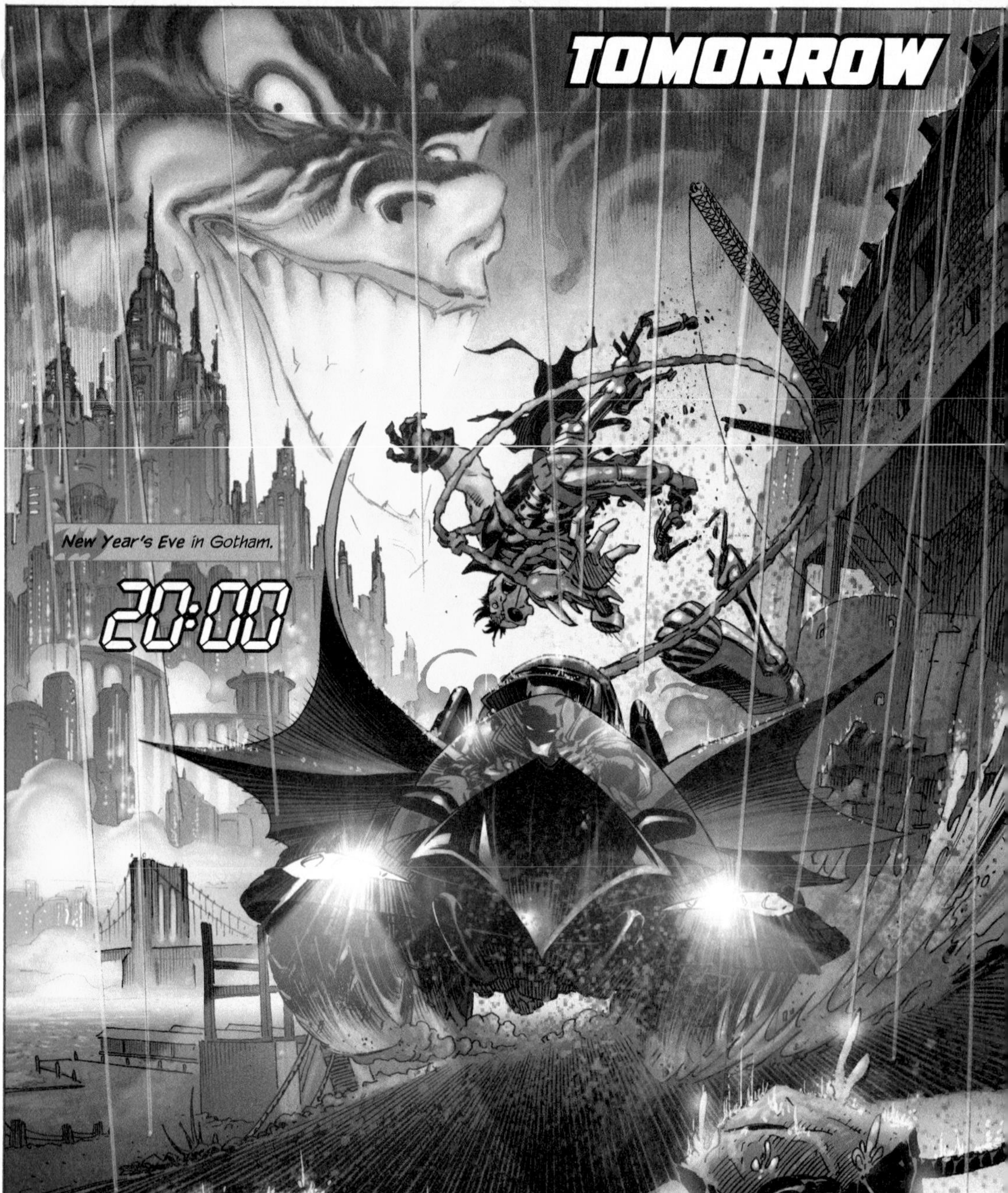
TOMORROW
New Year's Eve in Gotham.
20:00

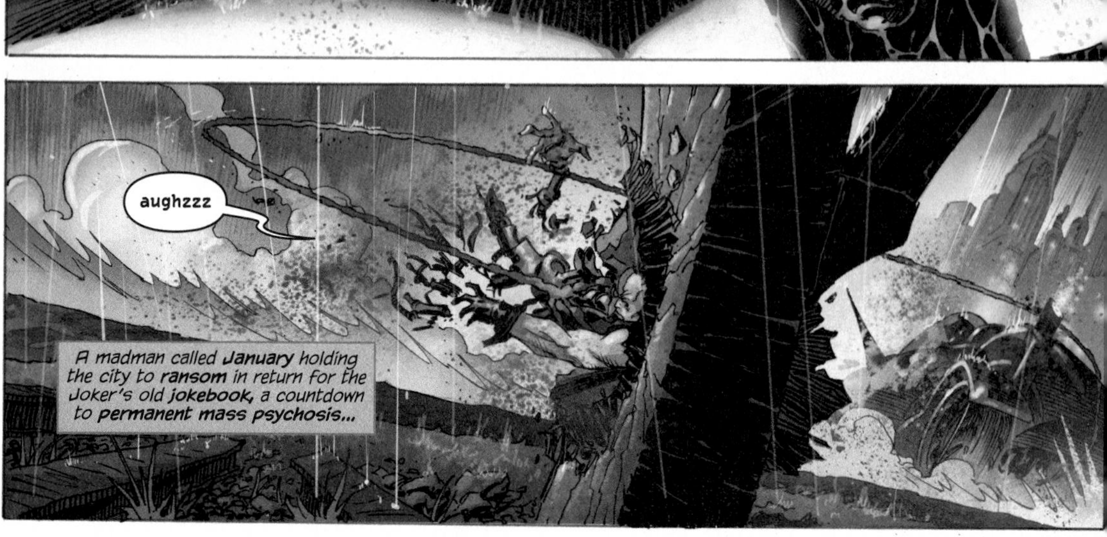
aughzzz
A madman called January holding the city to ransom in return for the Joker's old jokebook, a countdown to permanent mass psychosis...

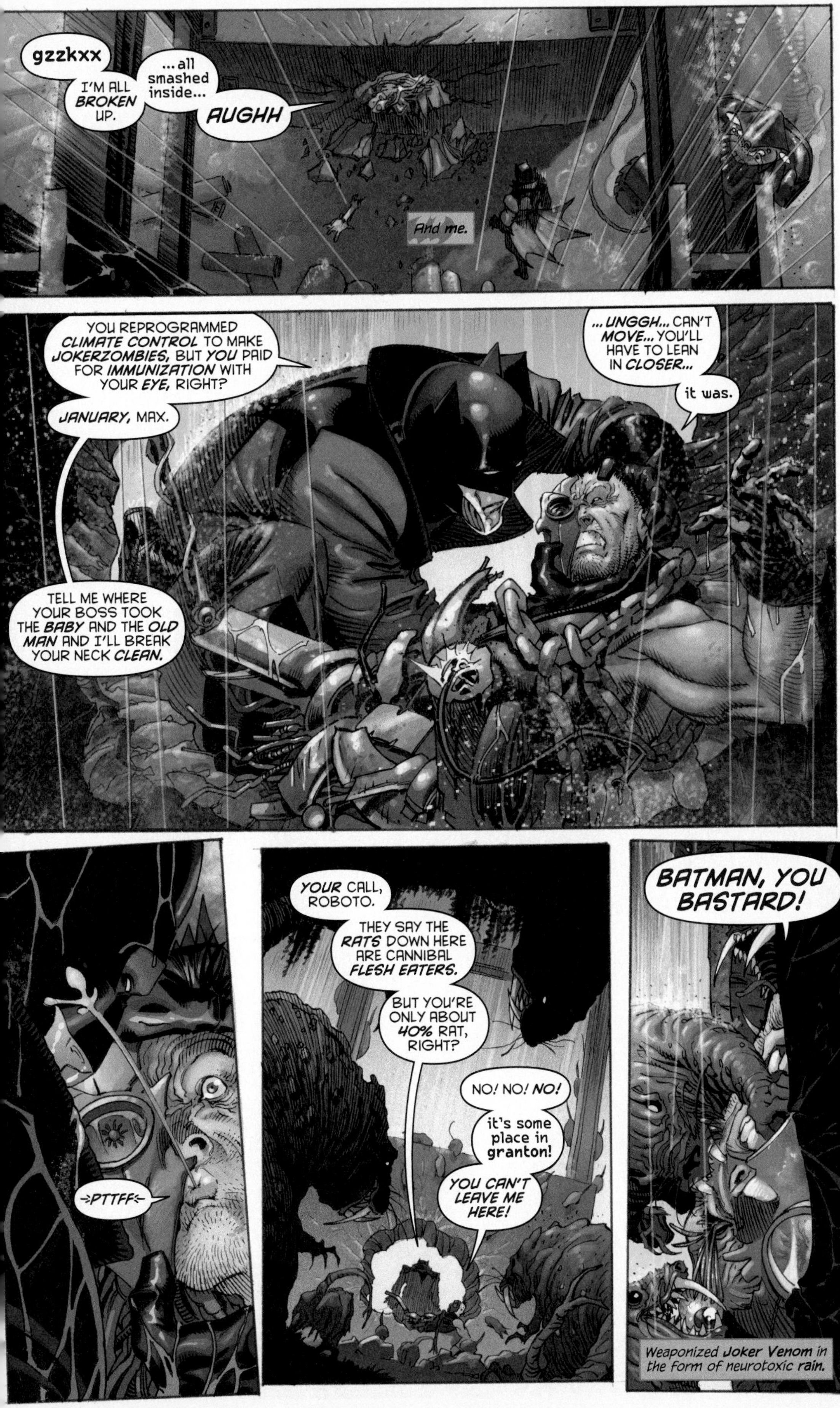
gzzkxx
I'M ALL BROKEN UP.
...all smashed inside...
AUGHH
And me.
YOU REPROGRAMMED CLIMATE CONTROL TO MAKE JOKERZOMBIES, BUT YOU PAID FOR IMMUNIZATION WITH YOUR EYE, RIGHT?
JANUARY, MAX.
TELL ME WHERE YOUR BOSS TOOK THE BABY AND THE OLD MAN AND I'LL BREAK YOUR NECK CLEAN.
...UNGGH... CAN'T MOVE... YOU'LL HAVE TO LEAN IN CLOSER...
it was.
PTTFF
YOUR CALL, ROBOTO.
THEY SAY THE RATS DOWN HERE ARE CANNIBAL FLESH EATERS.
BUT YOU'RE ONLY ABOUT 40% RAT, RIGHT?
NO! NO! NO!
it's some place in granton!
YOU CAN'T LEAVE ME HERE!
BATMAN, YOU BASTARD!
Weaponized Joker Venom in the form of neurotoxic rain.

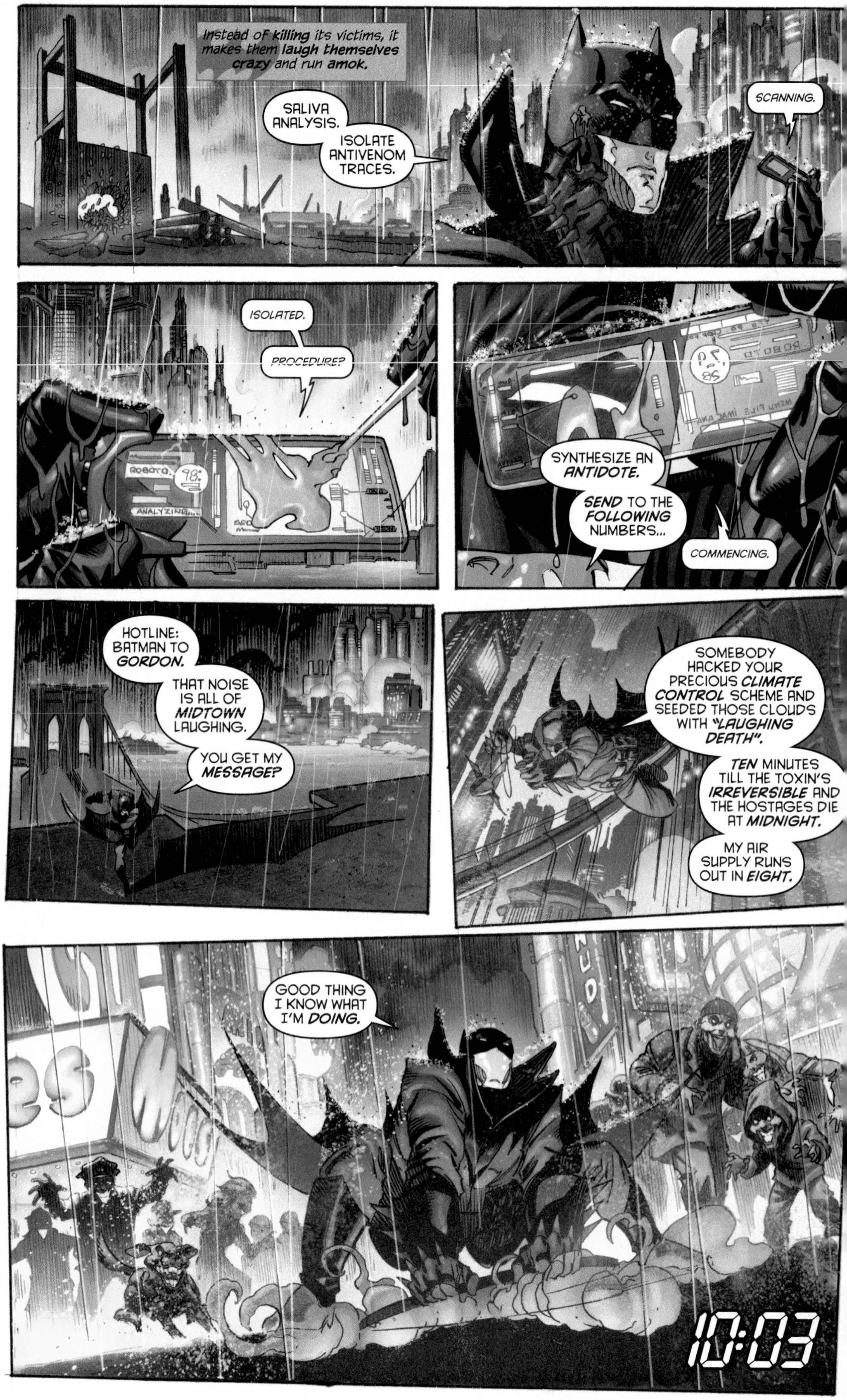
Instead of killing its victims, it makes them laugh themselves crazy and run amok.
SALIVA ANALYSIS.
ISOLATE ANTIVENOM TRACES.
SCANNING.
ISOLATED.
PROCEDURE?
SYNTHESIZE AN ANTIDOTE.
SEND TO THE FOLLOWING NUMBERS...
COMMENCING.
HOTLINE: BATMAN TO GORDON.
THAT NOISE IS ALL OF MIDTOWN LAUGHING.
YOU GET MY MESSAGE?
SOMEBODY HACKED YOUR PRECIOUS CLIMATE CONTROL SCHEME AND SEEDED THOSE CLOUDS WITH "LAUGHING DEATH".
TEN MINUTES TILL THE TOXIN'S IRREVERSIBLE AND THE HOSTAGES DIE AT MIDNIGHT.
MY AIR SUPPLY RUNS OUT IN EIGHT.
GOOD THING I KNOW WHAT I'M DOING.
10:03

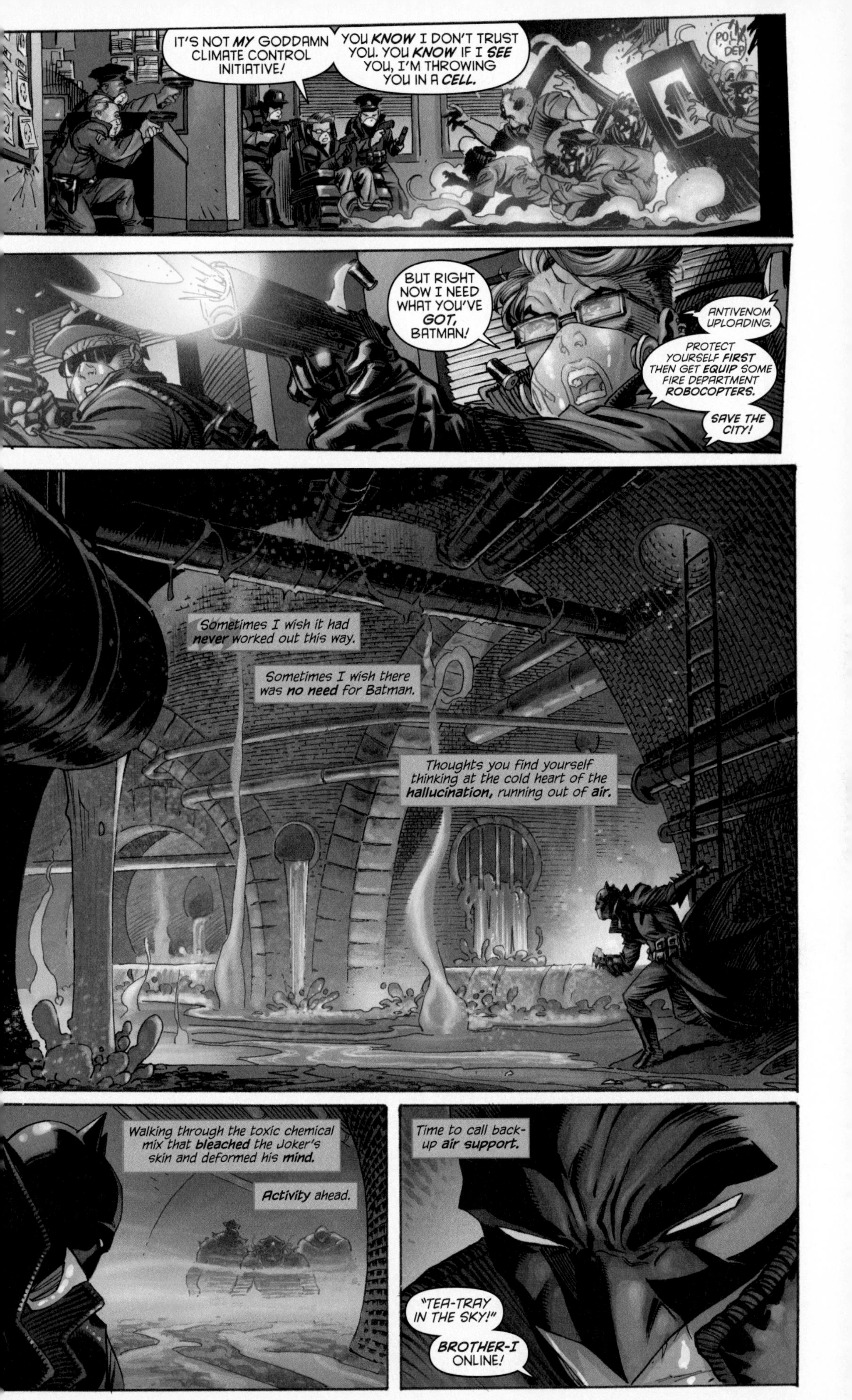
IT'S NOT MY GODDAMN CLIMATE CONTROL INITIATIVE!
YOU KNOW I DON'T TRUST YOU. YOU KNOW IF I SEE YOU, I'M THROWING YOU IN A CELL.
BUT RIGHT NOW I NEED WHAT YOU'VE GOT, BATMAN!
ANTIVENOM UPLOADING.
PROTECT YOURSELF FIRST THEN GET EQUIP SOME FIRE DEPARTMENT ROBOCOPTERS.
SAVE THE CITY!
Sometimes I wish it had never worked out this way.
Sometimes I wish there was no need for Batman.
Thoughts you find yourself thinking at the cold heart of the hallucination, running out of air.
Walking through the toxic chemical mix that bleached the Joker's skin and deformed his mind.
Activity ahead.
Time to call back-up air support.
"TEA-TRAY IN THE SKY!"
BROTHER-I ONLINE!

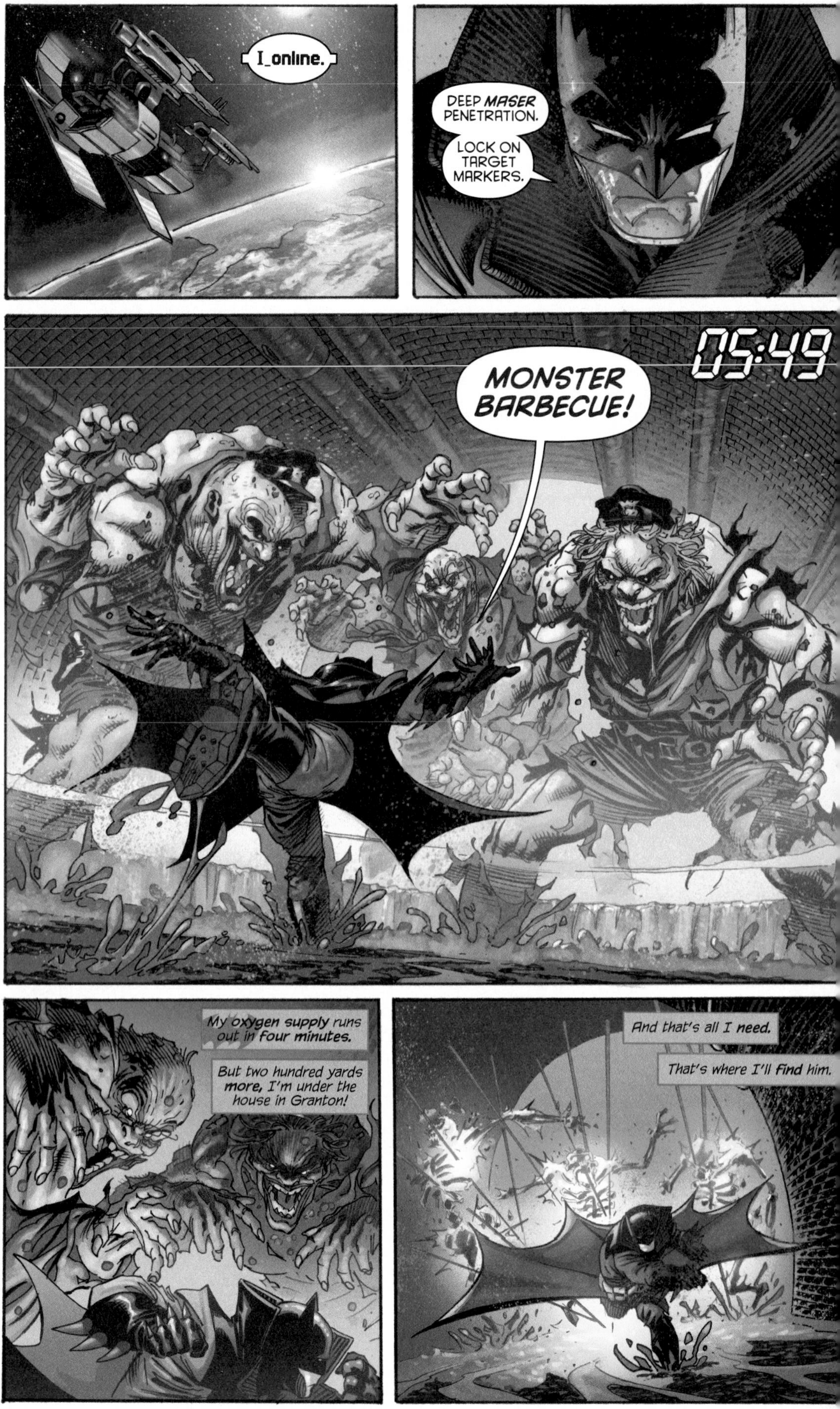
I_online.
DEEP MASER PENETRATION.
LOCK ON TARGET MARKERS.
05:49
MONSTER BARBECUE!
My oxygen supply runs out in four minutes.
But two hundred yards more, I'm under the house in Granton!
And that's all I need.
That's where I'll find him.

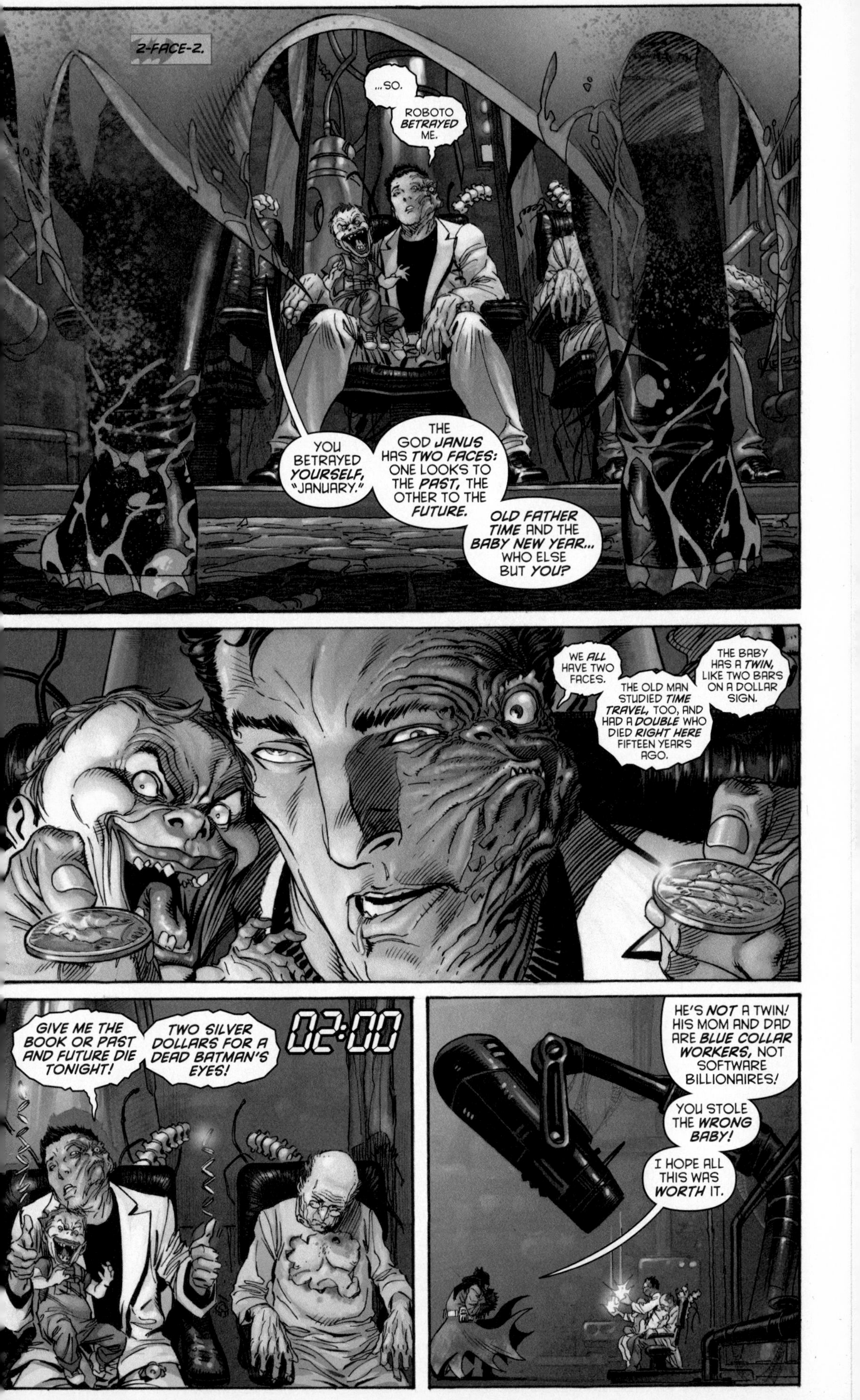

2-FACE-2.
...SO.
ROBOTO BETRAYED ME.
YOU BETRAYED YOURSELF, "JANUARY."
THE GOD JANUS HAS TWO FACES: ONE LOOKS TO THE PAST, THE OTHER TO THE FUTURE.
OLD FATHER TIME AND THE BABY NEW YEAR... WHO ELSE BUT YOU?
WE ALL HAVE TWO FACES.
THE BABY HAS A TWIN, LIKE TWO BARS ON A DOLLAR SIGN.
THE OLD MAN STUDIED TIME TRAVEL, TOO, AND HAD A DOUBLE WHO DIED RIGHT HERE FIFTEEN YEARS AGO.
GIVE ME THE BOOK OR PAST AND FUTURE DIE TONIGHT!
TWO SILVER DOLLARS FOR A DEAD BATMAN'S EYES!
02:00
HE'S NOT A TWIN! HIS MOM AND DAD ARE BLUE COLLAR WORKERS, NOT SOFTWARE BILLIONAIRES!
YOU STOLE THE WRONG BABY!
I HOPE ALL THIS WAS WORTH IT.

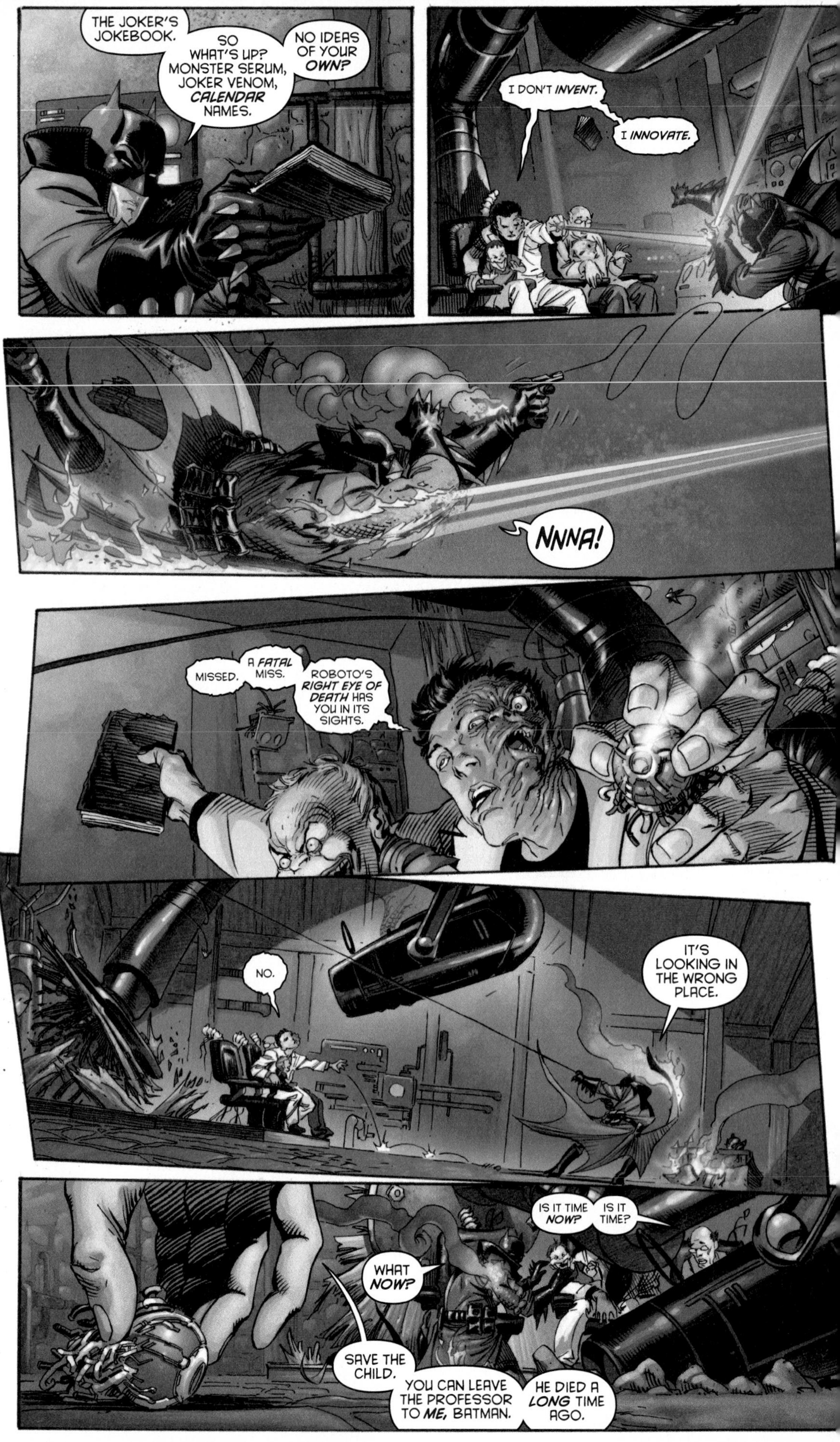
THE JOKER'S JOKEBOOK.
SO WHAT'S UP? MONSTER SERUM, JOKER VENOM, CALENDAR NAMES.
NO IDEAS OF YOUR OWN?
I DON'T INVENT.
I INNOVATE.
NNNA!
MISSED.
A FATAL MISS.
ROBOTO'S RIGHT EYE OF DEATH HAS YOU IN ITS SIGHTS.
NO.
IT'S LOOKING IN THE WRONG PLACE.
IS IT TIME NOW?
IS IT TIME?
WHAT NOW?
SAVE THE CHILD.
YOU CAN LEAVE THE PROFESSOR TO ME, BATMAN.
HE DIED A LONG TIME AGO.

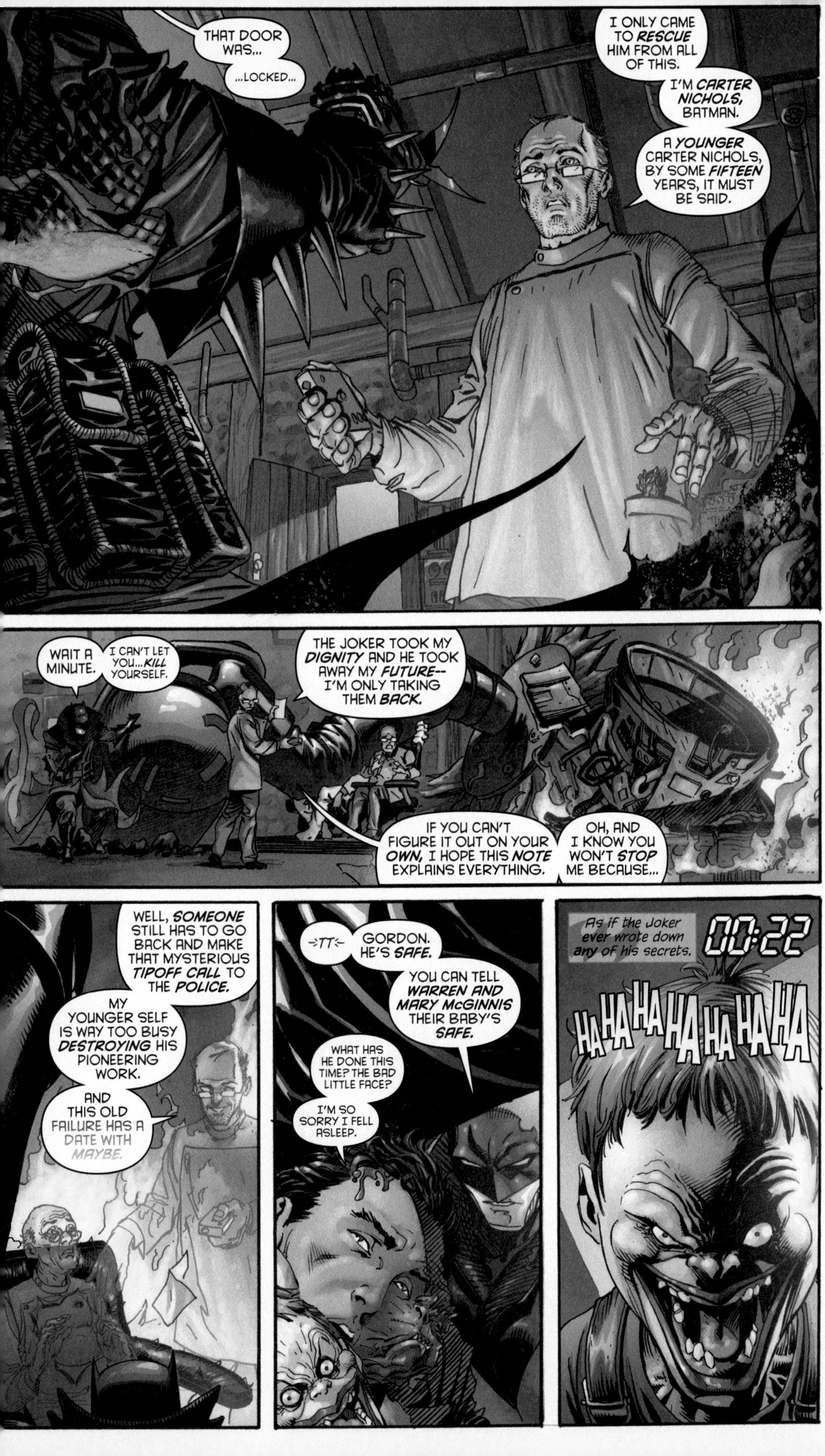
THAT DOOR WAS...
...LOCKED...
I ONLY CAME TO RESCUE HIM FROM ALL OF THIS.
I'M CARTER NICHOLS, BATMAN.
A YOUNGER CARTER NICHOLS, BY SOME FIFTEEN YEARS, IT MUST BE SAID.
WAIT A MINUTE.
I CAN'T LET YOU...KILL YOURSELF.
THE JOKER TOOK MY DIGNITY AND HE TOOK AWAY MY FUTURE-- I'M ONLY TAKING THEM BACK.
IF YOU CAN'T FIGURE IT OUT ON YOUR OWN, I HOPE THIS NOTE EXPLAINS EVERYTHING.
OH, AND I KNOW YOU WON'T STOP ME BECAUSE...
WELL, SOMEONE STILL HAS TO GO BACK AND MAKE THAT MYSTERIOUS TIPOFF CALL TO THE POLICE.
MY YOUNGER SELF IS WAY TOO BUSY DESTROYING HIS PIONEERING WORK.
AND THIS OLD FAILURE HAS A DATE WITH MAYBE.
TT
GORDON. HE'S SAFE.
YOU CAN TELL WARREN AND MARY McGINNIS THEIR BABY'S SAFE.
WHAT HAS HE DONE THIS TIME? THE BAD LITTLE FACE?
I'M SO SORRY I FELL ASLEEP.
As if the Joker ever wrote down any of his secrets.
00:22
HAHAHAHAHAHAHAHAHA

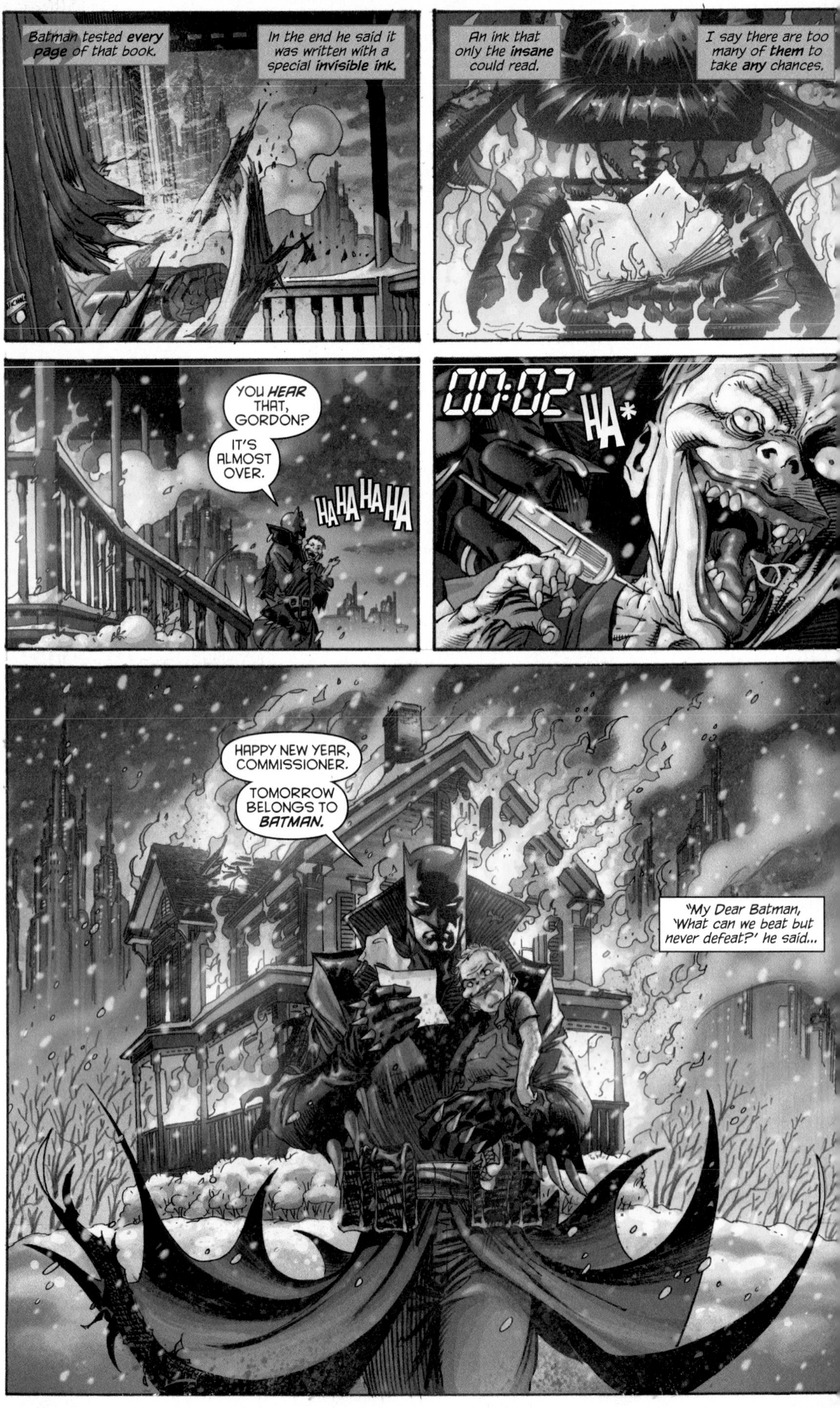

Batman tested every page of that book.
In the end he said it was written with a special invisible ink.
An ink that only the insane could read.
I say there are too many of them to take any chances.
YOU HEAR THAT, GORDON?
IT'S ALMOST OVER.
HA HA HA HA HA
00:02
HA*
HAPPY NEW YEAR, COMMISSIONER.
TOMORROW BELONGS TO BATMAN.
"My Dear Batman, 'What can we beat but never defeat?' he said...

GROWING PAINS

BEHIND THE SCENES OF DAMIAN SON OF BATMAN BY ANDY KUBERT

SON OF A BATMAN #1
GROUND
LOGO
DEAD BATMAN WILL BE DONE IN GRAY'S
STABBED JOKERFISH

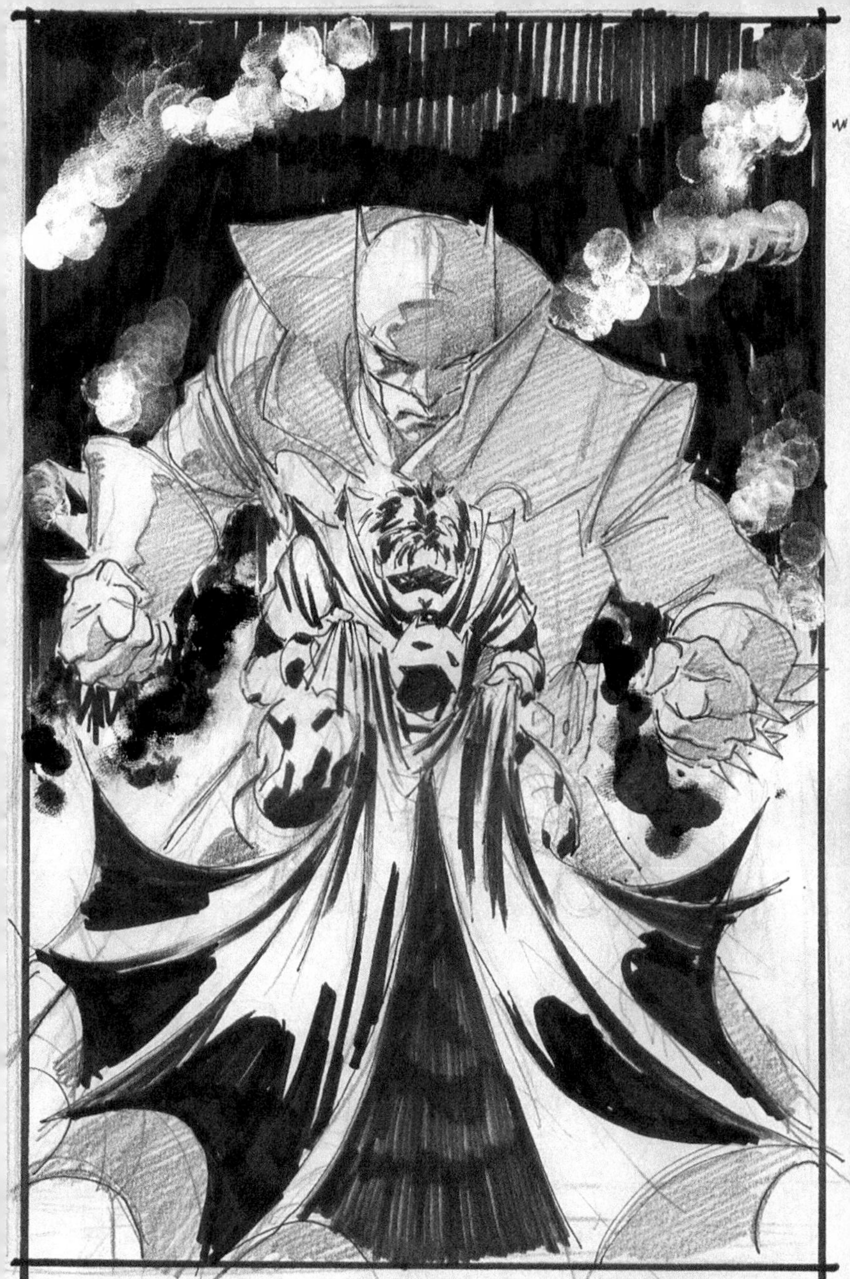

SON OF A BATMAN #2 COVER — Andy Kubert

DAMIAN DONE IN BLACKS / DAMIANBATMAN BACKGROUND IN WASHES VIA COVER #1

DAMIAN FIGHTING SHARPTOOTH AND JACKANAPES!

SON OF BATMAN #3

FLAMES
MAKE
BAT-
WINGS!

DAMIAN
STANDS
IN
BATCAVE/
FLAMES
COMING
FROM
BELOW

DAMIAN / SON OF BATMAN # 1

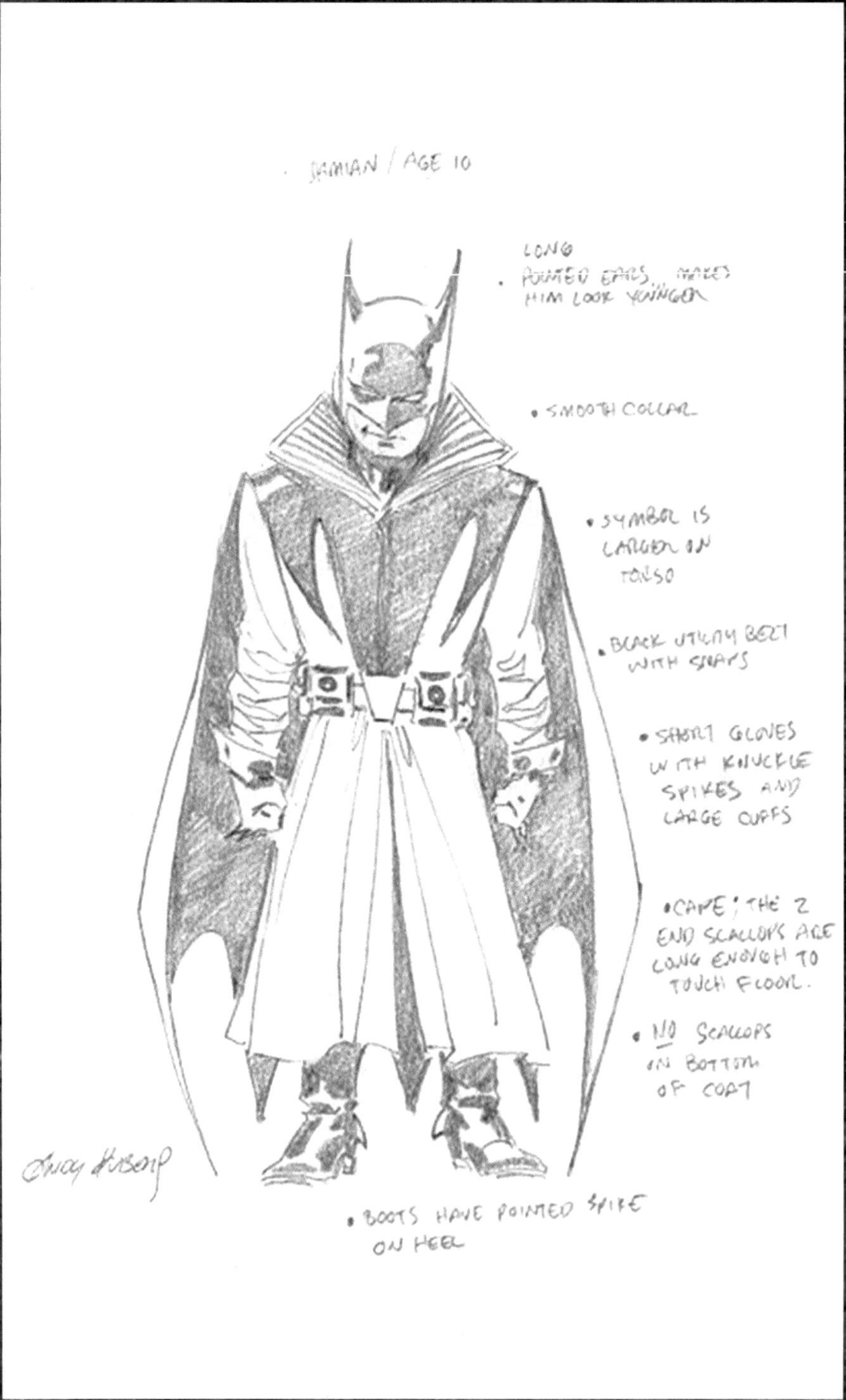
DAMIAN / AGE 10
• LONG POINTED EARS, MAKES HIM LOOK YOUNGER
• SMOOTH COLLAR
• SYMBOL IS LARGER ON TORSO
• BLACK UTILITY BELT WITH SNAPS
• SHORT GLOVES WITH KNUCKLE SPIKES AND LARGE CUFFS
• CAPE; THE 2 END SCALLOPS ARE LONG ENOUGH TO TOUCH FLOOR.
• NO SCALLOPS ON BOTTOM OF COAT
Andy Kubert
• BOOTS HAVE POINTED SPIKE ON HEEL

DAMIAN: SON OF BATMAN issue #4, pages 2-10 script

Pages Two and Three (double page spread)

Pan. 1 inset/

Close on Damian. He's looking right at us, all cut up and bleeding. Very determined, very pissed off.

Caption: ...when I wouldn't have gave it a SECOND THOUGHT...

Pan. 2 inset /

Close on screaming Jackanapes. We can see the Weasel, and Phospherous Rex.

Caption: ...to end their miserable EXISTENCE.

Caption: PHEW!

Caption: I don't think ANY of them has ever heard of mouthwash.

Pan. 3 large panel/

We are smack in he middle of the big fight inside the warehouse with Damian and all the colorful heavies. Jackanapes, Weasel, P-Rex and a couple of others that will look cool. We can see Bruce tied up in the chair as per last issue, and beside him is the Wannabe Joker. Damian has gotten the tar kicked out of him and is being launched across the spread by the jackanapes, crashing into some wooden crates, spilling fishing nets and lobster traps.

Caption: The Gotham City Dock Warehouse.

Caption: BRUCE is OUT of it. Haven't got much time...

Caption: Weasel... Jackanapes... Phospherous Rex... Tomahawks...

Caption: ...it wasn't that long ago when these guys would NEVER have

gotten this far.

Title and Credits
Title : Full Circle
Written and Drawn by : Andy Kubert
Colored by: A. Genius
Lettered by: Jared Fletcher
Edited by: Baxter Marts
Assited Editing by : J9
Batman created by: Bob Kane

Pan. 4 inset/

Close on Joker, screaming. His eyes are going wild.

Caption: ...and I would NEVER take the BEATING that I am.

Joker: RIP OUT HIS THROAT!!

Joker: Then make a NECKTIE with his TONGUE!!

Page Four/

The next 4 panels are quick action shots of Damian getting pounded by the baddies. We'll be panning in over the 4 shots.

Pan. 1/
Downshot. Baddies are leaping onto Damian. He's in the middle of the panel.

Caption: This WANNABE Joker is for real...

Pan. 2/
Downshot. We're getting closer in. Damian is getting belted in the face. Hands are all over him, grabbing and tearing.

Caption: ...albeit a bit UGLIER than the ORIGINAL, if you can believe
that.

Pan. 3/
Downshot. Closer yet. Clawed fingers are scratching at his face. He's cut and bleeding.

Caption: Someday, I'd like to hear HIS story...

Pan. 4/
Yet even closer. A Jackanape chomps down on Damian's neck. Damian's eyes are wide open... he screams!

Damian: AAAAAHHHH!!!!

Pan. 5/
Outside shot of the Batmobile with the mounted remote cameras aimed at the warehouse.

Caption: ...filthy ANIMAL!

Pan. 6/
C.U. on Alfred the cat watching the monitors sitting in the bat-con chair. We can see the Batman suit in the glass case beyond. A smashed wall in the warehouse allows the cat to watch the fight.

Caption: Glad my MONIKER doesn't follow a MONKEY!
Caption: Or a CAT...

Page Five/

Panel 1/
Large interior shot of fight... ground level. It's very dark, the figures would be edge-lit. All the

baddies are attacking Damian. Damian is all the way to the far
right of the panel, and to the left are all the baddies. The
Jackanape that bit Damian is now flying in the air, with his
teeth shattering out of his mouth.

Caption: These guys are NASTY...
Caption: ...and VICIOUS!
Caption: I'm gonna have to get ROUGH.

Panel 2/
Damian lunges after that Jackanape that
he just tossed. In the process, he is throwing off other baddies,
making a path towards that particular Jackanape.

Caption: My natural instincts are
kicking in...
Caption: Huge ADRENALINE rush...
Caption: ...pulse POUNDING...

Panel 3/
Close on vicious Damian. He looks like a
cornered wild animal.

Caption: I NEED...
Caption: ...to KILL!

Panel 4/
Close on Damian's hand, picking up a
fallen crowbar that lay in a pile of broken boards and lobster
traps.

Page Six/

Panel 1/
Damian jumps on the fallen Jackanape,
crowbar in his hand cocked behind his head ready to hit the
Jackanape. In the background, we can see baddies coming up
again after Damian.

Panel 2/
Close on the crowbar nailing the
Jackanape in the head.

Sound effect: THUUUD!!!!

Panel 3/
Angle on Jackanape. He's bleeding, eyes
barely open, cheek crushed in and missing a few teeth but alive.
Beyond, we can see Damian's arm cocked back again for another
blow. Damian is looking down intently.

Panel 4/
Close in on Damian. He's looking intent,
but a bit of gleam in his eye. Eyebrows are unfurrowing.

Panel 5/
Same angle on Damian, now he is looking

remorseful.

Caption: I made a PROMISE...

Panel 6/
Angle on Damian's hand, dropping the
crowbar.

Caption: ...and THIS wasn't part of it.

Panel 7/
Same angle as Panel 3 with Jackanape in
the foreground, but now, the baddies are tackling Damian taking
him towards the right side of the panel. Some of them have their
guns out.

Damian: UNNNH!

Page Seven/

Panel 1/
Damian, being inundated by all the
baddies, are crashing through a couple of pillars, broken boards
and nails, barrels and junk spill all over. In the background,
we can still see Bruce and Wannabe Joker. Joker is animated as
to what is happening.

SFX:
Joker: WeeeeHOOOOOO!!!!!
Joker: That looks like it HURT!
Joker: Now...TAKE HIM APART!!!
Joker: Then we'll do BRUCIE!
Joker (small): No, not like that, you sick
puppies!

Panel 2/
Damian rolls to the other side of the
room, away from the baddies. Some of the baddies point at him as
to not and let him get away.

Caption: Got to get some DISTANCE
between...
Pointing baddie: GET HIM!

Panel 3/
Tomahawk, a baddie that has a head
that's shaped like an axe, has his gun pulled out and is aimed
towards us (at Damian off panel). Behind him, we can see other
baddies.

Tomahawk: This is THE last stop for
him...

Panel 4/
Angle on gun firing bullets. Shell
casings eject.

Gun sfx: BLAM BLAM BLAM BLAM

Panel 5/
Damian has his forearms up, deflecting
the bullets off of his glove gauntlets. They're armored.

Panel 6/
Close on Tomahawk. Yelling and
pointing.

Tomahawk: He's ARMORED!!
Tomahawk: And OUTNUMBERED!
Tomahawk: Let's MOVE!!!!
Caption: I'm READY...

Pages eight and nine (double page spread)

Panels 1-6 will be vertical going along the 2 page
spread. Panel 7 will be inset at bottom of panel 6.

Panel 1/
Pull back. Damian gets overpowered by
baddies again. He's going down.

Damian: OOOF!
Caption: These guys are BIG...
Caption: I CAN'T let this happen...

Panel 2/
Close on Bruce Wayne. He still has
the make-up on, and is bruised and battered. His eye is barely
opened.

Caption: Not to ME...
Caption: Not to BRUCE...

Panel 3/
Closer in on the fight. Damian is
overpowered, even though he's just kicked Tomahawk in the
crotch. Owch.

Caption: Ever since I was a little kid
with a sword, I looked for APPROVAL...
Caption: And even though I showed
almost NO respect towards him...
Caption: ...doesn't mean that I didn't
FEEL it.

Panel 4/
Pull back from Bruce a bit. We can see
a little of the Wannabe Joker standing beside him.

Caption: Maybe that's the reason why I
became BATMAN...

Panel 5/
Closer in yet on Damian. Damian has his fingers firmly planted into a Jackanapes eyesockets. Damian is gazing off-panel (at Bruce) as he is still being overpowered.

Caption: ...because I'm still looking for that elusive APPROVAL from him...

Panel 6/
Pull back more from Bruce. We can see part of the wannabe Joker's face. He's smiling behind Bruce as Damian is losing.

Caption: ...and I'm not going to get it if these turds WIN.
Caption: 'Cause then, both BRUCE and I will LOSE.

Panel 7/inset
Close in on Damian. He's ripped and bleeding. He doesn't want to lose in front of Bruce. But he wants to stick with the way of the Batman. Damian is determined.

Caption: No way in HELL am I going to let THAT happen...

Page Ten/

Panel 1/
Pull back. Baddie bodies go flying in every direction. Damian is kicking butt!

Panels 2-6/ inset panels over panel 1, which is splash page panel.

Inset 1/Damian's fist connecting with The Weasel's face.

Caption: Seeing Bruce like this...

Inset 2/ Damian's elbow launching into a Jackanapes gut.

Caption: ...is tough enough...

Inset 3/ Damian bending back the arm of another baddie, breaking it.

Caption: ... have to exhibit...

Inset 4/ Damian's foot kicking in

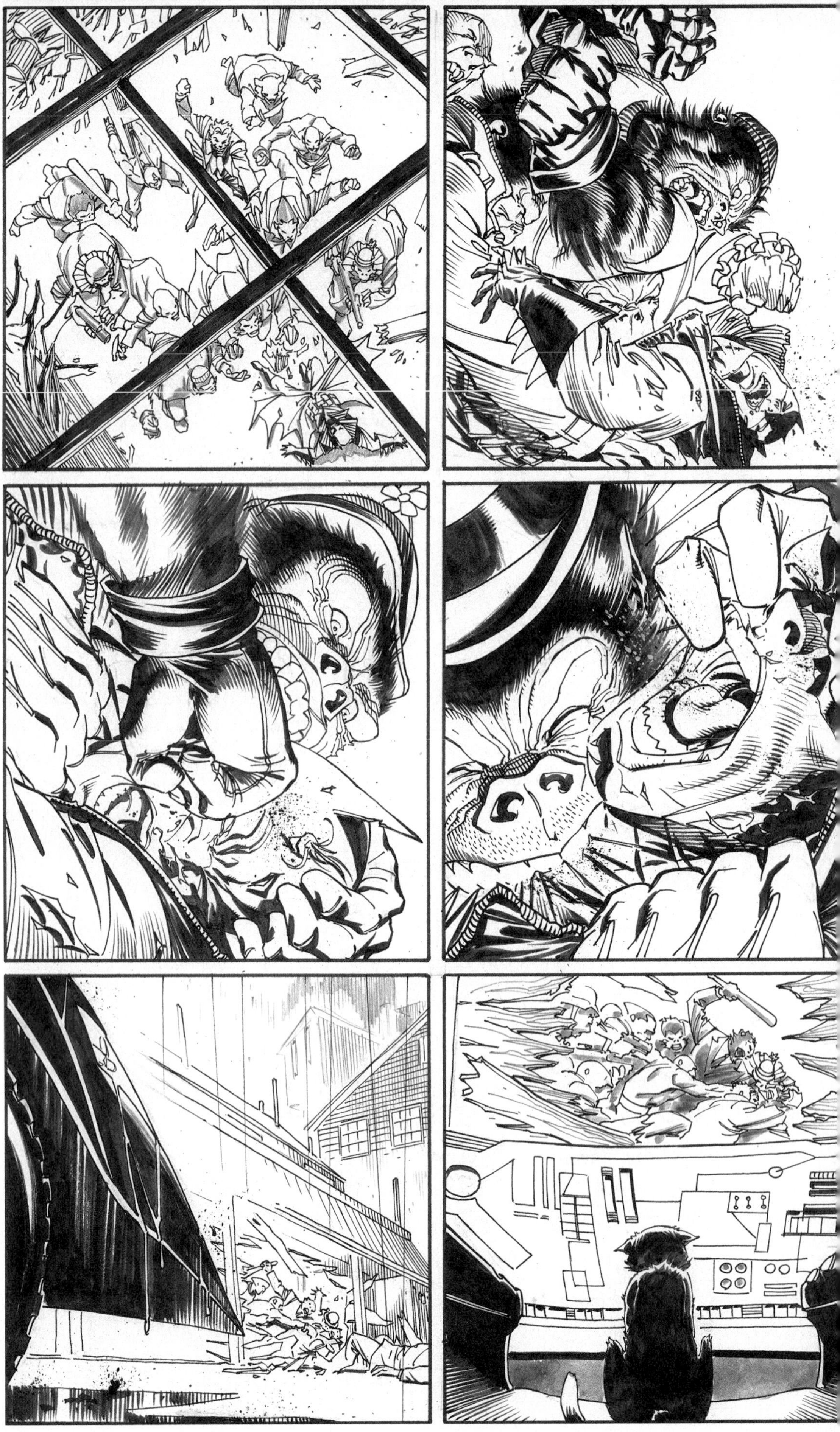

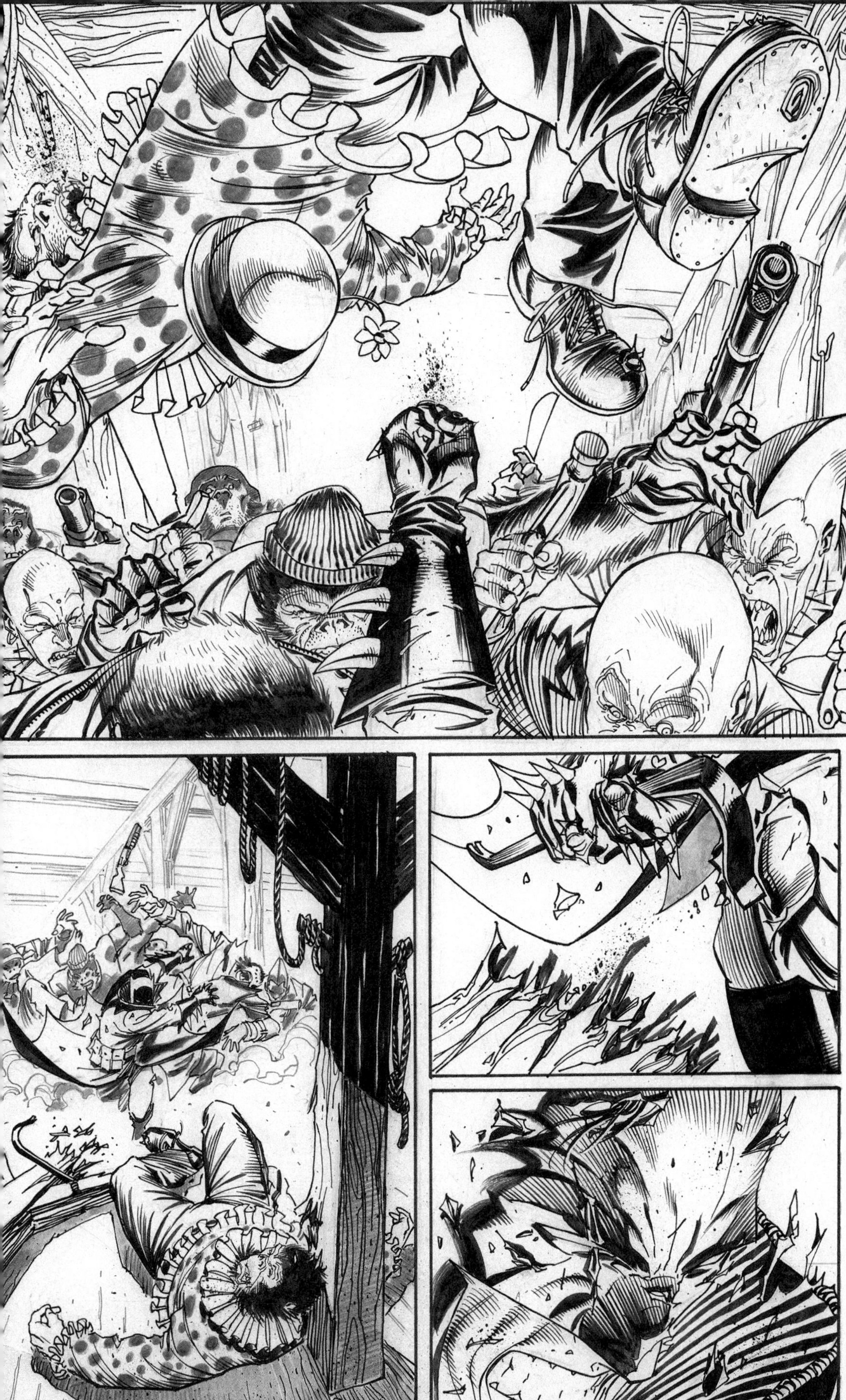

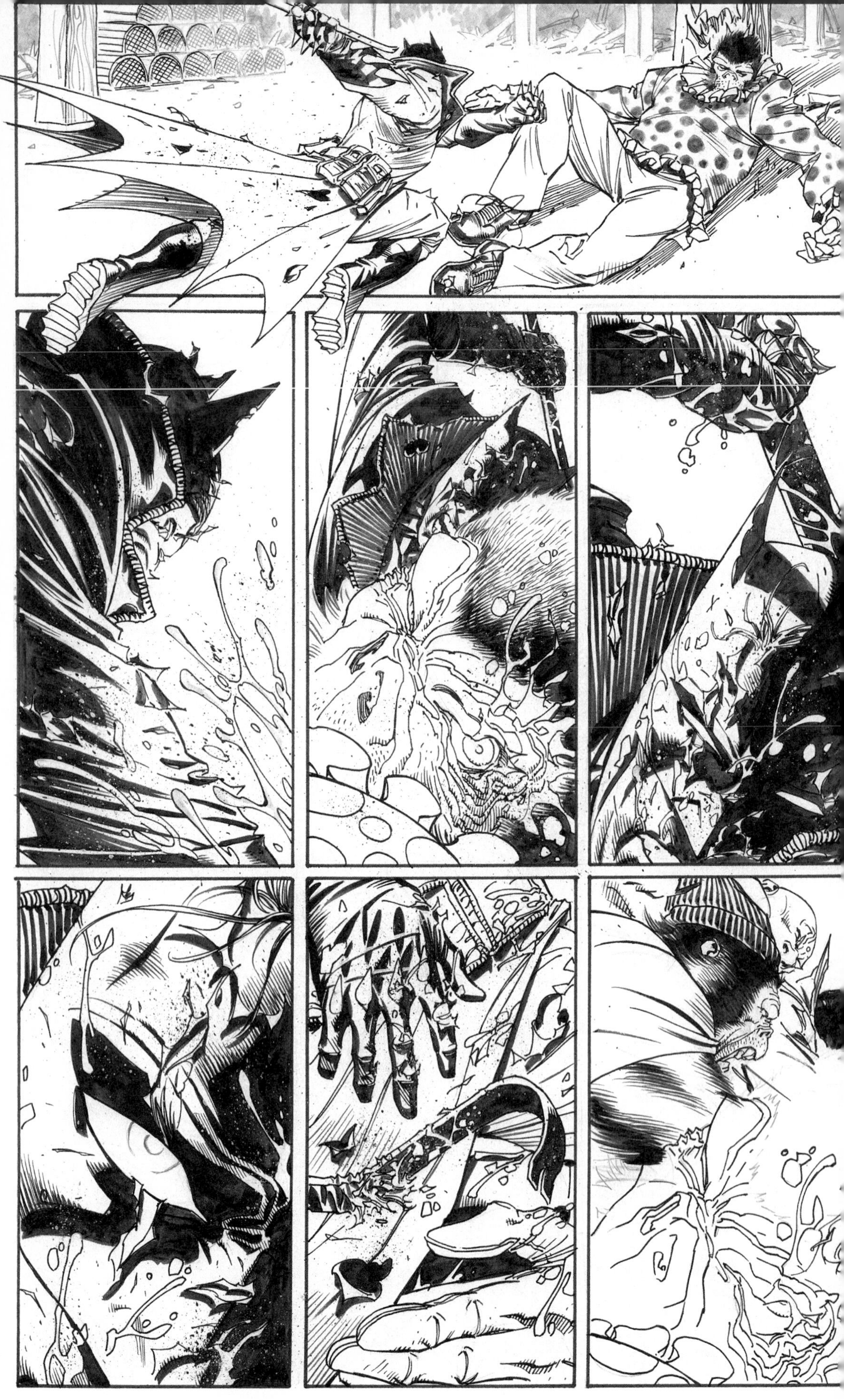

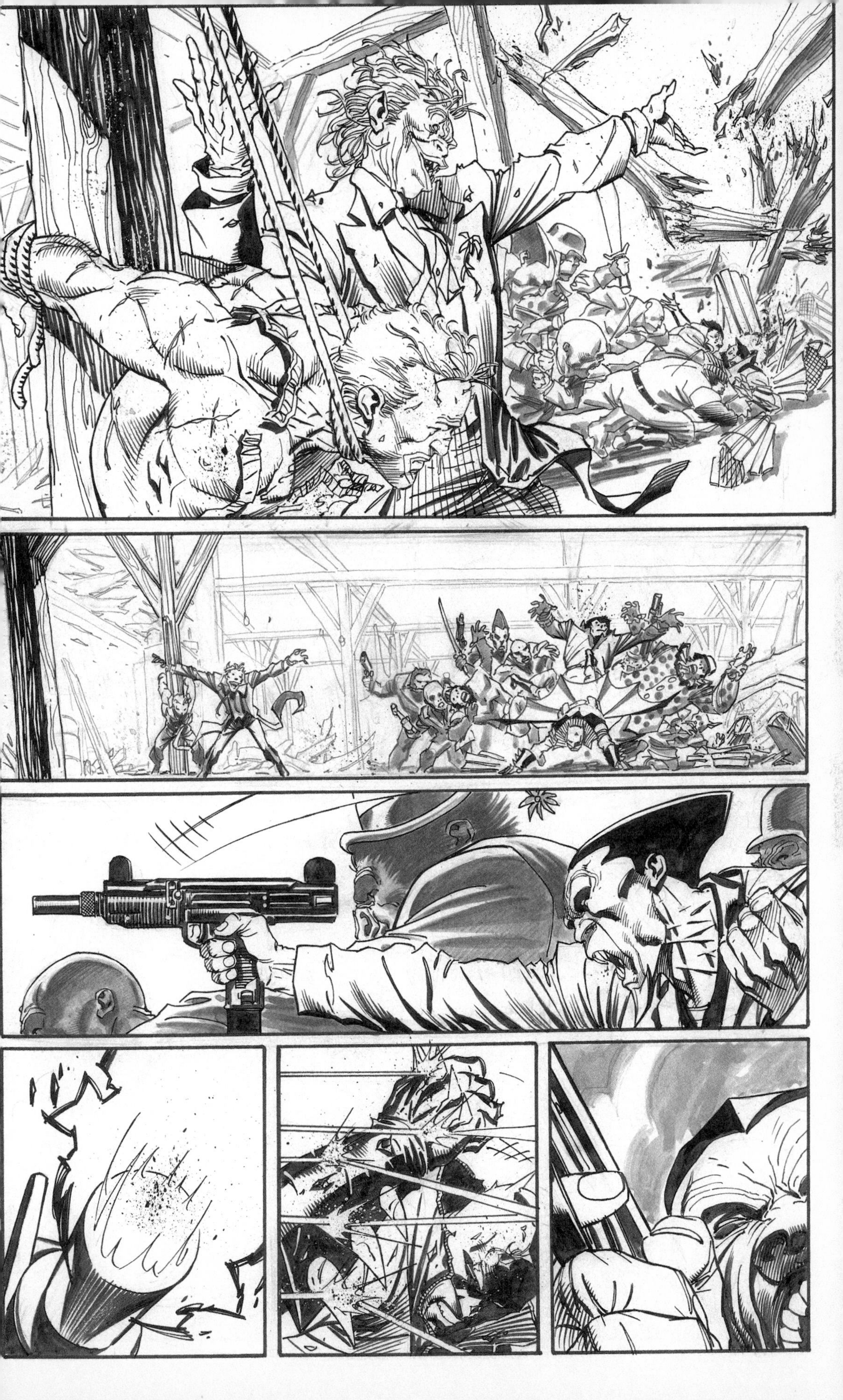

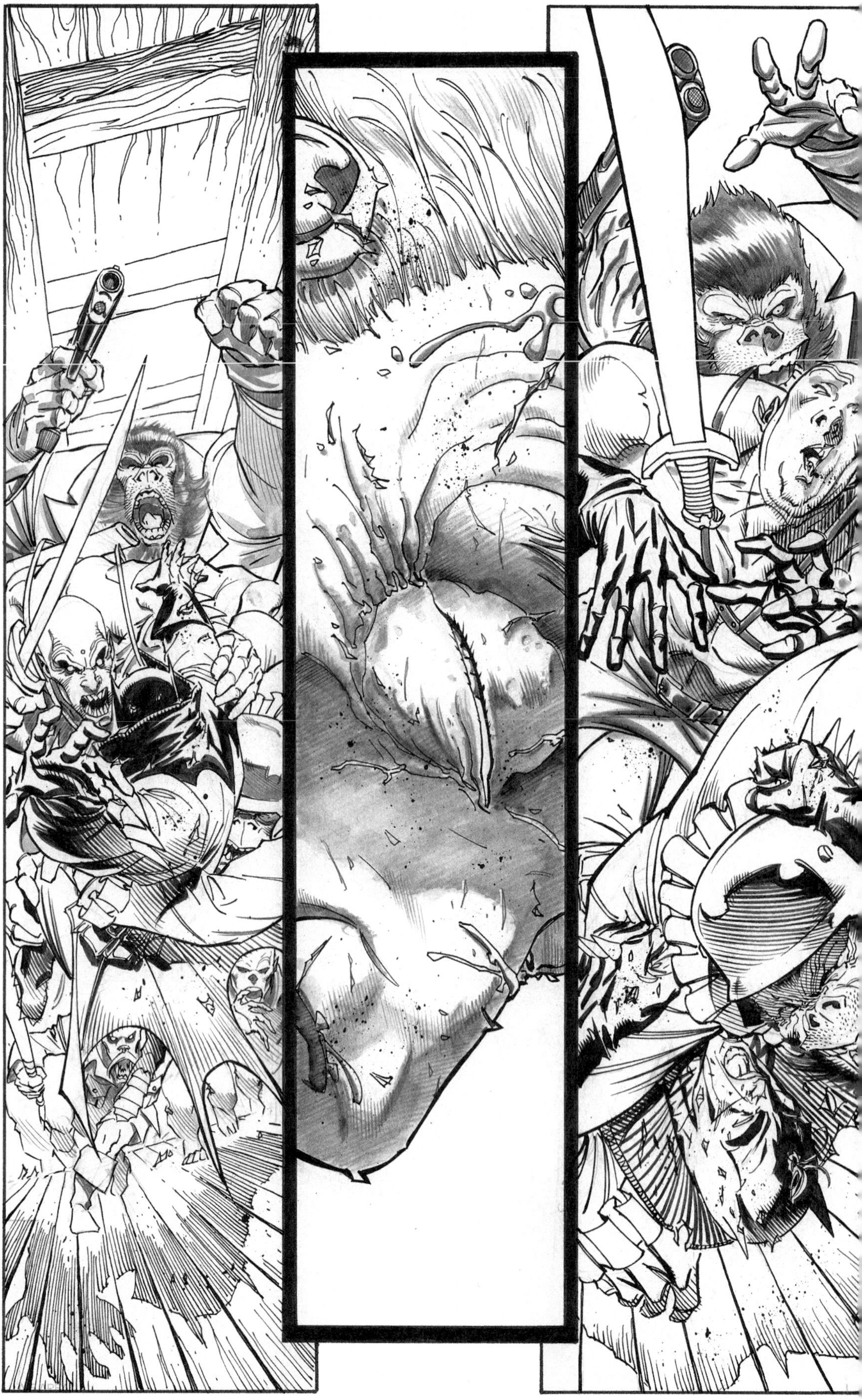

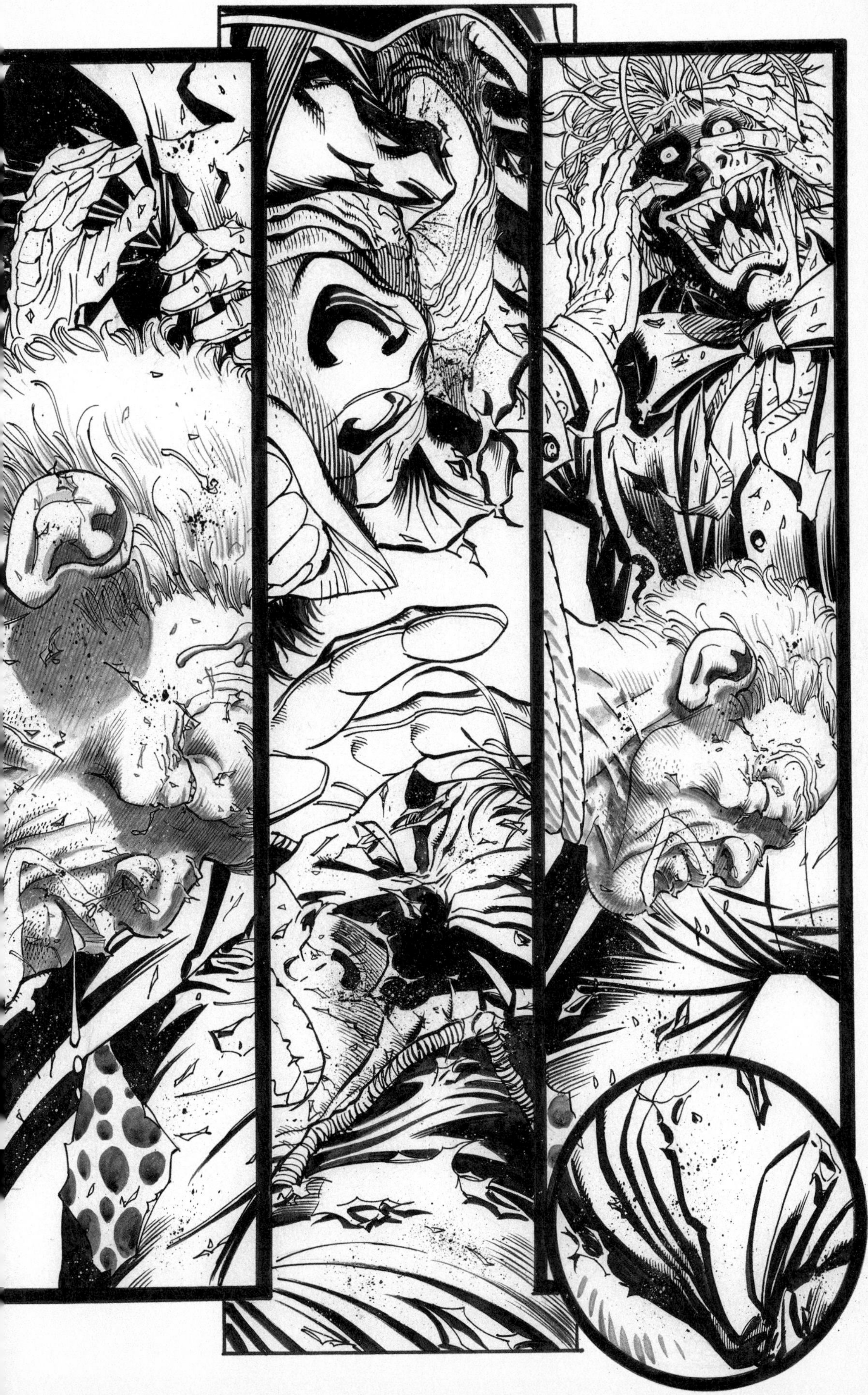

DAMIAN: SON OF BATMAN issue #3, page 10

Splash Page/

Damian comes crashing through the windshield of the school bus feet first kicking the Jackanapes driver in the teeth! We can see the Bat-Glider through the broken window heading up

over the front of the bus. Glass, teeth and the schoolbus cap go flying! Kids are screaming! Sharptooth reacts. The other Jackanapes do too, with one being able to point his gun

towards Batman.

Jackanape driver: -BATMAN?!?!
Jackanape driver: UUNNNHHH!!

PENCILLER Kubert INKER PAGE# 10 INTERIORS

TITLE ISSUE # 3 MONTH

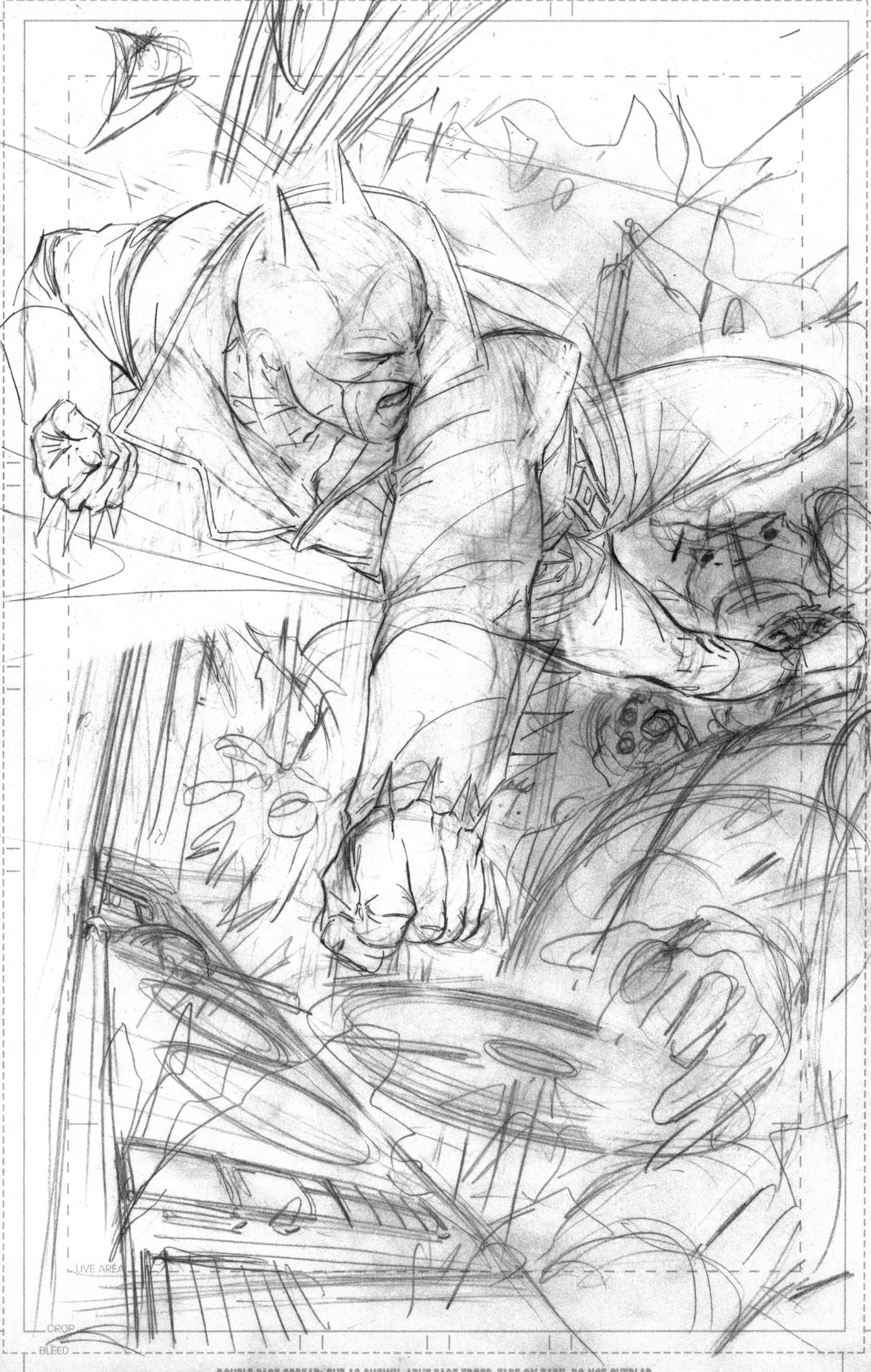

LIVE AREA

CROP

BLEED

← CUT RIGHT-HAND PAGE AT THIS LINE DOUBLE PAGE SPREAD: CUT AS SHOWN, ABUT PAGE EDGES, TAPE ON BACK, DO NOT OVERLAP CUT LEFT HAND PAGE AT THIS LINE →

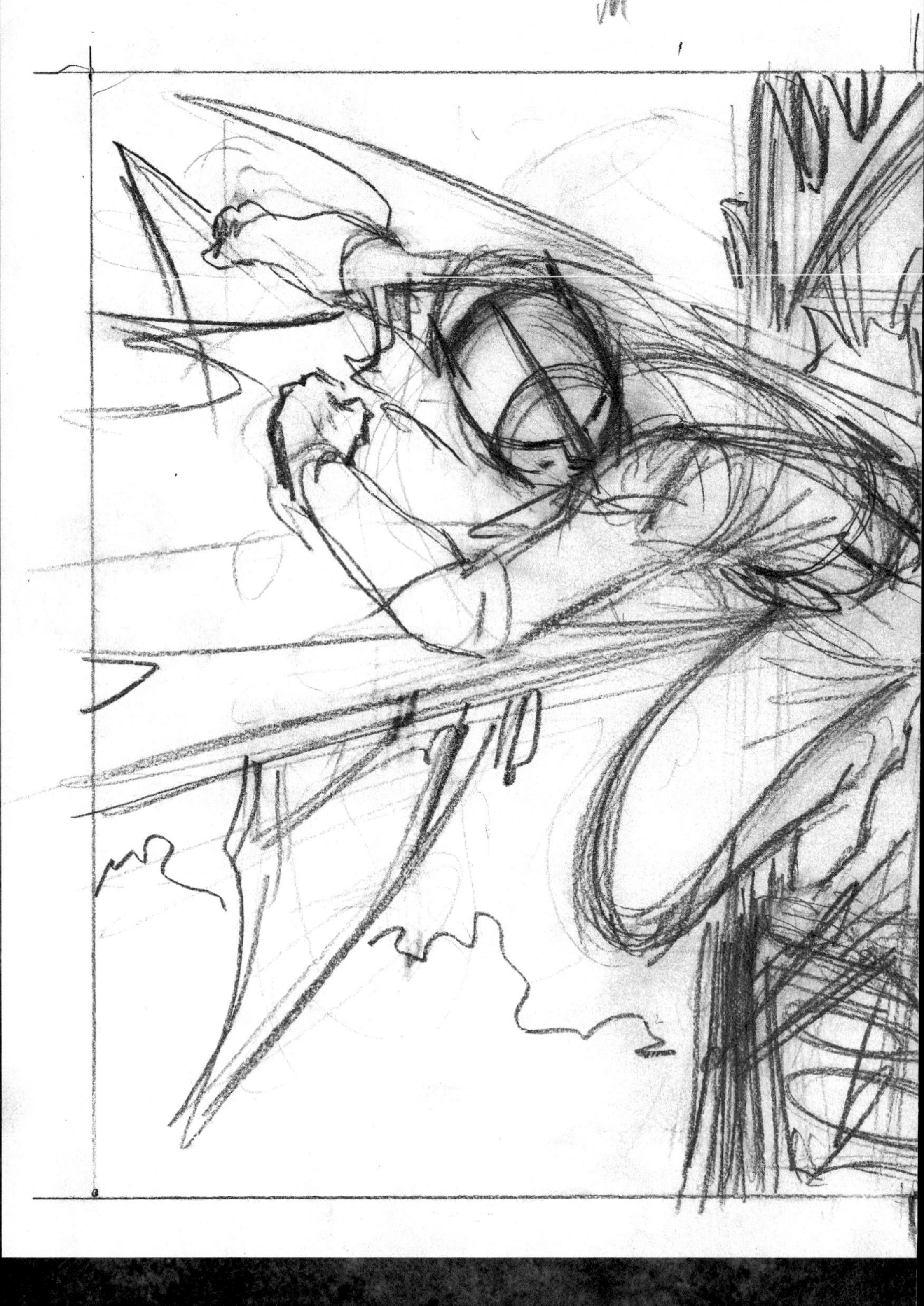

MIRROR

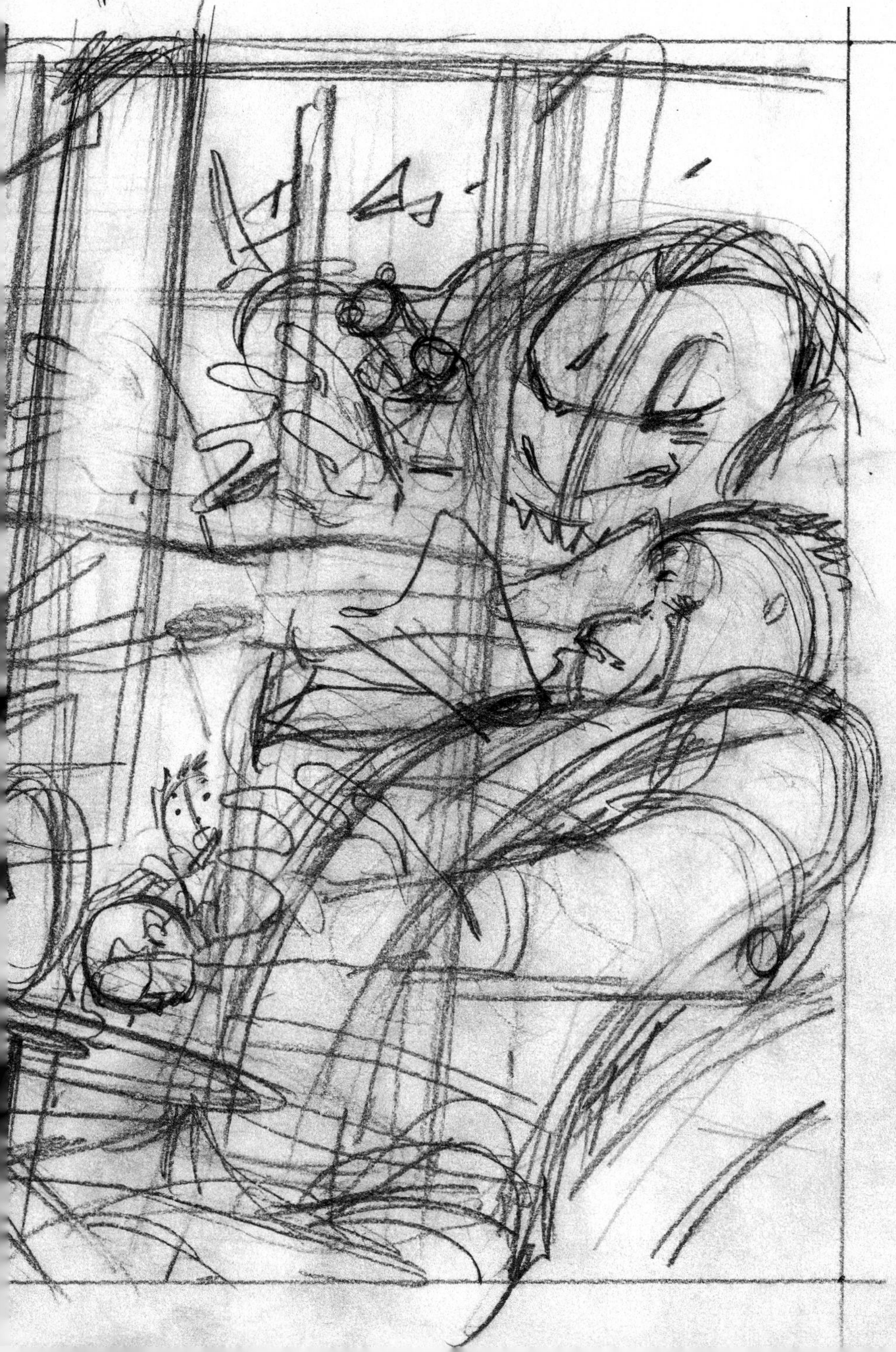

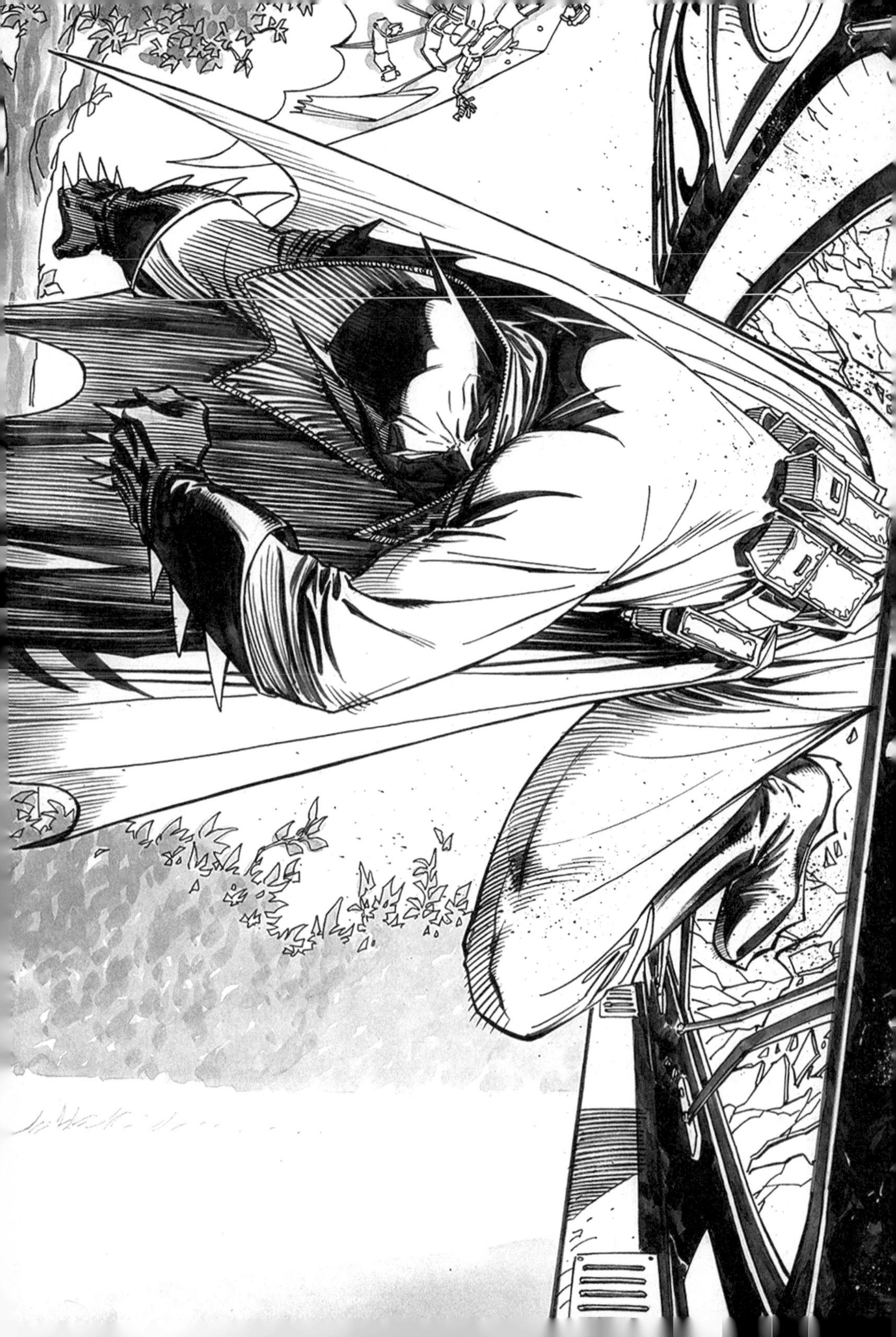

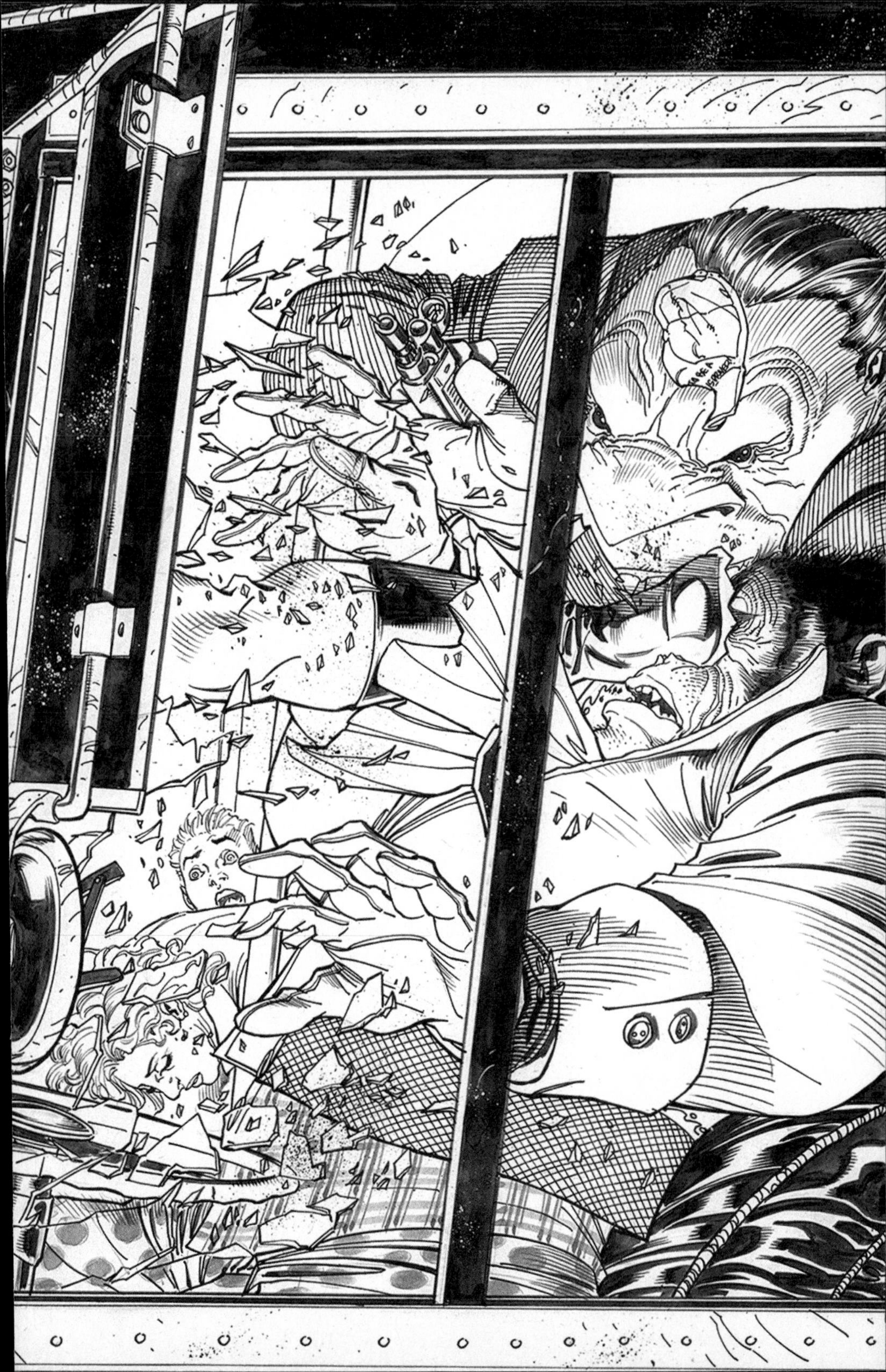

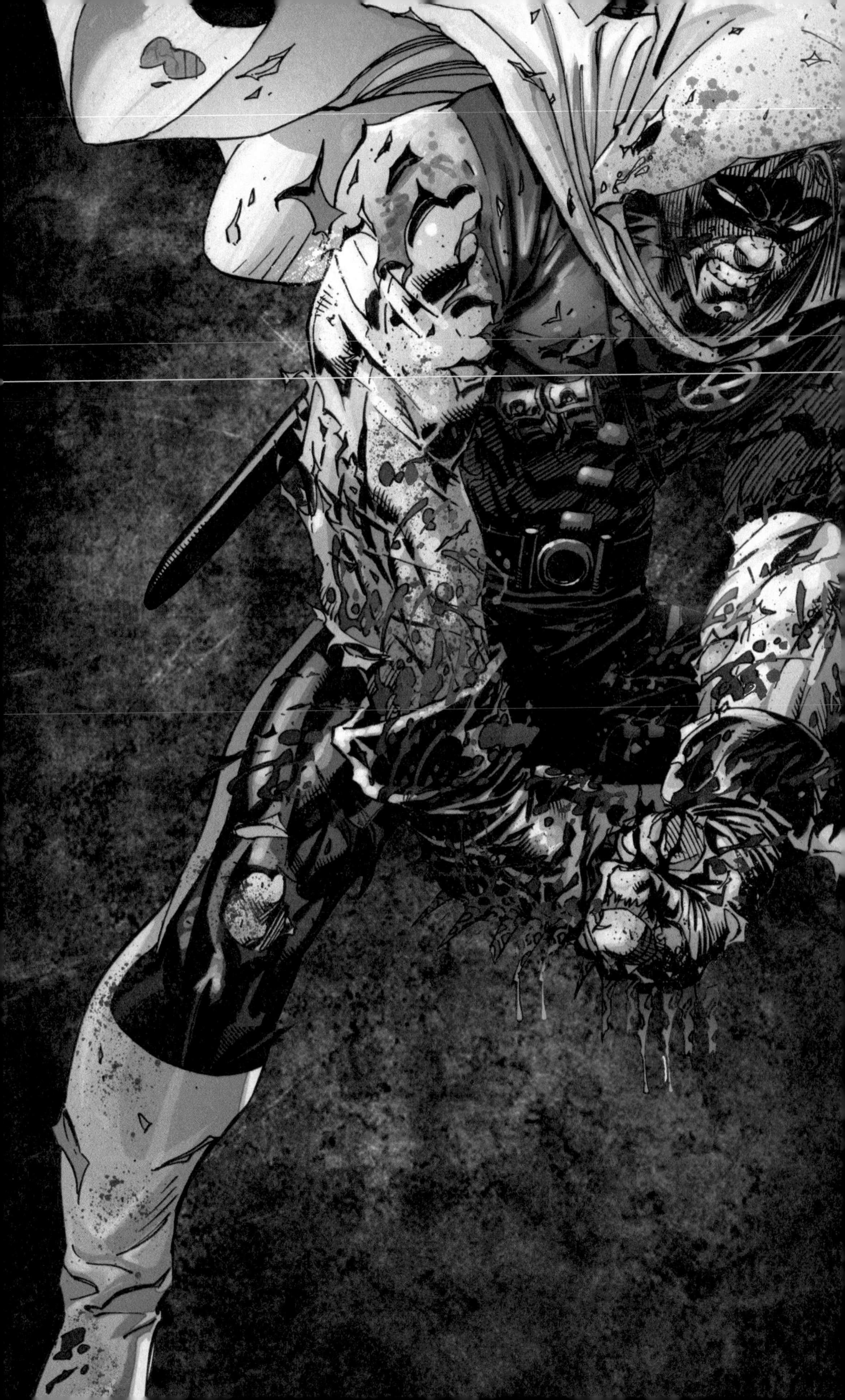

ANDY KUBERT

Andy Kubert began his career at DC Comics illustrating the first highly successful BATMAN VERSUS PREDATOR and ADAM STRANGE series. Andy went on to Marvel Comics' popular *X-Men* title, which was consistently a sales juggernaut and remained their top-selling comic during his six-year run. At Marvel he also illustrated such titles as *Ghost Rider*, *Captain America*, *Ultimate X-Men* and the *Marvel 1602* miniseries in which he collaborated with New York Times best-selling author Neil Gaiman and which earned a 2005 Quill Award for Best Graphic Novel.

For DC Comics, Andy has illustrated the best-selling BATMAN AND SON, FLASHPOINT and BATMAN: WHATEVER HAPPENED TO THE CAPED CRUSADER. His work has also appeared in other titles including ACTION COMICS and BEFORE WATCHMEN: NITE OWL. Andy is also an instructor at the Joe Kubert School of Cartoon and Graphic Art in Dover, New Jersey.

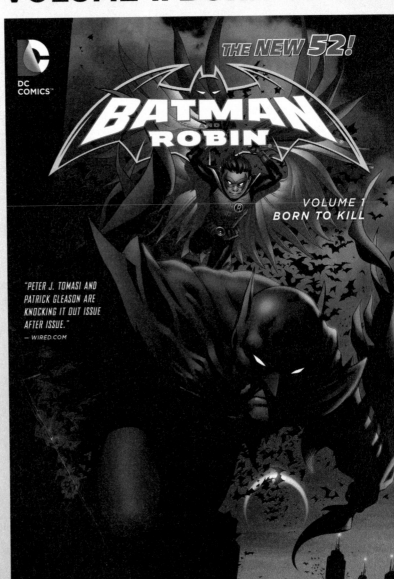